More
Frugal
Gambling

More Frugal Gambling

by Jean Scott
and Angela Sparks

Huntington Press
Las Vegas, Nevada

More Frugal Gambling

Published by
   Huntington Press
   3687 South Procyon Avenue
   Las Vegas, Nevada 89103
   (702) 252-0655 Phone
   (702) 252-0675 Fax
   e-mail: books@huntingtonpress.com

Copyright © 2003, Jean Scott

ISBN: 0-929712-41-2

Cover Design: Bethany Coffey Rihel
Interior Design & Production: Bethany Coffey Rihel &
Laurie Shaw

Cover Photograph by Sampsel Preston Photography
Hair by Cindy Chamberlain
Nails by Stella, Amp Salon at the Palms

Dedication

To all my faithful readers, who pressure me gently, but insistently, to continue giving frugal gambling advice and, much to my dismay, keep me from retiring.

Acknowledgments

I feel like a literary sponge: taking in gambling and casino information, thoughts, facts, ideas, and data from thousands of sources; mixing, sorting, and organizing this raw material; testing it in the heat of personal experience; then squeezing out words for a book to share with others, hopefully in a helpful way.

So many people inhabit these pages that it would take another whole book to list all their names.

It's nearly impossible to find the words to express my deep appreciation for all the help and inspiration I receive: from hosts, many of whom I call my friends, and other casino employees, who help me understand the always-complex inner workings of casinos; from fellow gaming writers, who provide valuable information that saves me much research time; from gambler friends, who share with me profitable new "secrets" they uncover; even from TV producers, who are always anxious to present the frugal story during prime time, and George Maloof, who is always willing to let the cameras come into his Palms casino.

I especially want to mention one group of friends and correspondents whose help and influence permeate this whole book: Skip Hughes' Internet video poker forum. Hundreds of members of Skip's List have given me helpful information throughout the years and scores volunteered to critique the rough drafts of many of the chapters in this book. I'd give names, but I'm afraid that I'd miss some, and I want everyone to know that all their efforts are greatly appreciated.

I do want to name a few people of special importance, because they've been major influences in the direction of my writing career. I want to thank Jim Wolf for choosing me to help market his software, which we named *Frugal Video Poker*. He provided the technical expertise that this amateur computer gal needed, including setting up a Frugal Gambler Web site, something I'd wanted for a long time.

I'm really glad my publisher, Anthony Curtis, keeps inviting me to stay with Huntington Press. I can always depend on his constant striving for perfection to make my book as good as it can be.

I could never leave out thanks to my dear friend and oh-so-capable editor, Deke Castleman. The day he's no longer willing or able to clean up the exclamation points in my rough drafts is the day I do retire from writing!

And then there's Brad. What can I say about a man who cheerfully makes my breakfast every morning, then takes the list I give him and dutifully runs around town while I'm chained to my computer writing: Earn 1,000 points at Casino A and get a coupon for free gas; drop clothes off at the dry cleaners; collect bounce-back at Casino B; mail book orders at the post office; use coupon to get gas; stop at grocery store last so milk won't sour sitting in hot car. You scared me to death with that gray face when I watched you being put in an ambulance in the middle of a heart attack last March. I can't imagine how I would live without you.

Lastly, I want to thank my daughter Angela, for agreeing to come on board for this frugal ride. Not only did she do the writing that shows, but she did a lot of the tedious behind-the-scenes work of tape transcribing, note organization, and proofreading. I would have been working on this another five years if not for her help.

Contents

I

INTRODUCTIONS—
The Queen of Comps
and The Frugal Princess

I *SO* DIDN'T WANT TO
WRITE THIS BOOK

When I started writing *The Frugal Gambler*, I was
sure it would be my first *and* last book about casino
gambling. For years, family and friends had encour-
aged me to write about how to gamble successfully, to
reveal all the techniques and tricks Brad and I had
learned, developed, and used—yet I resisted this en-
couragement. After all, I was retired from teaching and
wasn't thrilled about "going back to work." I finally
compromised: I'd write the book, but I'd cover my
ideas about smart gambling so thoroughly that I could
then retire again—and never have to think about grind-
ing out any more books.

Well, that notion didn't even last until *The Frugal
Gambler* came out. After I submitted the final draft to
Huntington Press, the red-pencil-wielding English
teacher in me drove my editors crazy. Every time Anthony Curtis and Deke Castleman thought the manu-
script was ready to be laid out, they'd receive another

e-mail from me with revisions and additions and suggestions and contentions … until they had to do something to stop my fine-tuning. Anthony finally put his foot down and told me that at the rate I was going, I'd be running alongside the postal truck that was delivering the book to the printer, yelling at the driver that I wanted to add just one more idea! He suggested that, instead of sending a constant bombardment of new material, I start making notes for the "next book."

So this second book almost started writing itself. And by the time *The Frugal Gambler* came back from the printer in 1998, those notes were piled so high on my desk that I knew I was a long ways away from retirement. Unfortunately, the book wouldn't *finish* writing itself. It needed me to help. So why did it take almost a half-decade? My explanation might seem a bit feeble, though it could probably win a prize for the Understatement of the Year: I've been one busy procrastinator.

Though I resisted the burden of writing another book with all my energy, in the end I felt I *had* to write this one. That half-decade has spanned two different millennia—and we're all living in a very different world today than the one we were in when I first decided to put my casino ideas down on paper. There have been many changes, both in Brad's and my personal lives and in the casino world itself.

Moving to Las Vegas

Probably the biggest change in our lives between the first and second *Frugals* has been pulling up our Indiana roots and becoming permanent residents of Las Vegas. Getting our own place and living here full time has definitely changed our casino emphasis. We especially like not having to play for our room; we can choose which casino to play in by its overall advantage, instead of according to where we can most easily earn comped accommodations. Plus, we can go home and sleep in the same bed every night, a welcome change after 16 years of traipsing from one hotel to another. Of course, we still play enough that we can always get free rooms for out-of-town friends and family.

One of the biggest advantages of being a Vegas local is that we can always find good video poker; we have hundreds of positive-expectation machines all over town to choose from, a luxury we could enjoy nowhere else in the world. We also have a never-ending choice of good promotions: tournaments, bonus-point days, giveaways, and drawings. And the opportunities to build up our comp bank are endless, meaning we never have to cook a meal at home if we don't want to.

Having a local address gives us the benefit of a constant stream of mailings from the off-Strip locals casinos that feverishly compete for our business with coupons for bonus points, gifts, shows, meals, drawing tickets, and best of all, bounce-back cash (vouchers for hard cash we can get if we return to the casino to collect it).

One of the most enjoyable benefits is that we meet a lot of people who share our interest in video poker, so we never lack for friends or social opportunities. Being in this local loop also allows us all to share our knowledge of good playing opportunities, some of which may not be generally known or well-advertised.

Moving Up in Denomination

Another change has been our move to higher-denomination video poker. Our usual wager up to 1997 was $1.25 a hand, which is full-coin on quarter machines. As I write this in 2003, you might find us playing anywhere from $5 a hand on the dollar machines or $25 on a dollar Five Play multi-line, all the way up to $50 per hand on Ten Play.

We can afford the higher limits now that our gambling bankroll is larger. This came about from success at the lower levels of video poker and extra income from writing projects and speaking engagements. We also keep adding to our bankroll, because our living expenses, now that we've moved to Las Vegas, continue to contract: Casinos feed us, provide much of our entertainment, even send us on comped vacations. We also earn gift certificates to buy essentials and extras at department stores, gas stations, and supermarkets. We'd be hard-pressed to spend our pensions if we didn't have grandchildren to spoil.

Another reason we've gone up in denomination is that we're getting older and no longer have the stamina to play for long periods every day like we did in our early gambling years. The higher denominations and multi-line machines allow us to take advantage of better promotions that would require more hours of play (at lower levels) than we're physically able to put in.

Finally, moving up in denomination has given us a lot more experience with the comp system, especially in terms of what slot hosts can do for us. We rarely used hosts before I wrote *The Frugal Gambler*. Now we interact with them all the time, so I'm able to help you navigate this tricky part of the comp system from personal experience.

Moving into Cyberspace

Buying and learning to use a computer has made major changes in my life. I truly love my computer. Brad is grateful that I don't take it to bed with me, but it's my constant companion at all other times. Sometimes I feel like a slave to it—what, I have only 50 e-mails to answer today? But the blessings it has brought by increasing our circle of friends far outweigh the curses. (Brad, on the other hand, won't clutter his life by learning to use it. He says he's lived quite happily for 71 years without one and has no desire to get on the information highway. Good thing, too—he's so relaxed, he'd probably fall asleep and get run over!)

The computer has improved my research and writing efficiency, so I can crank out more and better magazine columns, feature articles, and books (note the size of this one). Also, everything I write is much more legible—much to the delight of my poor editors, who no longer have to decipher my tiny scribbles.

However, the most important benefit of "getting connected" is that it makes us much better at our video poker "job." Tutoring programs, such as *Frugal Video Poker*, teach us to play new games and help us to stay sharp on the old ones. We now have software with the capability to quickly generate strategy charts for any new game we find—a definite time-saver. In addition, being on the Internet, especially Skip Hughes' video poker list, has allowed us to make hundreds of new friends who share information about playing opportunities and casino changes, helping to keep us up to date in a way that print never could.

Moving-Target Casinos

Sometimes it seems as if the only thing that's changed more than we have since *The Frugal Gambler* is the whole casino scene itself. Implode the old; build the new. More! Bigger! Better! The expansion of the casino industry is truly amazing to watch, especially when you live in the heart of it.

And not only is the total casino business changing, but each casino is continuously being transformed.

Buildings are expanded and renovated. Restaurants, even showrooms, come and go. Competition is forcing the casinos to promote like crazy and computerization is giving them the tools with which to experiment. Marketing policies change more often than the weather, and software allows for never-ending tweaking. Likewise, the comp systems have gotten bigger and more complex. Slot clubs are being modified and consolidated.

It also seems that a whole new generation of electronic gambling machines is introduced every year. Multi-line video slots are making nickel players valuable customers. The video poker universe is exploding with new variations: multi-game, multi-denomination, multi-line—you can now play *penny* video poker with a $5 max-coin bet, the same as the traditional dollar games.

I just *had* to write this book to help the poor players who are reeling in confusion in the midst of all these changes.

About This Book

Speaking of change, it's the one thing that stays constant in the present and you can count on in the future. So, although I've tried to be as up to date as possible in the pages that follow, remember that you shouldn't be surprised or disappointed if you find something in a casino that isn't exactly as I've described it. Always double-check before you depend too heavily on any one piece of my advice.

Another point I would like to stress is that *More Frugal Gambling* is *not* the advanced course for people who have graduated from *The Frugal Gambler*. This second book is merely a continuation of the first. It's written by the same "gambling grandma" for the same casino patrons. And while it contains useful information for players who are in a casino to make a profit, it will prove even more useful for those who go to casinos strictly for entertainment and want to make their money stretch so the fun will last longer.

Another thing that hasn't changed is that Brad and I still do everything together. Pardon me for this personal note, but I want to remind everyone that even though Brad often stays in the background while I'm attending to my "royal" duties, he's the one who not only does most of the legwork, but also gives our team heart. That's why his friends often call him the King of Kindness.

There *is* one important addition to this book. I'm proud to announce that my daughter Angela Sparks, the Frugal Princess, came on board to help me from the inception of *More Frugal Gambling*. As a beginning gambler, she provides a grounding perspective for me; I've been at this casino game so long that I often forget what it's like not to have it mostly figured out. Look for Angela's beginner tips that are peppered throughout the text, especially if you're a newbie just getting your feet wet in the casinos.

And so, after Angela gives you her history so you can get to know her better, we'll launch right into the art, science, and fun of frugal gambling.

FOLLOWING IN THE QUEEN'S FOOTSTEPS TO BECOME THE FRUGAL PRINCESS

by Angela Sparks

As the daughter of the Queen of Comps, I was destined to grow up frugal. But when I was a teenager I rebelled, as many young girls do, often telling my mother that I didn't want to be anything like her. However, now that I'm an adult with a family of my own, I realize that I'm more like the Queen than I could have ever imagined.

As you may have read in *The Frugal Gambler*, Mom had a puritanical upbringing in a minister's home. As well as stressing strict moral principles, my grandparents placed great emphasis on thriftiness. Although I wasn't raised in such a rigid setting, my mother continued the tradition of frugality.

In fact, I can't remember a time when I wasn't expected to be economical. My father was retired from the Air Force. So after my parents divorced when I was five, I had an ID card for the commissary on the military base close to where Mom and I lived. At first,

Mom was permitted to go with me, so as we shopped together she taught me how to use coupons, how to do price comparisons, and generally how to stretch our budget.

Once I reached the age of 10, however, I couldn't have a non-ID person accompany me, so I had to start doing the shopping myself. Mom sent me in with a list, an envelope full of coupons, and strict instructions to get generic items whenever possible. These early shopping lessons have saved me hundreds, even thousands, of dollars over the years, especially now that I have a big hungry husband and two children to cook for. And as fate would have it, I married an Army infantry sergeant and am back to economical shopping at military commissaries and post exchanges. I spend so much time in the store comparing prices and finding the best deals that sometimes my husband says he's tempted to call in a Green Beret search party.

While I was growing up, I had more fashionable clothes than I could ever wear out, but they never cost much. My mom shopped at thrift stores before vintage clothing became fashionable, she dragged me around to hundreds of yard sales, and best of all, we hit the mall sales like there was no tomorrow. We *never* bought anything at full price. An exciting outing for us was to find an end-of-season take-50%-off-the-already-marked-down-sale-price extravaganza at a department store. The supreme shopping experience was a 50%-off day at the thrift shop.

I didn't realize that Mom was being frugal—I thought everyone bought clothes this way. But as I grew up and began to hang out at the mall with my friends, I realized that they were spending a lot of money for their trendy outfits. Sometimes I wished that I could do the same, but I knew that mom's way ensured that I would always look stylish and still have money left over for other things. Because my mother pinched pennies, I could be involved in more activities than many of my peers. I took lessons of all kinds—gymnastics, tap and jazz dance, and flute and piano. I was able to travel all over the United States on school and church-group trips, and even to Australia to visit my father. You could almost say I was spoiled—but spoiled in a very thrifty way.

My mom loved to play games as a child, but because of her parents' religious beliefs she was limited to using a spinner in place of dice and wasn't permitted to play games with cards, not even Old Maid. She didn't learn the four suits until she was well into her thirties, but some of my earliest memories are of playing cards with her. I know now that she was teaching me card games like poker and blackjack at the same time she was learning them herself. We learned about straights, full houses, and 4-of-a-kinds by playing Yahtzee. I always wanted to join in whatever game my parents and their friends were playing during an evening get-together, so to pacify me Mom would promise to teach me the games the next day.

I was in high school when Mom and Brad, my new stepfather, started going on casino junkets to Las Vegas, Reno-Tahoe, and other casino destinations all over the world. I had no idea how they did it, but I knew they weren't losing the family's money and that the word "comp" was magic. Only later did I learn that comp was short for complimentary and meant "free," Mom's favorite word, which became mine, too.

Experiencing the Good Life First-Hand

My first trip to a casino was in the spring of my senior year of high school. Having heard so much about Mom and Brad's exciting gambling adventures, I was thrilled that my graduation present was a trip to

Las Vegas for me and a girlfriend, using—what else?—free airline tickets they'd earned after getting bumped off one of their previous flights. Back then, Mom and Brad were blackjack players and I knew that they considered anyone who played machines to be uninformed, as well as certain losers. Still, the video poker machines fascinated my girlfriend and me. We were too young to legally gamble, of course, but we'd sneak out to play the nickel video poker machines at another casino where Mom or Brad wouldn't catch us, hoping our $2 roll of nickels would last a long time.

Gambling wasn't our main interest. We were more concerned with getting a tan by the pool, attracting the attention of young men, and trying to order Long Island iced teas without being carded. For those few days we lived in hitherto-unknown luxury. We stayed in a beautiful room that I knew was free and saw shows with complimentary tickets. We could go to the coffee shop any time and just say "charge it to my room," without the fear of getting in trouble, because I knew it would be comped. Mom didn't have the title of Queen of Comps yet, but that didn't matter—all my friends and I knew was that we were being treated like royalty (especially when the hotel took us to the airport in a long stretch limo).

After high school I went to college at BYU in Utah. It's a mere six-hour drive from Las Vegas, so my friends and I made numerous trips to visit Mom and Brad when they were there, always staying in comped rooms and eating comped meals. I wasn't 21 yet, so I still had to sneak around to play the nickel machines, but sometimes we'd get brave and play a bit of quarter video poker. We were less scared of losing our tiny bankroll than we were of hitting a big jackpot. Mom had warned us that a big jackpot would lead to the casino checking our IDs and we wouldn't be able to collect.

Las Vegas was an inexpensive vacation for poor college students, as there was an abundance of free or inexpensive non-gambling things to do. We could window-shop at the expensive casino malls, hang out by the pools, and people-watch everywhere. Mom had discount coupons for the Wet 'n' Wild water park, miniature golf courses, and the movies. She always had a stack of coupon books that we could use in the casinos for free snacks and casino logo merchandise, such as key chains, T-shirts, and hats. And in the evenings we were never bored, because we had comped tickets to top-notch shows.

Finally, I Reached the Age of Casino Consent

I turned 21 while I was living in Australia with my father. There were no casinos around, so I had to make do with playing poker with my friends. I had to call Mom one night all the way from Australia to clear up an argument over whether a straight beat a flush. (In Australia, it did!)

A year later I returned to the U.S and started working as a secretary and saving for my next trip to Las Vegas. I was excited that I was finally of legal gambling age and actually had a small bankroll to play with. I'd been practicing basic strategy with a computer blackjack tutor on my lunch hour, so I was prepared to win a bundle.

When I got to Vegas, Mom took me downtown to play live dollar blackjack where I could practice at a low-minimum table. It was a good place to learn; the casinos weren't crowded and Mom could sit by me and do some coaching without more experienced players becoming impatient. I learned the little signals of live blackjack, like scratching the cards on the table when I wanted a hit and tucking my cards under my chips to stand. Though I didn't win that bundle, I did take home a few extra dollars and I was thoroughly convinced that being an informed player was the only way to go.

Husbands, Kids, and Coupons

My next trip to Las Vegas a few years later found me in a much different situation, now married to my soldier husband Steve, with toddler Zachary and baby Kaitlynn Starr in tow. Our gambling sessions had to be balanced with family entertainment. Las Vegas had become more kid friendly by this time, as casinos realized that many couples with children still wanted to spend their vacation in a casino town.

There was Circus Circus, where we could watch acts under the big top in between playing midway and video games. Zachary still imitates the howling wolf of the laser show he remembers from our first visit to Sam's Town; he also still loves to watch the volcano explode at the Mirage and the pirates beat the British at Treasure Island, as he did on that early trip. Mom had stacks of coupons, of course, and we literally strolled (and strollered) all around, coupons in hand, looking for the best free stuff in town.

Mom and Brad have always felt that couples with children need time alone, so they reserved a suite for Steve and me for one night while they baby-sat. Mom armed us with lots of coupons, while Brad palmed us each a small gambling bankroll. After a lavish dinner, especially tasty since it was free, and some wandering around, I found a low-limit blackjack table where the players seemed to be friendly. Steve didn't enjoy playing table games as much as I did, so he went in search of a lucky slot machine. In my mind he was just having fun while I was being the serious gambler! After a few hours, Steve and I were thrilled that we were both winners.

But I'd indulged in a few too many fuzzy navels and Steve had been tempted with too many free Buds at the machines. So on our way out we got greedy and decided to place our total evening's winnings of $50 on a single blackjack hand and try to double it. I was scared to death as I was dealt my cards and got very upset when I realized I didn't have any chips to double down when I was dealt an 11. I got so flustered that I tucked my cards under my chips and forgot to take a hit. The dealer just let me make this stupid mistake and I ended up losing. I learned an important lesson that night, somewhat painfully: Don't gamble when you're too tired, strung out, or have had too much to drink. In fact, I was so ashamed of making such a bad decision that I only recently told my mother about what happened that evening.

After The Frugal Gambler

Our next casino trip wasn't to Las Vegas, but to Biloxi with its dockside riverboats. It was a three-generation vacation, and Mom and Brad were going to get in some quality grandparent time. Previous to the trip, I'd transcribed *The Frugal Gambler* from tape onto a computer, so I was a much more informed gambler and now better understood the whole reality of what Mom and Brad did. But during the time between our last trip to Vegas and this Mississippi vacation, they'd made the complete transition from high-rolling blackjack players to low-rolling video poker players, so I had a new game to learn. I practiced video poker on our computer before we left, but relied mainly on strategy cards and personal coaching from Mom.

Our next casino trip was to a riverboat in Joliet, Illinois—this time without our children, who were visiting their other grandma. We stayed with Mom and Brad in a huge two-room suite that had a kitchenette and a Jacuzzi and we took full advantage of the indoor pool and spa. Again, Mom and I played side by side, especially important since we were playing a new-to-me variation of video poker. Brad kept up the tradition and slipped us a small bankroll so Steve and I could play on our own.

We were playing the Piggy Bankin' slot machines, one of the first slot games that had a positive long-term expectation if you could find one with at least 25 coins in the "bank." We then discovered a few video blackjack machines and played them heavily after Mom told us the payback was over 100%. We lost a little in spite of that fact, learning the important lesson that gambling percentages are based on long-term play and you don't win every time, even on a positive game. But we followed an even more important guideline and stopped playing when our designated gambling bankroll was gone. We went home with the great feeling that we had received good entertainment value for our money and hadn't lost more than we could afford.

Burning Up the Flight Paths

There are only two states where there is no form of legal gambling at all. I lived for two years in one of them, Utah, when I was in college. Then, ironically, with casinos springing up all over the country, the Army decided to send us to the other holdout, Hawaii. Mom wasn't going to be denied seeing her grandchildren by anything as trivial as an ocean, so two or three times a year, when she and Brad weren't crisscrossing the Pacific Ocean to visit us, we were on a plane coming to Vegas, where they now lived permanently. I practiced on computer software until I could play Deuces Wild accurately and it became my game of choice. I'll never forget the thrill of getting my first royal flush.

When the Army decided that three years was long enough for a soldier to be stationed in "paradise," they played a cruel trick on us and we ended up at Fort Drum, in upstate New York. But, as Mom says, "This is why airplanes were invented," and we still look forward to frequent visits to Vegas, especially during the long winters.

Boarding the Frugal Express

If you'd have told me seven years ago that I'd be helping to write a book with my mother on being a frugal gambler, I would have told you that you were nuts. For one thing, I never thought that my mother and I would ever be able to work together; I was still remembering how we clashed over everything in my rebellious teenage years, and even though we've become good friends, we still do things very differently. Furthermore, while my children were babies, I thought that I was never going to do anything except wash bottles, change diapers, and do laundry. But my kids are growing up now and are in school all day and I actually have some time to myself, so here I am. Actually, I can't think of anything more fun than writing about gambling with the Queen of Comps—unless it's doing the "research" in a casino.

II

THE CASINO GAME

1

The Pyramid Falls

"Different strokes for different folks."
—*Sylvester Stone of Sly and the Family Stone*

A Tale of Two Gamblers

In January 1998, Brad and I were playing $1 Double Bonus at a large Las Vegas resort-casino. We were just outside the high-limit area, where I noticed a man, sharply dressed, playing all by himself, at a $25 video poker machine. He looked so serious, like he was concentrating hard. I watched him out of the corner of my eye for a while and he looked like he was having anything but a good time.

Suddenly, I saw his machine light flashing—he'd hit a royal flush—for $100,000. Because it was the high-limit area, which was empty at the time, this man didn't have a crowd of onlookers around him, celebrating with him and congratulating him and getting a vicarious thrill by imagining what they'd do with that much money. He was alone, just sitting there, waiting to get paid, looking rather grim.

So I walked over and congratulated him on his jackpot. He didn't seem the least bit thrilled; he didn't even smile. I was more excited than he was just seeing a $100,000 royal on the machine.

I had to ask him, "Aren't you excited?"

And he answered, "Well, yeah, but I've dropped a hundred grand into these machines over the last few days."

I later talked to a host and she said that he was probably right: The royal had just gotten him even.

A few weeks later, we were in a tiny shabby casino in a blue-collar Las Vegas neighborhood, making a coupon play. Nearby was a man dressed in working clothes, playing a penny machine. With a woman on either side of him, he was laughing and joking, smoking cigarettes and ordering drinks for himself and the two ladies—just plain enjoying himself.

Brad is always interested in offbeat characters, so he walked over to see what was going on. Though you could play up to 120 pennies on this machine, the man was playing only one penny at a time. Brad commented, "You sure look like you're having fun." And the man replied, "We're having a blast! You know, your money lasts a really long time on this machine!"

The Pyramid Revisited

Some people have written to criticize my pyramid in *The Frugal Gambler*. (If you remember, this pyramid had four levels: "Clueless in a Casino" at the base; "Clear Thinking" one level up; "Balanced" on top of that; and "Pro" at the peak.) My critics claimed that it "labeled" people; therefore, they thought, it was a putdown. They said that they've known some rude and selfish pro gamblers who only rose to the top because they were "scum."

2

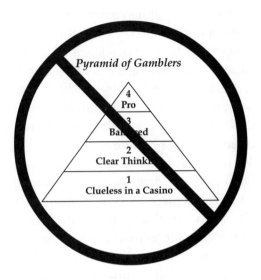

Whoa! I certainly didn't mean for that pyramid to be a barometer of character. I don't believe that a professional gambler, who happens by dint of personal choice and hard work to be at the apex of the casino pyramid, is a better person than someone who's unknowledgeable and wandering around lost in the casino jungle.

Perhaps a better way to categorize gamblers, if we can even do such a thing, is to talk about goals and personalities, instead of trying to find one neat all-encompassing illustration.

Goals

Goal Groups

Like the two players in the stories at the beginning of the chapter, casino goals fall somewhere between the extremes of getting the money and having fun. At one end of the spectrum is the professional gambler, who goes to his "job" at his casino "office" eight to ten hours a day, six or seven days a week, toiling away at a video poker machine or blackjack table. The former plays fast, sometimes banging away at two machines. The latter plays three hands heads-up against the dealer, with intense concentration. Neither is making small talk with other players and both often resent any interruption, social or business.

At the other end of the spectrum are the purely recreational players, dropping a few coins here and there as they carry their coin cups through the rows of slot machines, or drinking and whooping it up with friends at the crap table. I recall a scene at a riverboat-casino a few years ago. Four senior citizens, two couples, were crowded around one nickel video poker machine. All four would "vote" on which cards to hold, taking turns pushing the buttons and dropping in a single nickel for the next hand. Whenever they stopped to order drinks, there was a lot of chatter and laughter. They cashed out credits immediately after every winning hand so they could enjoy feeling like winners while the coins clinked into the tray.

The images of the pro and low rollers are extremes, of course. But they illustrate the two main reasons that people go to casinos—for profit and for fun, with the entertainment factor overwhelmingly more common. Even the most serious gamblers, those whose goal is to make money, will say that the entertainment factor is still very important. We often say that we can't help it that we like our "work" so much.

Goals have a way of overlapping, so there are many categories of gamblers intermingled between these two main goals.

• The largest group can be summed up as people seeking *occasional entertainment*. The typical member

4

of this group is a vacationer who goes on several-day sprees to casino destinations—Las Vegas, Atlantic City, or even the Mississippi Gulf area—once or twice a year. This might be coupled with a monthly trip to a nearby riverboat or Native American casino. This casual casino visitor enjoys the restaurants, the shopping, the shows, and the nearby sightseeing as much as, or even more than, the gambling itself. Some in this group play table games that look easy, such as roulette, but most are likely intimidated by blackjack and craps. Reel slots are the game of choice for most of these people, and many don't join a slot club, because they don't feel they play often enough to bother.

People in this group pay for their entire casino visit out of their entertainment budget; they don't differentiate between gambling and non-gambling expenses. Most don't read gambling literature, having more important interests in their lives. They think, "When I'm on vacation, my mind likes to vacation too." And most believe that luck alone will control whether they win or lose—so they mostly lose, but don't mind, since they'd be spending the same money on traveling or other entertainment choices anyway.

• More serious than those who go for occasional entertainment are those who want *frequent entertainment*. This group grows larger every year, thanks to the spread of gambling, which allows them to take several trips a year to casino towns and/or frequent daytrips to casinos within driving distance. This group still likes the non-gambling activities a casino provides, but their enjoyment of the games themselves is growing. The slots are popular with this group as well, but they join slot clubs and know how to accrue perks. Some learn the rules and etiquette of some of the more complicated table games and you might find them at the blackjack or crap tables.

Because they spend more time playing, many start to see the advantage of having a separate gambling bankroll to help them control their budgets. They also begin reading about gambling and casinos. Not only does the subject interest them, but they find the information can expand their gaming opportunities and make casino visits more profitable, and thus, more fun.

• Then there's a transitional group that thinks of gambling as an *inexpensive hobby*. These people still consider the casino a place of entertainment, but they're also willing to put forth some time and study in an effort to reduce their expenses so they can enjoy it longer. They go to a casino as often as their work schedule, family obligations, and bankroll allow.

Usually, people in this group have chosen one or two games that they enjoy, and have begun to study these games so they can play them with the largest advantage (or slightest disadvantage) they can. They often play blackjack and they've learned basic strategy. If they've chosen craps, they've studied which of the many bets available on the table have the lowest casino advantage. However, most of these players still choose machine play, although many are switching from slots to video poker.

Whatever their choice of game, this group quickly learns how to cover a lot of their losses by using the comp system. Those who play the machines become experts at using the slot club system, zeroing in on promotions such as bonus-point days, which helps them accumulate cash and comps faster.

This group usually consists of avid readers of gambling material; if they can't be in a casino, they want to read about being in one.

• The next group thinks a casino is a good place for a *profitable hobby*, and here is where the numbers quickly start to shrink. Many knowledgeable casino patrons develop gambling to the point where it becomes a low-cost hobby. But a few, in their search for information, come across an amazing concept: Some casino games can be played with the mathematical edge on the player's, rather than the casino's, side; and because of that, there's something called "advantage play." However, they soon realize that these opportunities are limited. And even when they're found, they all require strong motivation, dogged determination, an adequate bankroll, and extensive and continual study.

A select few of these hobbyists looking for profit can use their computer-driven research to do battle with the odds on their side in the sports and race books. A few succeed in the live poker rooms, where knowledge, experience, and patience are key requirements. A few can beat the casino by skilled card counting at the blackjack table. And a growing group of video poker players can end up in the black in their casino logs by skillfully choosing machines and applying accurate playing strategies.

These gamblers never stop studying. They soak up information like sponges—in written material, on the Internet, and from fellow gamblers. They hunt for good playing opportunities in any casino: on Native American reservations, aboard Midwest riverboats, on Mississippi boats that never sail and rarely even float, and along the Boardwalk or in the Marina in Atlantic City. But for many of them, Las Vegas is the mecca of advantage play—and they spend as much time as they can in this city.

• Without even realizing it, many advantage players cross over from treating gambling as a profitable hobby to making it a *part-time job*. Actually, these two groups do about the same thing, only the label is different. Some consider advantage play a part-time job if they need the income for necessary expenses; other part-time "pros" supplement their regular income this way. Some remain hobbyists due to geographical considerations: They don't have advantage-play opportunities within driving distance, so they have to save their passion for when they can arrange a trip to a good gambling location.

The dream, especially of many younger video poker advantage players, is to retire in Las Vegas. This group would love to turn their profitable gambling hobby into a part-time job to supplement their pensions, as many retirees in Vegas have done.

• The smallest group consists of the pros who make gambling their *full-time job*. This is a tough gig, no matter which of the five possible specialties are chosen: live poker, video poker, race betting, sports betting, or blackjack. It's not only hard work, but the opportunities for making a profit are very limited. You can find good plays in only a restricted number of casinos, and in some gambling locales there are no opportunities at all. Most pros live and "work" in Las Vegas, which offers the most opportunities. But even here they're becoming more rare as time passes, forcing some pros to travel extensively to find work, often on only a temporarily profitable job. Bob Dancer, a well-known video poker pro, describes his job as most professional gamblers would, "A hard way to make an easy living."

To Change—Or Not to Change— Your Goal Group

Although many people are quite happy to stay in one goal group their whole gambling life, there's frequently a natural migration from the groups with the most members to those with the least. And a single thing is responsible for most of these moves: study.

The occasional recreational player decides he enjoys gambling so much that he wants to do it more frequently and he begins reading his gambling magazines—the same ones that used to be just for entertainment—with his focus on information he can use to cut his losses. As he becomes more knowledgeable, he finds out his bankroll lasts longer, so now he considers gambling an inexpensive hobby, one that gives him more pleasure than, say, collecting stamps. He reads every word about casinos and gambling he can lay his hands on and perhaps goes online to access even more information. He's overjoyed to find out about advantage play, something he can do in some casinos if he's willing to study and work at it. Now his hobby doesn't cost him anything and can provide days and maybe even weeks of pleasure.

Most people have no desire to move from here into the part-time-worker or full-time-pro groups, and even for those who have considered it, there are a multitude of roadblocks, including family responsibilities, time constraints, job security, a low tolerance for ambiguity, and many lifestyle factors. You must always fit your gambling goals into your life goals. You might envy the player with an elaborate computer log that attests to his large income from gambling. But for most people, there's just as much merit in simply enjoying the casino experience at little or no expense.

I have an Internet friend who posted the following on a video poker bulletin board:

"The first time I played Deuces Wild, I'd stopped at Las Vegas on my way to a meeting in San Francisco. I played about 16 hours and won about $4. I spent $6 to call my wife from the airport to share my success with her."

A win—no matter how small—is a great thing for casual or recreational gamblers. They're not planning on making a living with this activity or even making huge profits. They talk most about the fun associated with the experience.

Personalities

Although most people enter a casino with one or a mixture of the two main goals I've discussed, profit and fun, each person is also bringing into that casino something unique—an individual personality, one that influences how he or she tries to reach those goals.

Some gamblers are slow and deliberate; some are rash and foolhardy. Some thrive on the challenge of taking a chance; others are scared to death of going broke. Some are frugal; some are spendthrifts.

Some players (like me) always hit the deal button to speed up the accumulation of credits on a Triple Play video poker machine so they can get on to the next hand more quickly. Others (like Brad) let the credits accumulate slowly so they can study the results that came up on each line. One guy feeds the bill acceptor like crazy, plays like he's possessed, doesn't cash out until he's ready to go, and hates when the hopper needs filling. The woman next to him stands in line at the change booth to buy rolls of coins, slowly and deliberately feeds them into the machine, cashes out frequently to re-feed them, and chats with everyone around her (except the speed demon at the next machine who is pointedly ignoring her).

Brad and I are very different from each other and it definitely shows in our gambling habits. When I study a new video poker game, since I'm a details person, I try to learn every penalty-card situation I can. Brad really doesn't care whether our playing opportunity is worth $15 an hour or $14.75. For example, he might ask me how much it's worth, theoretically, to remember an obscure penalty card. If I say something like, "five cents an hour," he reaches into his pocket, pulls out a quarter, hands it to me, and says, "Here. Now you won't have to stress out for the next five hours." I'm lucky that Brad's laid-back attitude toward life keeps me from being totally nutty.

I know a millionaire senior-citizen gambler who carefully guards her modest hundred-dollar bankroll at the nickel and quarter machines so it'll last through her whole three-day Vegas vacation; she gives herself a daily allowance with no thought of ever dipping into the next day's reserve. I also know a kamikaze gambler who comes to Vegas with a couple thousand dollars he gets from draining every bank account he has, then starts blasting away at the $1 machines. If he hits even a mini-jackpot, it's time to take a shot at a $5 game. A little win there and it's straight to the $25 machines—where a short losing streak wipes out his whole bootle and he's back on the plane home in record time. (This guy says he doesn't recommend his style of play for people who can't be "Zen-like in the face of brutal ups and downs." Amen!)

Some people think that if they study gambling it won't be exciting or suspenseful; it'll ruin the thrill of playing with wild abandon. Brad once had a friend who said he wanted to gamble at a game where he didn't have much chance of winning, so if he did win, he'd feel as if he'd really pulled off something.

Some gamblers think that living on the edge makes things fun. But many eventually discover that playing around that edge may be fun for a little while, but that it's sharp and makes them bleed—or worse, that it's a long way down when they fall. The ones who've experienced a few of those falls often realize that doing a little studying and playing smarter may be the most fun of all.

Are You Ripe for a Type?

I often thought that there was likely a correlation between personality types and the games people choose to play in a casino. But I never realized how specifically they could correspond until I read an article by Henry Tamburin in the August 2000 *Casino Player* called "Choosing the Right Game for Your Personality." Henry came up with a clever typology (a system for classifying behavior based on universal characteristics) that casino patrons can use to determine if they're playing the game that best suits their psychology.

Henry identified ten personality types, then matched them up with the best casino games for them. I was interested to see a category called "Frugal," which Henry defined as "someone who hates to spend money and wants to get as much value as possible." (Hmm. Henry and I are good friends. Was he thinking about me, I wonder?) And which games do you suppose best suit the frugal gambler? Brilliant deduction, Holmes: video poker and slot club promotions. (He definitely *was* taking my picture.)

For "Extrovert," Henry recommends craps. I would add Let It Ride, where all the players are rooting for the dealer to turn up good cards, and the big six, which is so mindless that there's nothing else to do but cheer for everyone's number. "Introvert" types, according to Henry, do better at slots, video poker, roulette, and mini-baccarat. I might add table poker to that list.

Henry also lists "Risk Taker" (keno, progressive slots, and crap prop bets), "Competitive" (poker and tournaments), "Flamboyant" (baccarat, blackjack, craps), "Intuitive" (Let It Ride, Three Card Poker, Caribbean Stud, and new slot machines), "Thinking" (blackjack, video poker, live poker, and tournaments), "Insightful" (card counting, video poker, and comps), and "Feeling" (slots and video poker).

With which of these gambler profiles do you more closely identify? Or do you fall somewhere in between? Are you an Extrovert who simply loves to play, whether it's penny slots, craps, or the big six, always rooting loudly for your money and making fast friends with other players at every turn? Or are you an Introvert, cool and calculating, playing blackjack, video poker, or baccarat on your own terms for your own reasons?

Perhaps you're a grim Introvert, who stands dark and determined at a crap table while everyone else is cheering and hooting, slapping high fives with their friends, and swilling and spilling beer after beer. Or maybe you're a flamboyant Extrovert, trying to yuk it up with a blackjack tableful of players concentrating on basic strategy or the count.

Some of these categories, of course, overlap. Thus, Henry's typology would identify the $25 video poker player I described at the beginning of this chapter as a Risk-Taking Thinking Introvert, and our penny slot gambler as a Feeling Flamboyant Extrovert. Both were certainly playing the right games for their gambling types.

I'd describe myself as a Frugal Insightful Extrovert, since I like to play video poker, focus on promotions and comps, and am friendly and outgoing to my fellow players—both at nearby machines and anywhere else on the casino floor I might wind up during my wandering breaks (as anyone who's ever met me in a casino will surely testify!).

But what about you? Are you playing the right game for your personality type? If you can apply the above typology to yourself in such a way that it fits, then you're on the right track. If, however, you think of yourself as a Flamboyant Competitive Risk Taker and you're playing roulette or slots, it might explain why you're not getting as much enjoyment as you want from a casino.

Extreme Gamblers

Unfortunately, some gamblers find themselves in a class they can't control. These are problem gamblers, men and women who become addicted to the action and go a long way toward ruining not only their own lives, but also the lives of the people closest to them.

Some psychiatrists consider an addiction to gambling the most dangerous and deadly psychopathology of them all—much worse than an addiction to cigarettes or alcohol or drugs. No one knows what causes one person to turn to gambling as an escape, then become addicted to it. What's well-known, however, is that some people should not gamble, because it causes problems in their personal lives. Many of these types can simply choose to eliminate it from their list of recreational activities. However, some gamblers—I've seen estimates anywhere from two percent of gamblers to five percent of the general population—find it difficult to make this choice on their own.

The purpose of this book is not to encourage anyone to gamble. What I try to do in these pages is to help people gamble smarter *if* they've decided to visit a casino and know they can handle it—which, after all, is 95% or more of all casino visitors.

The following is a list of 20 questions prepared by Gamblers Anonymous to help identify problem gamblers:

1. Did you ever lose time from work or school due to gambling?
2. Has gambling ever made your home life unhappy?
3. Has gambling ever affected your reputation?
4. Have you ever felt remorse after gambling?

5. Did you ever gamble to get money with which to pay debts or otherwise solve financial difficulties?
6. Did gambling cause a decrease in your ambition or efficiency?
7. After losing did you feel you must return as soon as possible and win back your losses?
8. After a win did you have a strong urge to return and win more?
9. Did you often gamble until your last dollar was gone?
10. Did you ever borrow to finance your gambling?
11. Have you ever sold anything to finance gambling?
12. Were you reluctant to use "gambling money" for normal expenditures?
13. Did gambling make you careless of the welfare of yourself or your family?
14. Did you ever gamble longer than you had planned?
15. Have you ever gambled to escape worry or trouble?
16. Have you ever committed, or considered committing, an illegal act to finance gambling?
17. Did gambling cause you to have difficulty in sleeping?
18. Do arguments, disappointments or frustrations create within you an urge to gamble?
19. Did you ever have an urge to celebrate any good fortune by a few hours of gambling?
20. Have you ever considered self-destruction or suicide as a result of your gambling?

This list probably will make most wise gamblers think, and perhaps even lead a few to change some of their gambling habits. However, most compulsive gamblers will answer "yes" to at least seven of these questions and, hopefully, realize they have a serious problem. Fortunately, help is available. Call the National Council on Problem and Compulsive Gambling's toll-free hot line (800/522-4700) and they will point you to a help program in your area.

Don't Change When You Walk into a Casino

Compulsive gamblers are an extreme version of people who undergo a personality change when they walk through the casino doors. But people who work in casinos, or play frequently, see variations on this theme all the time: the considerate person who becomes totally demanding of his host; the conservative businessman who loses control of his good financial sense at the high-stakes tables; the studious academic who plunges into playing a game about which he has never read one word; the ethical individual who suddenly decides that anything's fair in the gambling world; the dedicated mom and wife who begins staying too long at the video poker machines and neglecting her family ...

You're a pretty sensible person, right? You work hard at your job; you pay your bills on time; you shop sales; you budget your money carefully. Don't drop your common sense at the entrance to a casino. Take it inside with you and use the same careful consideration that you do in the outside world. Look before you leap; avoid making hasty decisions with your money. Guard against the temptation to abandon your conservative habits and the smart managing of your money.

Being in a casino is also not an excuse to lose your manners or become hard-hearted. Hang onto your human decency. An acquaintance of mine told the story of playing blackjack at a very crowded casino one New Year's Eve. People were standing around waiting for a blackjack seat to open. Suddenly, a man at the table next to his fell off his chair and clutched his chest in pain, obviously suffering a heart attack. Immediately, even before security arrived, a woman

King of Kindness Rules Even in a Casino

One day Brad was playing a 50¢ video poker machine when a woman came up to him with 10 pennies in her hand and asked if he would change them for one of the 50¢ coins that were filling his tray. He didn't know whether her math skills were weak or she was just desperate, but she looked so pathetic, he said, "Why sure, I really need some pennies for change anyway." He took the 10 pennies, put them in his pocket, and gave her one 50-cent coin. The lady was so happy she was crying and trying to hug him. That got to him—so he just reached into his tray, scooped out a whole handful, and put them in the lady's hands.

What happened next? She went her way, Brad kept playing, and in less than an hour he hit a royal. Unrelated? Probably. But who knows?

stepped over the man on the floor, put several chips on his blackjack spot, and proclaimed, "He's not playing anymore; go ahead and deal."

Of course, this is an extreme example of human callousness, but you might want to think about all your actions and attitudes in a casino and when you go home, look in the mirror. Do you like the person you become when you're gambling?

The Frugal Princess Weighs in on Serious and Casual Gamblers

Mom and I are very different when it comes to gambling. Mom is one of the rare few who are highly successful in this field, and she's taught me how to become a smarter casino visitor. However, as she's discussed above, she also knows that the vast majority of casino customers are recreational gamblers like me. Here's a quick look at how our individual situations differ in the casinos.

Priorities and Goals

My husband Steve and I go to gambling destinations once in a while for a few days at a time, so our goal is to have fun and be entertained. If it's Vegas or some other child-friendly area, we bring along our two grade-school kids. The whole family shares the common goal of getting as many amenities for free as possible. Our frugal and informed ways help us stretch the budget, but we still know we'll have to spend at least a small chunk of money on our vacation. Because we want to have a variety of gambling experiences, we sometimes play games that look interesting, even though we know the casino has the edge—something Mom and Brad almost never do. For example, we've been known to play those noisy Monopoly and Wheel of Fortune slot machines. But I'm well on my way to mastering the basics of video poker, which has become my main game of choice. I'm enough like Mom that the concept of losing less and winning more is as compelling as just having fun.

On the flip side, Mom and Brad play only the good games. Though they don't consider themselves professional gamblers, they know that they can make a modest profit by primarily choosing games with little or no casino edge, then combining them with promotions that will tilt the edge in their favor.

Visit Frequency

Steve and I get to visit a gambling venue for a few days at a time only a couple of times each year, so we have to cram all we can into short periods. We can take advantage of short-term promotions, such as scratch cards and double- or triple-point days, but not long-term opportunities. It takes us a few trips to build up slot club points at our target casinos, so we can qualify for fully comped rooms and meals.

Since Mom and Brad now live in Las Vegas, they have the time to rack up a large number of slot club points for comps and cashback. They can take utmost advantage of ongoing and just-for-locals promotions— for example, a casino may pay a bonus on quads collected over a whole month. They have the time to enter tournaments and can be present for numerous drawing dates. They can also establish long-term relationships with casinos and slot hosts.

Bankroll

In order for our itsy-bitsy bankroll to last several days, we look for things that help us stretch it, such as using coupons that give us a good edge on the house. Going on coupon runs keeps us busy and makes us feel like we're doing more gambling than we really are. We also feel that we must impose restrictions on how much we play at a given time. Hence, we ration our money, playing only portions of what we bring during any given session of play. This is not a strategy that enhances our expected return, but it works well for our limited bankroll and overall goals.

Having accumulated a large gambling bankroll, Mom and Brad are able to ride out the inevitable ups and downs of video poker and volatile short-term promotions. They can play until they get tired or have somewhere else to go, rather than having to quit because they run out of money. Even though Mom has been called the Queen of KuPon, it's often more profitable for her to play video poker where there's a good promotion than it is to run all over town chasing coupon offers, even good ones.

Our Shared Goal

Although I've been talking about the differences between Mom and me, there is one thing that she and I, and probably casino visitors in all categories, can certainly agree on: Casinos are exciting. And it's the hope of both of us that more and more gamblers will realize that, if you gamble smarter, you can stretch your time and money in these exciting places.

2

The Name of the Game—
Luck or Math?

"Luck never gives. It only lends."
                    —A Yiddish proverb

Defining the Term "To Win"

Everyone wants to get lucky and win. But not everyone means the same thing when they say, "I won."

Some mean that they've come out ahead in this particular gambling session or casino visit. But they don't say how much they've lost during other sessions or casino visits. Winners have a tendency to be talkative, while losers stay silent. A friend of mine takes a certain amount of money in his pocket when he goes to Vegas and expects to spend or lose it all. If he gets back home with any money, he feels he's "won."

Some people brag about their jackpots and conveniently forget about all the losses in between. I'm unimpressed by people who tell me they hit a $20,000 jackpot while playing $25 slot machines. It's very likely that if they'd played that denomination machine very long before the jackpot, they were in the hole more than $20K when it hit.

Newspapers, magazines, and casino newsletters publish all those photos of smiling "big winners." I skip right over them, especially those that say the winner had been playing only five minutes or had put in a single roll of coins. Did that jackpot get them even for all the years they've been gambling and losing? Is that a smile of relief that they'll be able to pay their bills that month? I wonder how long it will take before they feed all that money right back into a machine or lose it at the tables? Don't laugh. I heard that one Megabucks winner lost the whole jackpot trying to hit it again. The stories are rampant about big lottery winners who are broke or have to file for bankruptcy in just a few years.

The fact is, if you rely only on luck to be a winner all the time or in the long run, you're doomed. Luck is a phenomenon that can be identified in the past, but it's impossible to depend on it for the future. It's fitting—although a bit sexist—that a common metaphor for luck is a fickle lady.

Math, Not Luck—
Always the Eventual Winner in a Casino

Casino games are based on mathematical odds, usually odds that ensure that the casino will win in the long term. You may have been lucky and beat some of these odds in some past stretch of time, but that doesn't mean you'll continue to do so. The longer you play against the odds, the more likely you are to be a long-term loser.

Fortunately, this is not a hopeless situation, because you can gamble smarter, playing *with* the math instead of against it. One way is by choosing the few games and playing situations where the odds are with you and not the house. However, this takes a lot of serious study and effort, which many players don't want to put forth. Do you have to abandon math and go back to depending entirely on luck if you don't want to become a gambling scholar? Definitely not. Remember this: Losing less is a form of winning. If your main goal in a casino is having fun—and that's the goal of most people—then losing less will allow you to play longer and have more fun.

There are two very different mathematical ways to make smart decisions about what casino game you play: 1) by considering the house edge, and 2) by looking at the time element. If you have profit in mind, you'll be more interested in the house edge, while a purely recreational player will be looking more closely at the time element. Many gamblers wisely use a combination of the two.

Fighting the House Edge

Gamblers are not at war with the casino, but with the casino edge. Most games that a casino offers have the odds in their favor—after all, I've never known a casino to purposely be a non-profit organization. Therefore, most casino games are defined as negative-expectation games. That is, the long-term probable result for the player is that he will lose. However, there are a few opportunities where player skill or special knowledge can turn the math odds around, making a positive-expectation game where a player can have a chance of being a long-term winner. Opportunities may be found in a number of casino offerings:

Blackjack—Learn to count cards skillfully and you can get a small edge, .5%-1.5% on average.

Live poker—You're up against other players, not the house. Some of the opponents you encounter in poker games will be more ruthless than any casino in taking your money, but knowledge, experience, and patience can make you a long-term winner.

Tournaments that require skill—Often money-management (betting skills), more than playing expertise, is paramount. You're pitted against other players rather than against the casino. Although luck always plays a part in tournaments, the skillful players end up with more cash in the long run.

Race and sports betting—The spoils go to a few computer-savvy number-crunching experts.

Video poker—This is a fertile area where the odds can be in your favor, although not every machine you see will be a long-term winner. I cover this complex

---

Bingo

Bingo doesn't get the respect it deserves. There must be *some* reason why it's so popular, even in places where people can choose plenty of other casino games to play. There's a bingo game going on somewhere in Las Vegas any time day or night. And it's not just "grandma's game" anymore. You'll find almost an equal number of men and women playing in today's bingo games, and the bigger jackpots are pulling in a younger crowd to join the seniors who have always been the customer base.

What is the attraction of bingo? First, bingo is simple and takes no special skills—no study or practice required here. Second, it can be very inexpensive; you can play a long time by investing only a few dollars. The cost is a fixed amount that allows you to carefully control your gambling bankroll. Third, you have a shot at a big payoff. Finally, and probably most importantly, it can be a very social experience.

Bingo is not automatically a negative-expectation game. A savvy player in Las Vegas and other venues can watch for opportunities where high jackpots turn bingo into a positive bet.

subject in depth later in the book. You need to learn which machines to play, as well as the strategy for each type of game. This doesn't come easily—Brad and I have been video poker students the whole 12 years we've been playing the game. And you won't find "good" machines in every casino, or even in every casino area.

Slot machines—You can now find gold in a category that wouldn't even have been on the list just a few years ago. Slots of any sort used to be a sure-fire way to lose money. However, in the last several years, with the introduction of machines that have bonusing features, sometimes machines with "banked" credits can make a slot a positive-expectation play.

Negative games with a progressive meter—The jackpots can get high enough that it turns them into positive plays. This can include slot and video poker machines, Caribbean Stud (though the progressive has to be extremely high), and keno.

Any game with an extra—You might find a chance to turn the tables on the casinos and have the odds in your favor. This goodie list is endless: coupons, special promotions, cash or comp benefits associated with a slot club—I give examples throughout the book.

Iffy Ways to Get an Edge

There are some other ways people have been known to beat the casino legally. I call these the "iffy" techniques, because they present themselves so infrequently or take such an extreme amount of skill that they're useless for the average player. In some cases, it's controversial as to whether or not they're even possible.

Dice control—Craps is a game that possibly, for a very very few extremely talented and dexterous people, might be beatable by controlling the dice. It requires throwing the bones in a way that they can be controlled to a great enough degree to influence a small percentage of outcomes and produce an edge for the shooter. It's certainly not easy, as so many crap systems advertise. I think I'd have a better chance at becoming a world-class gymnast!

Wheel clocking—At roulette, some players have been able to clock a wheel and predict, with some accuracy, the quadrant of the wheel that the ball will drop into. They then load up the appropriate section of the layout with bets to get an edge over the house. This play might depend on the wheel having a "bias" (being out of whack in some way). Such conditions are very rare nowadays, as modern casinos spare no expense to calibrate wheels and eliminate biases. Some players knowledgeable in physics have tried, with some success, to apply high-speed computers to roulette to calculate where the ball will fall, but now computers are outlawed in all regulated casinos. Still others claim that it's possible to use a "dealer signature" method, which means finding a dealer who drops the ball and spins the wheel using the same routine all the time and using this information for prediction. The jury seems to be out on the effectiveness of this technique, though most experts appear to reject it.

The very fact that many casinos put up reader boards that track the results of past spins shows that they do not fear wheel trackers. Although all of these things may be possible, the number of people who have the skills is few, with even fewer having the patience to spend more time scouting and watching than playing.

Baccarat—Baccarat cannot be beaten by card counting and probably in no other way that would constitute a practical long-term system. Some pros, just as in blackjack, may be able to apply shuffle-tracking techniques (primarily in mini baccarat) and there are a few other super-sophisticated "moves" floating around.

But as in roulette prediction, these techniques can be mastered and applied by precious few.

Blackjack advantage play—Blackjack lends itself to many advantage-play techniques, among them various forms of shuffle tracking and "hole-card" play, as well as standard card counting. All of these strategies require copious amounts of study, skill, and practice.

Casino errors—Occasionally, a casino makes a mistake that allows players to get a big edge. I read of one extremely alert computer-savvy keno player who realized that a particular casino restarted its keno game each day at the same point of the computer program. He used this information to cash some very large tickets before the casino fixed its goof. A more common mistake and one that's more exploitable by us ordinary human beings, occurs when a casino offers a promotion that wasn't checked by someone knowledgeable in math—perhaps giving a bonus on certain video poker hands that gives players a juicy edge. This isn't really iffy, but you have to catch these mistakes early, because the casino usually finds and fixes them swiftly.

All the above techniques are legal, but they take special knowledge or extreme skill. In most instances, you would spend more time looking for such opportunities than actually playing them. Therefore, they appeal to few players.

Underhanded Ways to Get an Edge

All the techniques I've discussed so far are legitimate means to a positive-expectation end. But there have always been people, on both sides of the casino fence, who have tried illegal methods to achieve a win. Back when casinos were unregulated, operators would install roulette wheels with some sort of device under the table that controlled where the ball would stop. There has always been, and probably always will be, those who try to switch loaded dice in and out of a crap game. When the early slot machines appeared, cheats used mechanical gadgets to make the machines "pay on demand." When electronic machines showed up, the crooks also went high-tech, using electronic means to induce a jackpot. Someone makes a game, someone else tries to find its weak point.

Most illegal methods for beating casino games require inside information and surveillance countermeasures. In some instances, a cheat may work for a slot-machine manufacturer or a state regulating agency and have some inside information on, or even access to, the innards of machines. The casinos must be constantly on the lookout for employees who have a player partner they're "helping."

Notice that all of the above options, even the iffy and illegal ones, involve knowledge, study, and some kind of skill. There is no way to be a long-term winner at gambling by depending on luck alone!

Keeping the Edge Low

As I discussed earlier, many people are willing to budget some of their money to be entertained in a casino. They hope they'll win sometimes, but they're happy if their money just provides them with a long period of play. Still, "I would like to keep my losses down to an affordable level," they say. "Do you have any game suggestions for me?"

I'm so glad you asked. Here's a list of games and bets that keep the casino edge down to 1.5% or less— a long-term loss average that many gamblers would consider comfortable. That is, they're paying a price that's not too high for the entertainment it provides. The numbers in parentheses are the house edge for each game described.

Baccarat—Bet bank (1.06%) or player (1.24%). Don't

make the tie bet, which has a 14.4% casino edge.

Craps—Make pass/don't pass, come/don't come, or place bets on the 6 or 8 (1.5% or less). Adding single odds gets you down to .8%; adding double odds gets you down to .6%. Avoid all other bets, which can climb up to a wallet-emptying 16.67%.

Blackjack—Play according to basic strategy and the casino edge will usually be only about .6% or less, depending on the number of decks and the house rules. A couple of hints here: The fewer the decks being used, the less the house edge, and it cuts the house edge by about .2% if the dealer stands on soft 17.

Bad Blackjack

Special warning for blackjack players: Be careful and watch for blackjack tampering in casinos all over the country. Casinos might give the game a whole new name and throw in a bunch of new rules, but remove some cards from the deck (Spanish 21). Or they might give it a hyped-up name and more crazy rules, but pay even money on naturals (Super Fun 21). Both of these games put players at a greater disadvantage than standard blackjack. They might keep the same basic game, but add high-edge side bets to spice up the action (Royal Match). Or—the latest and most insidious move—they might advertise "single-deck blackjack" ("our players asked for it") but forget to mention, except for a tiny sign on the table, that they made one small change: They pay naturals 6-5 instead of the traditional 3-2. This seemingly minor change costs even a $5 player an extra $2-$3 per hour, depending on the speed of play.

Here's a money-saving rule of thumb to remember and heed: Any blackjack game with a new name, special new rules, or a side bet is almost sure to be the brilliant idea of some casino executive to increase a casino's bottom line. And you know where that extra money comes from—right out of your pocket.

Video poker—Many VP machines, if you learn even a simplified basic strategy, have a casino edge of only about 1%-1.5%. And this can be lower. For example, the casino edge in 9/6 Jacks or Better is .46% with computer-perfect play, 8/5 Bonus Poker is .83%, and 9/6 Double Double Bonus is an even 1%.

By using the slot club and comp systems heavily, playing the games listed above can get you pretty close to an even gamble. Better yet, players who are skilled in getting the "extras" can get into positive territory. Notice that the last two in the games list above require some skill. You have to study, at least a little, to learn basic strategy in BJ and for the VP games mentioned. Seat-of-the-pants play on either will increase the casino edge considerably to a bankroll-disaster level of 2%-4%, or even higher.

Other games or bets not mentioned in the list have edges large enough to ruin the budget of most ordinary gamblers if playing time is not limited. Remember, games of pure luck that have built-in casino advantages cannot be beaten over time. The longer you play them, the more likely you are to be a long-term loser. You have a much better chance to win at games that require knowledge or skill. But again, you have to study and practice.

Where the Casino Get Its Edge

Everyone knows that almost all gambling games are engineered so that the house has the advantage. Here are some of the ways the casino gets its edge.

• It pays off winning bets at less than true odds. The early gambling writer, John Scarne, made this amazing-but-true declaration: "Casinos do not make money from losers. The money it takes away from them is used to pay off winners. Their profit comes from paying winners less than correct mathematical odds."

For example, in double-zero roulette, the odds of the ball landing in any one slot on the wheel are 37-to-1, but casinos pay only 35-to-1 when you hit a number. On average, of every 38 chips you bet, the casino takes two as its "cut"—put that into an equation and you'll find that the casino has a 5.26% edge given this arrangement. Consequently, for every $100 you bet at roulette, over the long term you'll lose $5.26.

Sports parlay cards use this same method. For example, the true odds of hitting a three-teamer is 7-1. However, a common payoff for this bet is 6-1, giving the sports book a 12.5% edge on this wager.

• The rules are structured in the casino's favor. For example, blackjack rules require the player to act before the dealer. They also mandate that the dealer play in a prescribed fashion. These rules ensure that the casino has the advantage. Crap rules pertaining to which numbers are good or bad for you ensure that if you make 1,980 pass line bets, over the long run, you will win 976 of them and the casino will win 1,004. That's a differential of 28 bets, which is where the casino gets its 1.41% edge.

• The casino charges a commission or fee for making or winning a certain bet. This is sometimes done when the bet offered has no house edge or when the player has the advantage. For example, in the bank bet in baccarat, you have to pay a 5% commission if you win. Also, for all winning player bets in pai gow poker, a 5% commission is collected. The "juice" in sports betting comes under this category. In sports betting, you pay the fee up front when you make the bet: Put up $11 to win $10.

• The casino makes a pay schedule that favors the house—as is the case with most video poker machines. Sometimes changing a single payoff can turn a potentially profitable game into a sure loser. The classic example is changing the payoff for 4-of-a-kind in Deuces Wild from 5 to 4, which turns a full-pay schedule returning 100.76% to a pocket-emptying short-pay version returning 94.34%. Playing full coin on a quarter machine and getting $1.25 less for every 4-of-a-kind—a hand you make on average about every 15 plays—well, there's no mystery about where that extra 5.66% casino edge comes from on the lower-paying schedule.

• The casino programs a slot machine, with a particular chip ordered from the manufacturer, for a specific overall payback of less than 100%. You can't tell by looking at the name or denomination of the game what this percentage is. For example, two Blazing 7s machines in two casinos, or even in the same casino, may look alike, but contain two different chips and have different overall casino edges.

The Cost-Per-Hour of Gambling

Maybe you're less concerned about long-term profit/loss and more interested in trying to make your short-term gambling bankroll stretch as far as possible so you can have more hours of entertainment in a casino. If so, there's a better factor on which to base your choice of gambling game. You can look at the average loss per hour. This tells you the cost of your casino entertainment, allowing you to choose the activity that best fits your goals and your pocketbook. Recreational players, whose main purpose in a casino is to have fun, always look forward to a winning session. Even though they know that this won't always happen, they can still have fun if the loss, or *cost*, is affordable.

The table on the opposite page lists the average costs-per-hour for a number of casino bets, starting

Gambling Games Cost Per Hour

Sports betting/$11/$10 (4.5%) $0.25
Blackjack/$5, 1-deck, basic stragegy (0.2%) $0.50
Blackjack/$5, 2-deck, basic strategy (0.3%) $001
Keno/$1 (30.0%) $002
Craps/$5, place 6 or 8 (1.5%) $002
Craps/$5, line/pass or don't pass (1.4%) $002
Blackjack/$5, 4-8 decks, basic strategy (0.5%) $002
VP/25¢ Jacks, 9/6 perfect strategy (0.5%) $003
Craps/$1, hardway 6 or 8 (9.1%) $003
Pai gow poker/$5, player only (2.8%) $003
Big six/$1 spot (11.1%) $003
Slots/5¢ (9.0% average) $005
VP/25¢ Bonus, 8/5, perfect strategy (0.8%) $005
VP/5¢ Jacks, JoB 6/5 (5.0%) $006
Blackjack/$5, average player (2.0%) $006
Let It Ride/$5, base bet (3.5%) $007
Roulette/$5, Atlantic City dbl. 0 (2.6%) $007
Roulette/$5, single zero (2.7%) $007
Three Card Poker/$5, pair plus (2.3%) $007
Mini baccarat/$5, bank (1.1%) $007
Mini baccarat/$5, player (1.2%) $008
Video keno/5¢ (15.0%) $009
Let It Ride/$1, bonus (25.5% average) $010
Three Card Poker/$5, ante and play (3.4%) 0010
Caribbean Stud/$5, ante (5.3%) $011
Blackjack/$5, poor player (3.5%) $011
Caribbean Stud/$1, bonus (27.5% average) $011
Roulette/$5, double zero (5.26%) $013
Craps/$5, field pay 3x on 12 (2.8%) $014
VP/25¢ 8/5 Jacks, perfect strategy (2.7%) $017
Craps/$1, any 7 (16.7%) $017
Casino War/$5, go to war on ties (2.9%) $018
VP/25¢ Atlantic City joker, average player (2.8%) .. $018
VP/25¢ Jacks or Bonus, average player (3.0%) $019
Mini baccarat/$1, tie (14.4%) $019
Slots/25¢ (7.5% average) $022
Video keno/25¢ (8.0% average) $024
VP/25¢ wild card game, average player (4.0%) $025
Craps/$5, field pay 2x on 12 (5.6%) $028
Slots/$1 (4.5% average) $054

with the frugal activities and going down to the highest-cost games. This chart was adapted from the more extensive chart published in *The Frugal Gambler,* which calculates these costs based on the house edge and the speed at which each game is normally played. The indicated betting amounts are the normal minimums that you can usually find.

Choose the casino entertainment that you can afford and/or that fits into your losing comfort range.

Can a System Help Me Win?

The word "system" connected with gambling has a negative connotation and is often paired incorrectly with the words loser or scam. However, you can't dismiss all systems. Blackjack card-counting and video poker correct-strategy play could be called systems— and they work. Even a system that tells you how to make the best bets in craps and which ones you should avoid would help you lose less. So some systems can be valuable to gamblers.

How can you spot the bad systems? This isn't always a simple task, but here are some of the characteristics of charlatan systems:

• *It's easy!* There is no way to beat casinos that's easy—never has been, never will be. If someone did happen to stumble on one that anyone could do, the casinos would change the games, the rules, or the policies to plug up the hole so fast your head would spin.

• *It's secret!* "Only 200 people in the whole world are being offered this surefire way to win at XXX." We get these letters in the mail frequently. Why us? As gambling-product buyers, we're obviously on a lot of direct-mail address lists. But I seriously doubt that only 200 people in the whole world are offered these "surefire" winning systems.

• *You'll win every time you play!* One ad on the Internet said its system was "like going to the bank for a withdrawal." Why is the seller sharing this information? Shouldn't he be out there madly making his own withdrawals before the casinos catch on?

• *It costs more than $50.* A number of years ago before computers were common in the home and not much was written about gambling based on sound mathematics, some good blackjack systems for counting cards were worth the $100 or $200 being charged for them. However, today a wealth of published information is available on every aspect of gambling and almost any of the really trustworthy materials (books, software, strategy aids) can be bought for less than $50, most of it much lower. Of course, you need to be a savvy consumer, because some of the stuff out there isn't worth the price of the paper it's printed on.

• *It's a money-management system that promises you can beat a negative-expectation game.* Most of these come-ons offer up complicated betting systems that don't (and can't) change the math over the long term. A few might change the win/loss pattern so you'll have lots of small wins. But if you continue to use these systems, you'll lose, as the fewer, but large, losing bets will wipe out all of those prior small wins.

• *It's a progressive betting system based on raising your bets after a loss.* In a popular version of this, called the Martingale, you double your bet after every losing hand. The dealer can't beat you every hand forever, goes the thinking. No, but there's a good chance he can beat you long enough for your system to crash, either by reaching casino bet limits or by your bankroll hitting zero. This is one of the surest systems to use if your goal is to go broke.

• *It's a progressive betting system based on raising your bets after a win.* Many progressive systems that require you to increase your wager modestly after a win can safely be used to break the monotony of flat betting. But they cannot move a negative-expectation game into positive territory in the long term. You may have winning streaks, but over time, most assuredly, you'll lose an amount close to what the casino edge says you should, just as you would have had you been flat betting.

• *It has quit-and-start-again requirements that ignore proven mathematical theories about the long term.* Short-term goals can be a way of managing your bankroll and your state of mind. However, short-term sessions, all taken together, *do* add up to the long term, whether you want to believe it or not. The machines or the cards or the dice don't know whether this is your first hand in a new session or your thousandth hand in a long ongoing one. So the odds of the game do not change.

• *It advocates changing your machine or sizing or placing your bets only at specific times, ignoring math principles.* There are some valid techniques with this "choice" feature—blackjack card counting, for example—but they're based on sound computer-validated principles of mathematics. The arbitrarily chosen systems have no math basis. Wait for a crapshooter to make three passes, then jump in? The odds against you are not changed. Switch machines after you've won $150? In four hours of play on a slot machine, whether done all at one machine in one session or over a whole day of jumping from machine to machine, the casino edge remains the same.

With all that said, I'll now state that as long as you aren't fooled into believing that these "wait" or "jump around" or "start-and-stop" techniques will make you a long-term winner at negative-expectation games, there's a redeeming factor in many of these snake-oil systems.

I hear you: "I can't believe you said that, Ms. Stick-to-the-Math!"

It's true. I'm in favor of any system that slows down your rate of play on negative-expectation games, because the more downtime you can schedule, the less you'll lose. When you're doing something other than putting money at risk, you're saving money. But you don't have to spend your hard-earned money for some complicated system advertised in a magazine to do this. Make up your own system. You'd be surprised how interesting your own systems can be.

Crapshooters, bet only when an attractive person of the opposite sex has the dice. An ugly shooter comes up—just stand by.

If you lose three spins straight on a slot machine, punish the machine by cashing out and looking for a friendlier one.

If you're playing Double Double Bonus (usually a negative video poker game) and lose your first bill in, put the machine in "time out" and play the next one for 15 minutes before you go back to the naughty one.

Play roulette only if there's a blonde dealer.

Sit down at a blackjack table only if the dealer looks older than you. Depending on where you are, you might have to shop around a long time.

The point is, whenever you aren't actually in action at a negative-expectation game, you're "winning."

I've seen scores, maybe hundreds, of systems over my 19 years of casino gambling. A few are useful. Some are harmless, but a waste of money to buy. But most of them are cruel, giving false hope that will be disastrous to your wallet. Don't be taken in; most of these system promoters are selling dreams and fantasies. Nothing takes the place of study and practice and discipline.

How to Lose Less and Play Longer

Several common-sense rules can be applied to stretch your play time.

• Drop down in bet size. If you're losing too much or too fast on the dollar slots, switch to quarters—or switch from betting green ($25) table-game chips to red ($5).

• Change your game to a similar one with a lower house edge. If you switch from video keno to video poker, you can probably halve the usual casino edge (8% to 4%), even if you haven't studied proper video poker strategy.

• Play the same game, but look for a better version. Change to a single-zero roulette game where, over the long run, you'll lose about half what you would on a double-zero game.

• Stick with the same game, but choose better bets. In craps, bet the pass line with odds. This keeps the house edge under 1%, opposed to the potential double-digit disadvantages associated with hardways and proposition bets. You can still scream and holler just as excitedly when there's a good roll!

• Keep the same game, but study to play it more skillfully. Learning basic strategy at blackjack will cut the casino's edge against "seat-of-the-pants" players from 2%-3% to .5% or less.

• Look for gambling opportunities where you can make small bets at a very slow pace. In the keno lounge, you average about seven bets an hour and you can bet just one dollar (or less in some places) for an average loss of $2 an hour. In the sports book, you can bet $11 on a football game and have three hours of entertainment with an average loss of about 50¢. If you can't put away enough complimentary drinks to cover those losses, you aren't even trying!

• Take time to use gambling coupons. Yes, it's time-consuming, but you may find that the big edge that comes from coupons allows you to win more per hour than you can in any other casino activity. I'll be giving

Gambling and Life

Do you suppose you wouldn't gamble if there were no casinos or lotteries or other gambling opportunities? Think again.

Did you ever get married? Statistics say that one out of every two American marriages will end in divorce. Now those are some bad odds.

Have you ever ridden in an automobile? Worldwide, a half-million people are killed each year and 15 million are injured in traffic and road mishaps. The odds that you'll be one of them are low enough to keep you driving whenever necessary, but you're still gambling.

When you cross the street, you're gambling that you won't get hit by whatever might be wheeling around the corner. Of course, when you stay home, you're gambling that you won't fall down, get poisoned, drown, burn up, or die in bed (one in three do).

When you fly in an airplane, you're gambling that it won't fall out of the sky or be used as a terrorist weapon.

When you buy any kind of insurance, you're hoping that you won't need it, but gambling that you will.

Ever own a share of stock or a piece of a mutual fund? It's a form of gambling.

Ever had the urge to open a restaurant, a women's clothing shop, or farm the land? The litter of failed small businesses and bankrupt farmers is a blight on the landscape. These people gambled and lost.

The urge to gamble is one of the great conditioning factors of life itself. It's as central to the human condition as the urge to eat, drink, and procreate. The human race evolved in an environment of risk and danger and chance. And the physiological and psychological attitudes of readiness, the ability to take risks, to challenge chance, to plunge into uncertainty are survival traits favored by natural selection over something like 250,000 generations of Homo sapiens.

Life is a gamble. Casinos simply provide a way to gamble-without the risk of losing your life. As my friend Max Rubin likes to say, "Casinos give you a chance to dance with the Devil and live to tell the tale."

you more details on this in Chapter 7.

• Slow down your play. Sit at crowded blackjack tables, so you play fewer hands per hour. Pull the handles on slot machines instead of pushing the buttons. One slow-play technique I witnessed was classic: A couple hugged and kissed after every 4-of-a-kind in video poker.

Coming Up

I've talked about many different casino games in this chapter and ranked them in various ways. But slots are what the majority of casino visitors play the most.

So slot machines get the whole next chapter to themselves.

3

Not Your Grandma's Slots Anymore

"The casino of the future will look more like an arcade, full of complex entertainment devices that look little like present-day slots."
—*A slot machine industry executive at the turn of the millennium*

For many months, I thought I would just have to skip putting a chapter on slots in this book. I suffered severe writer's block every time I thought about the subject. For inspiration, I tried wandering around casinos, but there were too many new machines and they all looked so complicated. I read every book and article about slot machines that I could lay my hands on, but that served only to underscore the idea that they were getting more complex every day.

Finally, the Frugal Princess came to my rescue, pointing out that I was trying to write about something with which I really didn't have any hands-on experience. "You're always talking about how slots are such a losing proposition, Mom. But the truth is, they're *fun*. You shouldn't knock something if you haven't tried it."

"Ouch."

Not that Brad and I had *never* put money in a slot

machine. Brad had merrily played away at the slots the first time we went to Vegas 19 years ago, because he was under the impression—Lord have mercy!—that we were there just to have fun. As for myself, always too serious for my own good, I had just enough gambling knowledge to be dangerous. Thinking I was "too smart" to play slot machines, I chose blackjack, although I'd never heard of basic strategy, much less card counting.

Of course, we both smartened up after that and barely glanced at slots for many years, becoming, first, skillful blackjack players, then video poker students. Oh, we did some "wonging on piggies" over the last few years—translated, that means we played the Piggy Bankin' slots. We'd jump on these and other new bonusing slot machines when the bonus was high enough to make it a positive-expectation venture, not dissimilar from the video poker games we played. But even that wasn't just for fun, so it didn't count.

Anyway, at the risk of ruining my reputation, I'll just say that I finally took Angela's advice. Brad and I set aside a small "research" bankroll and used it to play slot machines. I talk about the nitty-gritty results of our research at the end of this chapter, but the most valuable effect was that my writer's block disappeared. Now I glanced around a casino and immediately saw unending subject matter. And the writings of slot experts suddenly became more understandable.

Speaking of slot experts, I want to acknowledge the tremendous help I received from so many gaming authors who lent their expertise on slots: Henry Tamburin, Dan Paymar, Frank Scoblete, Michael Shackleford, Bill Konad, John Grochowski, Charles Lund, and many others, writing in their own books or in magazines such as *Casino Player*, *Strictly Slots*, and *Midwest Gaming & Travel*. Fellow *Strictly Slots* writer

Frank Legato gave me a valuable "slot lesson" every month, explaining and chronicling the rapidly changing world of slots. And my special resource on gambling-machine technology was *The Slot Expert's Guide to Playing Slots* by John Robison.

A Short History of the Slot Machine

The birth of the modern-day slot machine is generally attributed to Charles Fey, a German-American who lived in San Francisco at the turn of the 20th century. Actually, Fey's Liberty Belle slot machine prototype didn't spring fully born from his imagination; Fey merely added some conveniences and extra touches to mechanical gambling devices already in existence. But for the most part, Fey's basic concept and design (single coin, fruit symbols, and stiff handle—the true "one-armed bandit") defined the standard slot machine for the next six decades. They're still beautiful machines—we have a Golden Nugget "Golden Doll" in our condo—and the grandkids think it's a real treat to be able to insert one quarter and pull with all their weight on the heavy handle.

In the mid-1960s, Bally's plugged slot machines into electrical outlets, providing the proverbial bells and whistles: light and sound effects and multiple-coin

---

Early Returns

In the early part of last century, some jurisdictions outlawed payoffs in cash, so slot machines often paid off in gum. The pictures on the reels indicated which flavor you won—cherry, lemon, watermelon, etc. That's where the fruit symbols originated. Other slots paid off in cigars. That's where the expression, "Close, but no cigar," comes from.

and multiple-payline capabilities. Though these electromechanical slots were the first real evolution toward today's high-tech versions, they still had a reputation as sucker bait: Quarter slots held upwards of 20% of the coin-in, and as late as the mid-'70s, slots accounted for only 25%-30% of casino profits.

Then, around 1975, dollar slots were introduced. Thanks to the higher handle (dollar value wagered), they could be set to hold a much lower percentage, paying off players more frequently and in larger amounts. By the early 1980s, the profit from slots had increased to nearly half of the casinos' total take.

The arrival of computers ushered in the New Age of Slot Machines. By the early '80s slots went fully electronic, first with a circuit board that controlled the actual reels, then with "virtual reels" that could hold untold number combinations, leaving the actual reels the players see with only a reporting function—telling them if they lost or won (and how much).

The '80s also saw the introduction of video slots. At first these were just video versions of standard reel slots—color video screens that simply pictured spinning reels. But they didn't catch on until the early '90s when Aristocrat, an Australian slot machine manufacturer that had popularized multi-line multi-coin video slots in its own country, introduced them to American gamblers in some Native Indian casinos. They spread from there to the riverboats. Now all major slot manufacturers are bringing out multi-line multi-coin (sometimes known as "Australian") video slots, and these colorful games, with entertaining animated scenes on the bonus screens, are the fastest growing type of slot machine in casinos today.

Slot machine developers have never stopped adding new features—credit play, bill acceptors, bonusing games, bigger and bigger progressives, creative themes, skill-based choices. The newfangled computerized slots have become so sophisticated that we recently saw a 20-line Australian video slot that can take up to 500 coins a hand! Change is the name of the game! Many new slot machines don't even have handles, just buttons to push. Should we now call them "one-button bandits"? In fact, the latest development, the coinless slot machine,

---

Slot Handle

"The slot handle itself is now a useless appendage, for practical purposes. It is rigged to feel like you're loading springs on the reels, but actually, you're only loading springs in the handle. When you've pulled the handle all the way down, regardless of how fast, slow, strong, or gingerly you've pulled it, it essentially touches its own "spin" button, activated when you let go ... [Most] slot makers have kept the handles on, because people still like to pull them—but it's tradition, nothing more."

— *Frank Legato, May 1999 STRICTLY SLOTS*

---

may cause a future generation to wonder about our name for this entertainment: slot machines that don't have a slot.

The ranks of slot players are growing larger every day. Slot machines account for upwards of 70% of both casino floor space and profits, earning more, much more, than all table games combined.

In *The Frugal Gambler,* I wrote that a slot machine is like a book—you must study it a bit before you can determine if you want to give it your time and attention. With so many new players and the increasingly complex games, there's an even bigger need for "library" skills as you browse in the slot machine aisles.

It's no longer a simple matter of dropping a coin into a slot and pulling a handle. You now have to be familiar with many different types of machines, their elaborate paytables, their added features, and yes, even strategies on some. Keep reading to find information that will help you navigate the new casino slot maze.

The Geek Talk— Machine Mechanics and Electronics

Meet the Slot Boss—the RNG

No, RNG aren't the initials of the human who supervises the slot department. The main internal electronic component of a slot machine is known as the RNG, short for random number generator. The RNG is actually a software program that runs inside the machine, continuously cycling through millions of numbers, even when a machine is sitting idle with no one playing. (That's why, contrary to popular belief, if you play a Megabucks machine for 10 hours straight, then leave, and the next person to sit down lines up the three Megabucks symbols on the first spin, it wasn't "your" jackpot.)

When you hit the spin button or pull the handle, you're stopping the RNG at a particular point in its incessant number-cycling activity. In that same split second the RNG is activating the external pieces of the machine, the parts you can see: the reels or the video screen. Slot machine reels, or the video images of them, do not decide whether you win or lose. All they do is show, visually, what combination the RNG was choosing the nanosecond you hit the spin button.

Actually, a slot machine doesn't really need to have reels or pictures of any kind. John Robison calls them "window dressing." A machine could easily be manufactured so that after you put your money in and pushed the start button, a message would appear on a little screen showing where the RNG was at that moment and what you won, if anything. I can picture a machine with an attitude: "Sorry, sucker, you didn't win a thing." Or, "You were lucky this time and won $10."

And to explode another myth, on most modern slot machines the RNG does not make different "decisions" based on whether you played one coin or full coin. This isn't the way it's always been; early machines made the choice when the first coin was dropped. However, most gambling jurisdictions now want the manufacturers to use what John Robison calls the "just in time" method. "Under this method," according to John, "the RNG is polled at the last possible moment before the outcome has to be decided"—that is, when the spin button is pushed or the handle pulled. So, it's true that you get a different result playing one coin than you would playing three, but this is only because the RNG continues to cycle while you're dropping coins. But it's the same random cycling that goes on all the time, so your result playing one coin won't be automatically bettter or worse than your result playing three.

Similarly, the RNG doesn't "care" if you have a slot club card in the machine or not, if you use bills in the validator or coins in the slot, if you push the Spin button or pull the handle, if it's your birthday or your anniversary, if you're feeling lucky, if you're carrying your rabbit's foot, or if you tap on the glass while the reels spin. Its job is simply to signal the reels where to stop based on the combination of numbers it selects the instant you play the game.

This "non-caring" RNG is what makes a machine random. Now, this isn't to say that a slot machine can't be programmed to be non-random. For example, a programmer can set up a machine to never line up the reels in a way that wins the top jackpot. This is illegal, however, in all regulated jurisdictions in the U.S. So it's extremely unlikely that any casino in a regulated area would risk losing its lucrative gaming license to do something of the sort.

Trying to Understand the Virtual Reel

Another important slot machine concept is the "virtual reel." In the old mechanical and electromechanical slot machines, the number of "stops" on the reels—the actual number of symbols and blanks—determined the odds of receiving a payout. You could count the number of stops to figure out the return percentages.

John Robison, in his book *The Slot Expert's Guide to Playing Slots,* has done the math for us. He tells us that the chance of hitting the jackpot on a slot machine that has only one jackpot symbol on each of three 22-stop reels is 1 in 10,648 (22 X 22 X 22 = 10,648). John continues, "The largest jackpot this machine could pay would be 10,648 coins." (He goes on to explain that it would actually be less, "because that number wouldn't allow for any lower-paying winning combinations or profit for the casino.")

So what if the casino wanted to make the jackpot higher? The slot maker could add additional reels to the machine: "By adding two more reels to the jackpot-only machine discussed above, the chances of hitting that jackpot decrease to 1 in 5,153,632." But there's a problem with adding more reels: "Slot players intuitively know that landing five jackpot symbols on the payline is less likely than landing three. Five reels may be the standard for most video slots, but reel-spinning slot machines with more than three reels never caught on."

So slot makers experimented with adding more stops to the existing reels. According to Robison, "By squeezing just three more stops onto each reel of the machine, the chances of hitting the jackpot drop to 1 in 266,200." But of course, there was also a limit to how many physical stops the manufacturer could jam onto a reel.

Enter "virtual reels." I like how John describes them. He says that in computer science, "virtual" means pretending you have something you don't have, but really need. "Hence, the computer program in a slot uses a virtual reel in its memory to pretend that the slot machine's reels have more than 22 stops."

Today, slot machine software provides for billions of possible outcomes, as if, in the words of machine expert Frank Legato, "The reels are miles long and have hundreds of thousands of symbols." According to John Robison, "The virtual reels in a slot machine contain from 32 to as many as 256 (or even more) virtual stops. Each blank and symbol you see on the real reel corresponds to one or more virtual stops on the virtual reel."

In addition, the reels can be "weighted," meaning that the programmers can tell the slot machine to favor some stops (the no-payout or even-money payout) more than others (the jackpot payout). This weighting feature gave rise to the "near-miss" controversy, in which the RNG was configured to select an above-average number of losing spins that gave two winning symbols and then a third one landing just above or below the payline.

Nevada regulators outlawed this practice, but slot manufacturers found a way around the restriction. According to Legato, the way this works is through a programming technique known as "reel mapping."

In most programs, each number selected by the RNG equals a complete reel result—for example, blank-blank-7. The programmer maps the position of symbols on each reel so certain results will show the jackpot symbols lining up just above or below the payline. The programmer then loads up the program with numbers that achieve the near-miss, thus increasing the odds that the RNG will select a number resulting in the near-miss. (That way the actual selection of the number corresponding to a result remains random.)

This is a good example of adhering to the letter, though certainly not the spirit, of the law. Regulators are beginning to examine all types of near-miss programming, which slot manufacturers are defending vigorously. The manufacturers maintain that near misses are necessary so that players will see "proof" that winning jackpots are possible

Payback Percentages

Discussions about the RNG, which cycles in a random fashion, and the virtual reel, which can be weighted to favor certain outcomes, seem to cause confusion about the meaning of the word "random." And random does have a different meaning when talking about slot machines than when talking about video poker machines. Video poker must, at least in Nevada where it's law, pay off according to the mathematical odds implied by the listed paytable.

Gaming regulations in each jurisdiction set the odds parameters on slot machines, which includes mandating the number of spins it takes, on average, to hit every possible payoff on the paytable. This is called the machine cycle. You cannot tell what these odds are, however, by reading the paytables. On slots, there is no way to know the odds of how often the top jackpot will hit. However, you can be sure that, in regulated jurisdictions, it is possible on any one hand to

get any pay listed on those paytables. This fact
the requirements necessary to make the machir
dom. That is, it's not programmed to give yo
particular payoff on any predestined hand—there is
no set "pattern" of payoffs.

What *is* programmed into a slot machine (and not
into video poker machines in most regulated casinos)
is the long-term or overall percentage of the action a
slot machine returns to the player. This is set at the
factory according to what the casino orders. According to John Robison, industry "percentaging models"
account for the different average paybacks that are
made available to the casinos by the manufacturers
for a particular slot game. Robison states that a two-
coin Wild Cherry machine, for example, has 11 different percentaging models available, with average
paybacks ranging from 75% to 98% and hit frequencies ranging from 16% to 20%. The importance of this
fact for slot players cannot be emphasized too strongly.
Though they pay back at different percentages, the
machines look exactly the same. *You can't determine a
slot machine's payback just by looking at it.*

It's important to keep in mind that this percentage
is averaged over the long term. As I've repeated many
times, the term negative-expectation, which applies to
almost all slots, means that you can't beat the casino
in the long term—though a player can and does sometimes get lucky and win in the short term.

All regulated casino jurisdictions set minimum
payout percentages for slots. In New Jersey, for example, the minimum allowable return is 83%; in Nevada, it's 75%. But because of heavy competition, almost all casinos offer much higher percentages than
these. If you're a Vegas local or live near a group of
riverboats and play slot machines several times a week
(and God help you if you do!), it would be wise to

consult the charts of return-percentage statistics in gambling magazines such as *Casino Player* and *Strictly Slots* to find the geographical location near you that has the best paybacks.

Some states break down the percentages by individual casinos, while others, such as Nevada, report only by regions. The monthly charts in *Casino Player* demonstrate, for example, that casinos in downtown Las Vegas and outlying locals neighborhoods usually have better overall payback percentages than the Strip. This general-area information is about as specific as you can get for Nevada and some other jurisdictions.

Interestingly, for the occasional recreational player, it doesn't really matter whether you're playing a machine where the payback is 94% or 96%, since even if you play every day, it would take you a very long time to notice a 2% difference in your results. John Robison says that it would take 10,000,000 spins before you could be reasonably sure of being within even one-half percentage point of that average payback.

Hit Frequencies

Hit frequency is different than payback percentage. Some people, when they refer to a machine being "loose," are confusing the two. Return percentage, as we've seen, determines how much of the customers' coin-in a machine retains long term. Hit frequency, on the other hand, tells you what percentage of spins returns something, even one coin.

Note that this doesn't mean the number of "winning" spins you'll get; many of the new video slots will give you lots of little returns that are only a fraction of the original bet. Thus, hit frequency is more connected to the perception of winning, than actual winning. There is no correlation between hit frequencies and payback percentages on most slot machines.

They may go together on some machines—high hit frequencies and high payback percentages—but you can also have a high hit frequency on a machine that overall has a low payback percentage, and vice versa.

When playing slots, it's a good idea to choose a machine with a hit frequency that matches your goals, so let's talk about the general categories of hit frequencies.

The traditional one-liner reel machines, which have a simple paytable with only seven or eight winning reel combinations, have the lowest hit frequency. You might hit a payout every seven or eight spins. But when you do hit, it's a true win, where you get back at least as much as you wagered on that spin. If there are wild symbols, your hit frequency will actually go down a bit, maybe hitting only every eight or nine spins, but your wins will often be higher.

You can tell the reel slots with higher hit frequencies by their more extensive paytables with more winning combinations. These can be one-liners, such as Red White & Blue, or multi-line reel spinners, such as Diamond Line Blazing 7s. They hit more often, every five or six spins, but you pay for the higher frequency with many little hits that are less than your original bet. When you see a slot machine with five payout lines or more, you know you have a frequent-hit machine, whether on video slots or the newer reels.

Which is better to play? If you have a large bankroll and a lot of patience and want a reasonable chance of hitting a fairly big jackpot once in a while, stick with the traditional low-hit-frequency reels that have the less-complicated paytables. However, if you want to stretch your time in the casino and like your slot sessions to have high entertainment value, choose the new multi-line video slots, many of which will give you a hit 50% or more of the time.

The Types of Slot Machines

Multipliers

Sometimes called equal-distribution slot machines, multipliers come in three varieties: single payline, multiple payline, and straight.

A single-line machine usually has three reels, accepts multiple coins, and pays off when the winning symbols line up on a single (center) payline. The payoffs are proportional (each payoff is multiplied by the number of coins played), except for the jackpot, which comes with a bonus when you play max coins. Double Diamond is an example of a single-payline multiplier.

Multiple-payline multipliers have more than one payline. Playing one coin activates the center payline. A second coin activates the top payline. Additional coins activate the bottom and diagonal paylines. Again, the payoffs are proportional, except for the top jackpot.

Straight multipliers can have either single or multiple paylines. The difference here is that there's no non-proportional payout for the top jackpot. If you bet one coin, the highest payout might be 1,000 coins; two coins pays out 2,000 coins and three pays out 3,000 coins. Straight multipliers are good for players who want to go from quarters to dollars to try for a higher jackpot, but want to play only one coin. They're not penalized for less than full-coin play.

Buy-A-Pay

Buy-A-Pay machines are tricky. Here, instead of activating different paylines, each coin you play activates a different set of payout symbols. For example, if you feed a single coin into a Sizzling 7s slot, you qualify to be paid off when certain combinations of bar symbols line up on the reels. But to qualify for a payout when the 7s appear, you need to play the second coin. With Buy-A-Pay machines, you should always play max coins—and study the payout display carefully so you know what you're shooting for.

Hybrids

These slot machines combine elements of the Multipliers with elements of the Buy-A-Pays. They always take at least three coins. Usually, if the second coin multiplies the payouts, the third coin activates additional winning combinations on the reels, and vice versa.

Progressives

Progressive machines are a casino's answer to the lottery. Although there are progressives with small jackpots, like Blazing 7s, the word conjures images of those with life-changing jackpots, such as Quartermania and Megabucks. Since a portion of every bet goes toward the big payday, less money goes toward funding the lower payouts along the way, so the "drain" on your bankroll—the amount you lose when you don't hit the top jackpot—is severe and fast. Frank Scoblete wrote these sobering words in the May 2000 *Casino Player:* "In order to generate such huge jackpots, in order to pay for the various licensing fees and profit-sharing arrangements, a Megabucks machine (or any large progressive) must return anywhere from 5 to 10 percent less than a comparable-looking stand-alone machine in a given venue."

Most people who play progressives such as Megabucks do so with a small part of their bankroll set aside for "taking a shot." They may not know the math, but they know from experience that their money evaporates far too fast to make these machines their regular choice.

There are different kinds of progressives:

Stand-Alone Progressives—People just won't believe that slot machines are random and that machines never become "due," even though the jackpot is higher than usual. On the other hand, I see people, especially with Blazing 7s, repeatedly pass up identical progressive machines with higher jackpots to play their "favorite" machine at close to reset (the point at which the progressive jackpot begins). I recently saw someone playing a $5 machine that had a $9,532 progressive jackpot, while on either side of him, identical machines had jackpots of $65,098, $39,247, $27,065, and $13,369. I'm sure this player hoped to hit the progressive. If I were playing these machines and hoped to hit the jackpot, I think I would at least try for the biggest one available. Wouldn't you? When lightning strikes, I want to be the happiest I can be! This reminds me of the advice I was given (and rejected) a long time ago when I was just a young girl: It's just as easy to fall in love with a rich man as a poor one!

In-House Progressives—These are progressives branded for a particular casino, or several casinos under the same corporate umbrella. For example, all the players at a bank of slot machines with a progressive meter at the Sahara in Las Vegas will be contributing to the same progressive jackpot.

Wide-Area Progressives—Megabucks is an example of a wide-area progressive: Upwards of 800 machines, owned and operated by International Game Technology (IGT), are scattered around casinos in most of the gambling jurisdictions in the country. The host casinos rake a cut of the action, but IGT pays off the progressive jackpot no matter where it's hit.

A common myth about wide-area progressives is that they're programmed to hit on weekends, or on holidays, or at newly opened casinos. Megabucks (or

Are You Sure You Want to Hit Megabucks?

Those of you who play Megabucks and dream of hitting a multi-million jackpot might want to read a book called *I Did It! My Life After Megabucks,* by John Tippin. Tippin is the "postal worker from Hawaii" who hit an $11.9 million Megabucks jackpot at the Las Vegas Hilton on Jan. 27, 1996. Though at the time it was a world-record jackpot and irrevocably changed the lives of John and his wife Stella, it's not a particularly pretty story.

Not only did John and Stella lose their trust in other people, including close friends and family (always suspicious of their motives), but those other people also lost their trust in John and Stella (thinking they'd become snobs or cheap). John and Stella had to deal with overt jealousies: "What did they do to deserve their wealth? Pulled a stupid slot handle!" And not surprisingly, since neither John nor Stella ever had to work again, they describe how they lost their sense of purpose (doing their jobs to earn their pay) and their sense of belonging (fitting in with their co-workers).

There were also the beggars, camping out on their doorstep with their hands out—some with terrifically heart-rending hard-luck stories (whether they were true or not was impossible to discern). And the thieves. Someone even tried to steal Tippin's identity by putting in a change of address in his name and rerouting his mail to a Las Vegas mail drop (Tippin's connections at the post office caught the scam in time to prevent a serious problem).

Of course, this is just one couple's story (though it's the only book by a Megabucks winner I know of). But it's an excellent cautionary tale, in case what you desperately wish for when you're playing for a huge progressive jackpot actually comes true.

The moral? If you do hit a once-in-a-lifetime life-changing jackpot, think long and hard before going public with your "good" fortune.

any slot machine in a regulated casino) is not programmed to hit at any certain place or time. More people play on weekends and holidays and at new casinos—so that's when and where the jackpots are more often hit. But once such a myth starts, it tends to perpetuate itself.

One final note about playing progressive slot machines. I want to ask this question of all of you who I see playing short coin (less than the maximum) on a progressive. Why would you ever play anything but max coin, unless you're a masochist and would enjoy suffering the pain of hitting the big one and not being able to collect it?

Special-Feature Machines

One of the earliest features added to the basic machines described above was the multiplying wild symbol, which doubled the posted payout when one wild symbol appeared and quadrupled it when there were two. This addition to Double Diamond, still the single-most popular machine on the casino floor, was the start of a trend to add something extra to a basic vanilla slot. Not content with these smaller multipliers, the slot manufacturers kept increasing them until we ended up with Ten Times Pay. People loved the illusion of getting paid extra, although this multiplication added nothing to the total payback.

Then there's the nudge feature. The most common example is a special breed of Double Diamonds—the old slot machine that has gotten more complicated. The original Double Diamond was a single-payline multiplier, a two-coin machine where the second coin had to be played to hit the big jackpot. Now there's Double Diamond Deluxe. Here, when diamonds stop just above or below the payline, they sometimes automatically "nudge" half a click up or down to land on the payline. This provides an extra bit of suspense at the moment of truth.

A newer nudge machine is the Big Cheese. When matching jackpot symbols line up on the first two reels and the third symbol lands one stop above or below the payline, that third reel nudges up or down to form the winning combination.

Lock and Roll is an interesting special-feature slot. These machines are found in Harrah's Cherokee Casino in North Carolina where, according to gambling writer Henry Tamburin, they "satisfy state laws requiring video games with a skill or dexterity feature." You can also find similar machines in Nevada and other states, with Hot Reels being one of the most common of these, which are sometimes referred to as "hold-and-spin" machines. With hold-and-spins, you're given a second chance to re-spin individual reels. They're similar to video poker, in that you hold the reels you don't want to re-spin and discard the reels you do. If, for example, the first two reels have jackpot symbols, while the third doesn't, you can hold the first two and discard the third, getting a second chance at hitting a winning combination.

"Pay-repeaters" are now being introduced as specialty slots. On Haywire machines, certain symbols lining up on the reels not only trigger a payout, but also "haywire" the machine, which repeats the payout. This gives you the illusion that you've been paid twice on the same jackpot.

Slot machine manufacturers are constantly adding new features to create excitement. But remember, no matter what these features are called or how much they sound like they'll give you extra chances for a jackpot, they do not increase your long-term payback—they simply distribute the same amount of money in different ways.

The Multi-Line/Multi-Coin Craze

Video slots are the new darlings of the casinos. First popularized in Australia, they were introduced to American gamblers in Native American casinos about 10 years ago. I remember seeing some of the early ones years ago at a riverboat casino, with their complicated pay schedules covering every inch of the glass payout display. I remarked to Brad at the time, "Those will never catch on; Grandma won't be able to figure out how to play them."

How wrong I was! I first noticed my error by observing the frantic rush of riverboat patrons to reach these machines. Many riverboats have special times to board, and even if you're young and strong and first in line during daytime cruises with senior citizens behind you, you could get run over by little old ladies and stooped-over men dashing up stairs to get to the nickel video slots. I watched in amazement as people waiting in wheelchairs in the handicapped line (they get to board first) got past the guards and jump out of their wheelchairs and start running! Once all the available machines filled up, I saw people two and three deep waiting and praying that someone would go broke and have to leave.

It's estimated that video slot machines account for about 30%-35% of all the machines on the floor of America's casinos. Many in the business think that, although reel slots will never disappear, video slots will eventually displace them as the primary type of gambling machine, attracting all kinds of players by the droves.

True, they're more complicated than most reel slots. So I suggest new players do as we did when we started our slot research—press the help button before sliding money into the bill acceptor and read about the game. Of course, you can just start playing and the machine will rack up the proper credits whether or not you know why, but we found that a little study of the help menu added to our enjoyment, since we then knew the best symbols to root for.

The experts tell us that it's better to play all the lines, even with just one coin per line, than to play only some of the lines with max coins. You don't want to see the symbols line up for a big payoff, then realize you didn't play that line. With these machines, however, unlike progressives, you can forget the mantra to "always play max coins." On these machines, the payouts are proportional, so you're not penalized for not playing max coin on each line. Furthermore, many of these machines have bonus screens, which is the reason I and most people play them. If you bet at least one coin on each line, you'll be sure to get to this fun action no matter what line brings up the bonus-game trigger symbols.

Penny Craze

Part of the allure of the multi-line/multi-coin machines is that some can be played for pennies. But don't let these penny slots bankrupt you! You may think you're safe from betting too much, but think again. Today's new penny slots often have only two denomination choices—a deceivingly low 1¢ or 2¢ game. The danger is that many machines allow you up to 250 of those 1¢ or 2¢ bets. Even at the 1¢ level, if you play max coin, that's $2.50—you're betting twice as much per hand than you would playing a regular single-line five-coin quarter machine. I recently saw an Aristocrat slot machine ad in a magazine for casino executives that touted its new 1¢ or 2¢ 20-liners that had a

500-credit-in capability. That means at max bet you could play $10 a hand, five times more than a dollar two-coin reel machine. The ad says: "Once again, Aristocrat leads the way with innovative products that increase your bottom line—these games are sure to enhance your profit." Remember, the ad was being pitched to casinos, not to players. When the casino is making more profits, guess where they're coming from. That's right—straight out of your pocket.

Penny games are great if you're a low-budget player, but only if you can discipline yourself. Don't be lulled into forgetting that credits are money—figure out how much money you're betting per hand, not how many credits. To keep your credits from getting so large that you're tempted to feel (and act) rich and invincible and bet too many of them, use only one small bill at a time to feed the machine and cash out when you accumulate a bunch of credits.

Also, keep in mind that these can be "fooler" machines, because of their high hit frequencies. You'll often get back something on every two or three spins. Note that I didn't say you'd *win* every two or three spins. If you're betting nine coins, one on each of nine lines, getting back three coins is a hit, but it's not a win. The danger here is what Frank Scoblete calls the "hanging-in-there" principle. "The unwary player will tend to hang in there longer, figuring he's bound to tag the big ones, since he's been hitting so often."

These new slots will give you more "time on device," the expression the slot machine industry uses to describe the length of time the gambler can enjoy the casino atmosphere by playing a game. And most people feel that they're getting good value for their gambling dollar on these new slots. Why? Because they can play—that is, be entertained—longer.

But remember that even though these video slots

often allow you to play longer on the same bankroll than the ordinary reels, ultimately they'll still swallow that bankroll. I remember reading a quote from a slot-manufacturing executive saying that these types of games are designed to "suck the blood out of the players slowly." Therefore, I give you the same warning that I give someone playing any casino game: Never bet more than you can afford to lose.

Fighting Slot Boredom with Bonusing

The new breeds of slots are also very big on bonusing. Bonusing is probably the most important feature ever to come down the slot pike and it has changed the total look and play of all kinds of machines. The plain-old reel-spinning slot machine—put in some coins, pull the handle or press the button, and see what the reels say you won—will probably never disappear completely. But as soon as the first "extra" appeared on a slot machine—a spinning wheel that landed on a bonus jackpot—slot machine players fell in love with bonusing. Wheel of Gold, introduced in 1995, was the first bonusing game and started the flood of creative bonus features we see on today's casino slot floor.

Although the spinning-wheel bonus is still used on many slot games—witness the continuing popularity of Wheel of Fortune—slot designers are thinking up new and creative techniques all the time for machines that give you a bonus chance at a bigger payout. There are large plastic bubbles on top of machines where the bonus amount is chosen, lottery-style, by bouncing ping-pong balls, as in Slotto, or tumbling dice, as in Roll the Dice. There are tall meters of bonuses on slot machines with a carnival look, like the Betty Boop Love Meter or the Bell Ringer. A game called Empire King has a tiny 3-D King Kong figure climbing up an Empire State Building to choose the bonus.

On some bonus slots, sometimes called "game-within-a-game" machines, the longer you play, the more bonus credits you accrue. Piggy-Bankin' was one of the first of these, as coins were "banked" during play and paid as a bonus when you got a "break-the-bank" symbol. The game Buccaneer works the same way, only you collect daggers and get the bonus when you complete the whole set.

It's very important to understand the bonusing feature on these machines, since you might be playing along, accruing credits, then inadvertently leave just when the bonus is about to pop. In fact, savvy advantage players often loiter near these slots, waiting for unwitting players to jack up the bonus, which they jump on and grab if the previous player leaves at an opportune time (see "Slot Wonging," page 67).

Although bonusing is popular on reel slots, it's on video slots where it has become a major draw. Second-screen bonus action with crisp graphics and a themed storyline is what makes video slots so popular. It's fun to try to catch a bigger fish to get a bigger bonus (Reel 'Em In), to collect more oil wells (Texas Tea), or to get more for an item we auction (Winning Bid).

Although bonusing makes a game more exciting, it's also popular because it provides a way to stretch your bankroll. You get additional entertainment for free, since you're not feeding a hungry machine more coins during the time you're watching the bonus. Every minute you watch a bonus instead of risking money, you're saving money!

Of all the changes in slot technology, bonusing has been the most firmly embraced by players. And it may be the one thing that will break down that tall wall between traditional reel-spinning slot players and those who play those newfangled multi-line video slots. Most slot machine manufacturers are bringing out hybrid machines that combine elements from both types, usually with a traditional reel spinner as the main game and a bonus game that acts more like a video slot. IGT has introduced the ultimate "teaching" machine for the I-don't-want-to-change reel lover, Double Diamond Run. The base game is the familiar five-reel Double Diamond and the top bonus game is a screen with the exact same symbols, but in video slot form.

Now comes the moment of truth regarding bonusing and the bottom line. I need to clear up a couple of common misconceptions. For starters, the word "bonus" here does not mean you'll win more. In order to award that bonus, the return on the base game has to be lowered. The total payback, base game plus bonus game, of these machines is in line with the other slots of like denomination in the casino. The bonus game probably provides more excitement and might allow you to stretch your fun time out a little longer. But it won't put any more money in your pocket.

I really hate to have to write about this next misconception; I feel like I'm telling a room full of kindergartners that there's no Santa Claus or Tooth Fairy. If

---

The Frugal Princess on Arithmetic

Here's a hint that will help those (like me!) who have a hard time doing the math in their heads when they want to convert credit totals to dollars and cents on nickel machines. Drop the last zero on the total and cut it in half. Did you just hit a 5,000-coin jackpot? Make it 500, then divide it by 2, and you immediately know you are $250 richer! How about a 4,000-coin royal? Make it 400, then divide by 2 to determine that you've just won $200.

you don't want to have your dreams spoiled, then you'd better skip these next few paragraphs.

Let's examine the Wheel of Fortune for a lesson. I often stop to watch when the bonus is activated on this machine; I bet you do too. You see the player and the watchers with big eyes, holding their breath as the wheel slows down near a big number. And when it just misses, you can hear the collective sigh of disappointment. I know most people think that the player almost had that big payoff, that if the momentum of the wheel had been just a little more, or less, the player would have hit "the big one." Casinos—and slot manufacturers—understand human nature; they know that furthering this perception will get people to play longer. "I'm getting so close! I can just feel that I'm going to hit the big payoff soon."

The fact of the matter is that the player had no chance of getting the big bonus on that particular spin, even though the wheel almost got to the largest number. Bonus wins are chosen the same way the base game chooses outcomes: by the random number generator. The bonus had already been chosen by the RNG before the wheel began turning. There's not an equal chance of the wheel stopping at any one of the bonus numbers. This isn't a mechanical wheel governed by the laws of physics; it's an electronic device governed by the RNG, operating the same way I talked about earlier in this chapter.

Frank Legato explained this in an informative article titled "Slots 101," in *Casino Player:* "The bonus you are getting has already been chosen by the RNG when you enter the bonus round. Some games even use a separate RNG program for the bonus round, and choose the result as soon as the bonus trigger lands. Either way, your bonus has already been determined."

True, there are some games in which your choice

does make a difference. The RNG picks a selection of bonus amounts on games like Jackpot Party, Little Green Men, and The Addams Family, and you get the bonus that lies behind the screen you choose. However, even with this system, there's no way for you to know which is the highest one, so there's no information that's usable.

This is true even on bonus games that seem to require some skill, e.g., the pinball slot. Frank Legato says that this is "perceived skill," because "it would be illegal in almost all gaming jurisdictions for skill and dexterity to gain a higher bonus; a level playing field is required."

Okay. All you dreamers can start reading again.

Slot Wonging

Long-time blackjack guru Stanford Wong popularized a technique of "back counting" decks by standing at a table without playing, counting the cards, then jumping in when the deck became rich in high cards, giving the player an edge over the house. This technique was dubbed "wonging" in his honor. In the recent past, since bonusing games have been introduced, the term "wonging" has migrated to slot machines.

In *The Frugal Gambler*, I wrote about how to wong Piggy Bankin' machines. To review, these bonusing games have a banking feature: As you play, credits build up in a bank and it's advantageous to play only when the bank reaches a certain level. On Fort Knox, Lady of Fortune, and Buccaneer Gold machines, unlike Piggy Bankin', the bonus doesn't increase. On these games, you look for machines where the steps you need to take to get to the bonus are fewer.

You can't necessarily tell just by looking at a bonusing game how it works or how wongable it is. This is why Charles Lund wrote his book, *Advantageous Slot*

Machines. In it, he tells you how to recognize when a particular bonus gets large enough to be advantageous to play, the best strategy to use, and when to stop playing. This is an extremely fast-changing area and most of the people who are successful playing these machines have joined a network with other people who do this in order to stay up on the new machines, changes, etc. Other than networking and Lund's book, where the information gets more dated by the day, I don't know of any other resources for getting information on wonging.

Unfortunately, many incidents have been precipitated by wongers turned "slot vultures." These are players who get a bit too aggressive in the pursuit of abandoned bonus machines—playing two machines at a time, burning out promotions by overplay, and even engaging in actual shoving matches and fist fights with other vultures when more than one of them is going for the same machine in bonus mode. I've heard about these treasure hunters pushing little old ladies out of their slot machine seats!

What's been the fallout from this behavior? Not only are some casinos taking the wongable games out, but most manufacturers are also actually redesigning their machines to limit the amount of wonging possible. So there are no longer as many opportunities as there were when these machines first appeared.

Still, I know of some people who do nothing but wong machines, and some make good money at it. It takes energy and patience and the right temperament, since you must continuously circulate around casinos, while spending a lot of time waiting and not playing. The average slot player will probably not be interested in wonging, although, if your bankroll is limited, it can be a good option to pass some time in a casino. Plus, you can sometimes use this wonging information to make more intelligent choices about which bonus machines to play. For example, from a row of Bingo slots, you should choose the one with the most bingo cards partially completed, or look for a Boom machine with the most firecrackers already displayed.

We don't make an effort to wong anymore, because we'd rather play than wait, and we find our hourly rate (machine return and slot club points and promotions) to be much higher when we concentrate on one high-paying video poker play. Still, we automatically check out the "piggy bank" when we pass one of our old favorites.

Slot Concepts

The False Concepts

More so than most gambling advice, many of the "insider tips on slots" you see are total bunk. Although much of this bad advice comes by mail in long letters with lots of bold type, I've seen too much of it in print and online by self-styled slot experts. The following is some of the more egregious slot advice I've read.

• "Try to find a machine that has had a lot of play, but hasn't paid out, so you'll be the one to get the jackpots, while the previous players have filled the slots full—just for you."

The fact is, what happened on the previous one spin or previous thousand spins makes not one whit of difference on a slot machine. Each spin is an independent event. Over the long term, the jackpot will hit a certain number of times, but you have the same odds of hitting it on the first spin after it's been hit as you do if it hasn't hit for several days. There's no chip (or conscience!) in the software that says, "Well, we haven't given out a jackpot for a while; let's do it now!"

A slot machine in regulated jurisdictions has to be random and random means you can't tell in advance what's going to come up on any one spin.

• "When a progressive is much higher than usual, you have a better chance of winning."

No, no, no! You never have even a good chance of winning a progressive. It's always a long shot! Your potential return improves as the jackpot rises, but you're fighting the same long odds on every spin, whether the jackpot is at reset or at a "life-changing" level. A progressive (or any other kind of slot machine) is never "due."

• "A slot will pay more if you pull the handle, rather than hit a button." Or, "You'll win more if you feed coins rather than use credits."

These (and, in fact, their opposites) are very old myths that will not die, no matter how many times gambling writers tell people that it's the random number generator inside the machine that dictates whether—and how much—you win on any one spin. However, believing these two myths could save you money! It takes more time to pull handles and feed coins, and the more time you spend with the mechanics of playing, the less you will lose.

• "Systems will help you beat the slots."

Go back to Chapter 2 and read again: No system can turn a negative-expectation game—and that includes slot machines—into one you can beat over the long term. A few money-management systems might

---

Did You Know?
A dollar slot player is as valuable to a casino in terms of expected win as a black-chip ($100) blackjack player.

---

help you lose less, mainly because you spend a lot of time doing everything but feeding a machine. But the majority of these schemes aren't worth the paper they're printed on. The only people making money on them are the charlatans who sell them. Don't waste your money.

• "You can make an informed guess about where the best-paying slots are located in any given casino."

I've read many varying opinions on this subject, even by respected authors, some of whom have interviewed slot managers. The advice for years has been to avoid the machines near the table games, the show and restaurant lines, and the casino entrance. Why? Because people tend to throw a few coins at them as they wait or pass by, so it doesn't matter if they're "tight." But I've also read just the opposite: The loose machines are placed where a lot of people can see them hitting frequently—yes, near the table games, the showroom, the restaurants, on a raised platform, or at the edge of high-traffic aisles. The idea is that this makes players stay to play the machines, because they think, "This casino must have loose slots—I've seen a lot of hits."

Some players believe that the good- and bad-paying machines are mixed together evenly, so if they aren't winning on one machine, they can move over to another that's probably looser.

The truth is, there's no generally accepted notion of machine placement. Each slot manager has his own ideas, nowadays more likely taking into consideration casino traffic patterns and eye-appeal of the machines. A casino does sometimes move machines around after looking at past results, but this is usually based on how much play the machines get, not on the payback percentage. A machine set at a higher overall return (for the customer) that gets played a lot will often make more money for the casino than a low-payback machine that doesn't get as much play. But there's no sure way for a player to know which is which.

The Be-Careful Concepts

Unlike the patently false slot concepts listed above, the advice that follows can be somewhat ambiguous. There might be a grain of truth in these statements, but you certainly can't count on them to be absolutely true 100% of the time. That's why I call them "be-careful" concepts.

• "You can usually assume that the better the paytables for video poker in a casino, the higher the payback from its slot machines."

Notice the word "usually." This correlation doesn't always exist. And, obviously, it isn't at all useful in selecting specific machines. But making this assumption can come in handy for selecting a particular casino, especially when there are several in an area to choose from.

• "The lower the coin denomination, the lower the percentage payback."

This is usually true. However, the more important consideration, especially if you have a limited bankroll, is money-lost-per-hour. So you need to consider more than just the lower return percentage. Slot machines have ravenous appetites and they like to eat fast. Obviously, the lower the denomination, the less you'll be feeding into the machine (on a per-coin basis).

• "Always play max coins."

As I've mentioned elsewhere in this chapter, this is correct advice on some slots and incorrect on others. John Robison has done a lot of groundbreaking work in this area and it's interesting to learn that you often aren't getting as much for a second or third coin as it seems, even on non-proportional pay schedules. However, even John admits that it's a psychological downer to line up the jackpot symbols on short-coin play and not get the big win that's displayed so prominently on the front of the machine. Sometimes psychological reasons override mathematical reasons.

• "You can trust casino signage and advertising."

This is another concept that falls into the maybe-yes maybe-no category. For example, if you find, in a casino in a regulated jurisdiction, a carousel with a sign saying that the return for all the machines is 98% or higher, you can trust this information. In regulated areas, gaming inspectors test machines to see that this is true. However, remember that this 98% return is over the long term and does not assure that you will not lose as much money in one short period as on any other machine in the casino. Similarly, if you see a sign on a machine claiming, "These machines paid back over 100% last week," that too can be trusted as fact. But again, it has no bearing on how anyone will do this week.

A story from an e-mail correspondent provides a good example of a notice on a sign atop a machine that was entirely true, but misleading. My correspondent was playing a nine-line quarter machine under a sign claiming, "Guaranteed Winner Every Time." Curious, he dropped his first nine coins into the slot and pulled the handle; the machine returned 15 coins. He dropped another nine coins in, and this time the machine returned two coins. When he asked a change person about the short pay, it was pointed out that he'd "won" two coins. Even though he'd lost the other seven, the casino considered it a two-coin player win.

Another misleading casino advertisement I once saw read, "Triple your chances to win! We've set our progressive Double Diamonds to pay three times as many jackpots!" Well, in the first place, casinos do not "set" their slot machines (neither the return percentages nor the hit frequencies). Manufacturers set the machines at the factory. Technically, the casino ordered special game chips from the slot maker. Semantics aside, however, this casino may have upped the number of jackpots, but to make up for it, they'd reduced the frequency of the smaller payouts. No matter what the ad said, you can be sure that the casino had set the total return to a percentage similar to other slot machines of the same denomination. Thus, you would not win three times more on this machine than on any other one. What would happen is that you would hit the top jackpots more often, but the drain in between them would probably break you before you could capitalize on the additional jackpot hits.

Trends— What the Future Holds

The slot universe is changing faster than an Indy 500 pit crew changes tires. Bill Fishman, a Mississippi casino executive, was quoted in *Casino Executive Reports* as saying, "Slots have changed more in the last five years than in the last twenty." It's fascinating—from both a writer's and a player's point of view—to track the changes and innovations in the slot machine industry and to try to guess where these trends will lead.

• Trying to explain the differences between a high roller and a low roller is getting more complicated. Once upon a time, a high roller played table games; slots were definitely for low rollers. However, slots are fast gaining prestige among high rollers—check out the $500 and $1,000 reel machines in some casino high-limit areas.

And wonder of wonders, those 45-coin video slots so popular with nickel players are popping up in the same areas, pumped up to the $5 denomination, with a max per-spin bet of $225! A high roller sitting at such a machine is playing at the same level as he would at a standard 3-line reel slot that takes $100 tokens. In fact, a slot whale making $225 bets per pull for *one* hour provides the casino with the same earning power as a $250-per-hand blackjack player playing for upwards of *nine* hours. You already see high-limit slot-salon players in their penthouse suites and long limos, right along with players from the velvet-roped table areas—and you'll see even more in the future.

• Since the new multi-line games allow for high numbers of coins to be bet, some casinos are starting to give better payoffs for lower-denomination games. As has been discussed, traditionally, the lower the denomination of a game, the lower the payoff percentage: Quarter games paid better percentage-wise than nickel games, casinos took a smaller percentage on dollars than on lower denominations, and so on.

But now a few casinos are taking into consideration that many nickel video slot players are risking more money per hand than those on quarter single-liners, so they've upped the payback percentage. This will be a boon for lower-level players who have the discipline to bet minimum amounts on these higher-paying multi-line slot machines.

• It doesn't take a genius or a clairvoyant to know that branding and theming will continue to be one of the major trends in slots. Slots based on nostalgic family games, such as Monopoly and Yahtzee, along with those based on game shows or an old TV series, such as "I Dream of Jeannie," "The Addams Family," and "I Love Lucy," are hot items today. When I wrote the rough draft of this chapter many months ago, I wrote next in this spot: "You will probably soon see machines based on new TV shows, like 'Survivor,' 'Who Wants to Be a Millionaire,' or—God help us—'Friends' in the near future." Well, I haven't seen any announcement of a Friends slot machine (although you may by the time you read this), but one company already has a Survivor slot and just a few days ago I saw Regis looking down at me from a big machine faceplate. Hey, I wonder if there will ever be a Frugal Gambler slot!

Humor is one of the best things the new slot machines brought to gambling and I see this continuing. For many years, gambling was fun, but it wasn't funny. Now our funny bones are tickled by an old wise-cracking codger with an attitude (Winning Bid), comical animated hayseed characters cavorting with background music from the old sitcom "Green Acres" (Cash Crop), and the ultimate in humor, a Three Stooges machine, with all the eye poking, slapping, and Curly Shuffles that have always made us laugh.

• I predict the further deployment of what I call the MMM Effect—multi-denomination, multi-line, multi-coin machines. The casinos love to mix different kinds of games so players who get bored easily don't have to move so often. And with these space-savers, one machine can give the player choices that only recently would have taken a hundred or more machines on the floor. Though it's a slam-dunk for the casinos, this can be a net loss for the majority of players, who'll play more in a specific period of time than was their usual habit. Also negative is the fact that it's far too easy to yield to the temptation to go up in denomination with just a touch on the screen, rather than having time to think about what's really best during the downtime when you cash out or move to another machine.

• I see the rise of more risqué themes. After a short

to-do about "kiddy slots" (Nevada gaming regulators squelching "South Park," for example), slot manufacturers may have decided to go the other way with definite adult themes. Aristocrat Technologies, an Australian slot maker, has introduced a game called Keep Your Hat On. It's a game-within-a-game slot, where a symbol of two screaming women (complete with sound effects) triggers the bonus screen that shows a male stripper surrounded by zippers. You touch a zipper, which reveals a piece of clothing tied to the bonus amount. What you try to do is pick zippers that remove the male stripper's clothes, in sequence (you can't take off his socks before his shoes, and so on), until all he's left wearing is his hat. (If you get to the end, the stripper discreetly turns his back as he removes his G-string, then turns back, with his hat covering the Little Fireman!) In mid-2002, the machine was available only in Atlantic City, and strangely enough, not in Sin City, but it's bound to spread to other jurisdictions soon. I imagine that there will be controversy over "adult" themes; as I write this, there's a fracas brewing over the possibility of a slot that features a popular brand of beer.

• Interactivity. No question about it, slot machines are becoming much more complicated in terms of player involvement. Instead of machines sticking to their reputation as no-brainers, slot developers are beginning to offer games that require some thinking. The lines between slots and video poker and between slots and popular non-casino video games have already begun to blur. Earlier in this chapter I talked about slots that require you to make a video poker-like decision; you hold certain symbols and take a second spin for others. And soon, machines might have multiple bonus screens triggered by specific combinations, not unlike video games with many different levels.

And the ultimate surprise? The introduction of slots that involve a skill factor, something that supposedly had been a no-no because of regulations that seemed to require an even playing field. I'm not sure how slot manufacturers are getting around this, but some new slots now give an advantage to the tactician or the knowledgeable. There's Ripley's Believe it or Not!, with a bonus-game trivia quiz. In this game, people with more trivia knowledge will do better than those (like me) who can never remember obscure facts.

Then there are games that by their name would seem to require skill. I had high hopes for the slot machine based on my family's long-time competitive passion, Scrabble, but I found no way to use my honed word skills; everything was controlled by that pesky random number generator. On the other hand, Cash King Checkers gives you a chance—not always, but sometimes—to think ahead and figure out moves that will give you more bonus credits.

Battleship, based on the children's game in which you have to sink a fleet of ships by shooting at squares on a grid, is the most fun for many because of the nostalgia factor, but it also attracts because you have a chance to use your brain. According to Frank Legato in an article in *Strictly Slots*, "A chart shows you how many grid squares each type of ship occupies. Once you find the first ship, you use the process of elimination to predict where other ships are likely to be hidden, based on the number and position of the remaining squares. This game employs abstract thought, short-term memory, even math." What shocking concepts for the player of a "mindless" slot machine!

• It could be said that today's gimmicks are just a glimmer of future possibilities. On a new machine based on the "I Love Lucy" show, when the bonus screen features Lucy in the famous chocolate assembly line scene, the odor of chocolate wafts through an opening in the machine. That machine might send you to another unusual slot machine I saw being test-marketed in a casino, called Pedal 'n Play. This game marries a traditional slot machine to a stationary bicycle that monitors how many calories you've burned. All the buttons to activate the slot machine are on the handlebars of the bike. The bike only works if the rider is playing the slot machine at the same time. Talk about sweating your losses!

Heavily themed casinos are the rage now. In the future, this same gimmick may be applied in a greater degree to areas within a casino, where change people, slot attendants, hosts, and floor managers dress in costumes that match a particular theme. There's already been a "Family Feud" area at MGM (though it's been removed). And at one time, the once-sedate Las Vegas Hilton actually fixed up a whole barnyard area, including real bales of hay, to contain all their Piggy Bankin' games.

• Another strong trend is group participation. Gambling machines are becoming less and less of an individual solitary preoccupation and more of a community experience. Of course, this is not a brand-new idea. I remember one of the first of these group-participation slot machines, the "world's largest slot machine" that used to attract crowds at the Four Queens in downtown Las Vegas. It's no longer there, but if I remember correctly, there were seats at six stations where people could bet credits or coins, then all root together as the eight giant reels spun on this huge machine. I also remember how much fun the big horse-race machines were, all of us sitting around the "track" cheering for our horses. And for years, the Big Bertha machines found at the entrances of some casinos always drew a crowd.

Now we have new games that continue this trend. Wheel of Fortune has become a group-participation slot machine; I've noticed that there are often as many interested watchers as players. People playing together on a bank of Elvis machines often stop, listen, and cheer whenever Elvis starts singing on any one machine. And there are "bonus zones," banks of machines or whole areas where everyone feels a kinship while waiting for bonus times or a secret progressive bonus to hit on one of their linked machines.

Remember the gimmick slot hooked up to the stationary bicycle? I can envision a whole health club full of them—Stairmasters, treadmills, rowing machines; you can't gamble unless the attached exercise equipment is in action. How about a virtual racetrack where everyone powers their cars with credits from slot play? The player with the most credits has the most power, so his car wins, triggering a bonus event. The sky's the limit!

This interest in group participation has already started to create a blending of table games and machines. Although video blackjack has been available on individual machines for a number of years, now popping up in casinos in many areas are large machines, such as Blackjack Blitz, that accommodate a number of bettors all playing their virtual cards against the same hand of an electronic dealer. There are also large video crap and roulette machines that allow this same group participation and camaraderie. The development of this "group slot machine" will grow quickly as long as there are jurisdictions that don't allow live table games.

• Space-age and computer technology will certainly lead to changes on the casino floor that I haven't even thought of. Virtual reality and laser games have already arrived at some of the most cutting-edge arcades and will probably make their way into the casino in my lifetime. And the possibilities that the Internet has already given us a glimpse of—well, I just don't have the imagination or the knowledge to predict the future of slot machines or the vocabulary to describe it. But Tony McAuslan, CEO of Next Generation Gaming, does: "Twenty years from now, you can expect the slot cabinet to be history. You'll probably be able to sit in a sort of 'Entertainment Pod' that features full sense-around sound and images, and maybe even a body suit with thousands of sensor points. The game will be a full-on assault of the senses." As strange as all this may seem, he adds one concept that we can see now very clearly: "The entertainment factor [will continue] to outstrip the gambling factor."

• The present trend that may represent the biggest technological change up to now is the recent rapid move to coinless slot machines. Again, as with so many trends, this concept is not brand new. Coinless slots were introduced at the MGM Grand in Las Vegas shortly after it opened in 1993, but players didn't like them. The ostensible reason was that they wanted to hear the sound of coins dropping into the hopper and they preferred to handle coins rather than receipts. Recently, however, coinless machines have been catching on, particularly with Vegas locals. People who play more often are willing to forego the sound of coins cascading into hoppers in return for the convenience of cashless vouchers and clean hands—although some coinless systems have added a very realistic coin-dropping sound effect when you cash out a ticket.

The standard belief has been that tourists coming for the total traditional experience are less likely to play more complicated new games or to accept coinless machines; they want the old standards and they want to keep their coin buckets. And in polls, people overwhelming say that they want to keep coins in their slots. However, wherever coinless machines are installed, they're very popular, even with tourists. Only time will tell whether the artificial sound of coins dropping will satisfy old-fashioned slot players who want to cling to the old ways. I'm guessing that most will welcome the transition after they've experienced the convenience of coin-free play for a while.

The casinos love coinless machines. The benefits to them are legion. They need far less floor personnel to fill hoppers and unjam coin dispensers. They need fewer employees to count, wrap, and move coins. The hard-count crew that exchanges full buckets for empty ones in the wee morning hours can be eliminated. The casinos can even reduce their coin inventory.

We didn't really understand all the benefits coinless machines have for players until the primarily coinless Suncoast opened in Las Vegas in 2000. To begin with, these machines save us time; there's never any waiting for non-W-2G handpays or hopper fills. In addition, there's no time-consuming scooping of coins from the tray and racking or dropping them into buckets when you want to quit, take a break, or change machines. (A useful hint: If you're cashing out a small amount that will be paid in coins, feed a bill into the machine to get to the voucher-only level.)

Coinless machines, believe it or not, also save us money—lots of it. That's because the tipping occasions are cut way down for our $1-$2 machine play. Likewise, they save us aggravation, because we no longer have to wait for a $1,000 handpay at the end of a $3,000 losing session and deal with phony congratulations from hustling employees. They also eliminate inconvenience: You can take a bathroom break, quit temporarily for a drawing, or meet someone for dinner without having to make major advance plans for cashing out. We don't have to carry heavy coin buckets and racks from machines to cashiers. And they keep our hands clean and my nails intact.

On the negative side, the vouchers are bearer instruments and they have expiration dates. In order to ensure that old tickets don't expire, we always make sure we cash our machine tickets before we leave the casino each day. And don't lose that voucher. Whoever finds it owns it.

Bad Idea

Not every new idea for slot machines is a good one. I've heard there is technology, already developed, that would allow players to insert their credit cards directly into the machine to buy machine credits. This is one future possibility that reaffirms my belief that just because something *can* be done does not mean that it *should* be done.

The Results of Our Slot Research

Now for the nitty-gritty results of our slot-playing research I promised you at the beginning of this chapter.

We set aside $200 for our bankroll and played four hours on various slot machines on a riverboat, over a period of two days. Not only did we not lose our entire $200 stake, but much to our surprise, we won $60.25 due to several small jackpots and one large one on Brad's favorite game, Filthy Rich.

We actually look back on those four hours with pleasure, but not because we won. The amount of that win was insignificant compared to the $7,050 we won playing $1 Five Play video poker those same two days. But what we remember is how much fun we had playing the slots, even on those machines where we eventually lost.

And—I might as well tell all—that isn't the last time we played the slots. No, we haven't given up video poker. That's still the casino game that entertains us 99.9% of the time—it's hard to beat having fun *and* having the expectation of winning over the long term! (I'll cover video poker in detail beginning in the next chapter.) But we still have some of that research bankroll left and it's provided some fun video poker rest periods since the research period ended more than a year ago.

When our brains need a rest from thinking about proper VP strategy, we can check out all the new video slots that are being introduced in the casino. We can avoid the frustration of waiting for friends delayed in Vegas traffic by turning to the casino version of the newspaper puzzle Jumble. If we find ourselves in a casino where there is no over-100% VP, we would definitely have more fun risking a small amount of money playing Battleship or Easy Street than a VP machine with an abysmally poor pay schedule.

And when our research bankroll is all gone, and it will go, I think I will make up a new gambling bankroll category. Maybe I'll call it our Just for Fun Casino Fund.

The Last Word on Slots

Although Steve Wynn is indisputably one of the most creative and successful casino developers in the world, having built the highly admired and much-visited Mirage, Treasure Island, and Bellagio, I have to be presumptuous and disagree with one quote attributed to him: "We are looking for reasons to make Bellagio and this town attractive to people who will think of Las Vegas as a deeper and more meaningful attraction. Because, let's face it, slot machines don't mean a damn thing anymore."

To borrow a phrase from the Three Stooges machine: "Nyuk, Nyuk, Nyuk!"

The Frugal Princess' Hints for Playing Slot Machines on a Budget

Play with Budgeted Entertainment Money—As with any gambling, my husband and I play the slots only with money we don't expect to have returned. No matter what anyone says, slots are programmed to give the casino the edge. We know we can't come out ahead in the long run, so we earmark some of our vacation budget for the entertainment of playing slot machines. It's no different from spending discretionary funds on going out to eat, seeing a show, or taking the kids to the movies. We save our main gambling bankroll for video poker, where we have a good chance for a long-term win. If we get lucky and win a few sessions at the slots, that's a nice little bonus.

Play With a Slot Club Card—We mainly sightsee and people-watch when we go to the megaresorts. We rarely play in them, though it's fun to slow-play nickel machines while sipping tropical drinks and eyeing all the beautiful patrons. We reserve most of our play for smaller casinos where we have a better chance of generating mail offers for free rooms or meals.

But regardless of the casino size, we always take the time to join the slot club, even if we're planning to play only a short time. You never know when you might hit a winning streak and play much longer than you expected your bankroll to last. You'll often be surprised by all the slot club goodies you can earn, since many casinos reward slot players by setting the slots to accumulate points up to twice as fast as VP machines. Taking advantage of all the slot club benefits, such as cashback, comps, and mail offers, helps offset some of your losses. If you like to switch back and forth between two machines, be sure to get two players cards so you'll never be playing without earning slot club points.

Study the Different Types of Machines—As Mom has alluded to, there are two different types of slot machines—reels and video slots. Each has its advantages and disadvantages, so it's a personal preference as to which you choose. Steve likes the one-line three-reel machines. He got lucky on these once and made his $40 session bankroll last all night while he tried to win a Harley-Davidson motorcycle parked right above his machine. On these types of reel machines, we play full coin unless we can find one where all the payoffs are equally proportional to the number of coins bet, so we can play only one coin without a penalty. If there's a jackpot or a bonus in the payout schedule, you need to play full coin, as Steve did while playing for the motorcycle. It's much too disappointing if you miss a big jackpot on a progressive or don't get to play the bonus game on a machine like Wheel of Fortune because you were playing short coin.

On the other hand, I think reel machines are boring, even if there's a big jackpot. I know these machines won't give me as many small hits and I know I don't have a very good chance of hitting the big one. If I'm going to risk (and probably lose) my money, I want to at least have some fun doing it—and watching reels go round and round isn't my idea of fun. So I mostly play nickel video slots, with their usually humorous and always entertaining bonus games. The first video slot I ever played was Little Green Men, where during the bonus round you might be abducted by aliens. It's still one of my favorites. Other particularly fun slots include Yahtzee, with the dancing dice; the kooky Addams Family; and Fortune Cookie, spiced up by the jokes of Mr. Lucky, the Chinese restaurateur.

Steve, on the other hand, likes the fact that although his three-reelers don't hit as often as my video slots, when he does hit he gets back at least the amount of his bet. He doesn't like getting so many hits on video slots that don't pay even as much as he put in for the hand. "That isn't a win in my book," he says. But he agrees with me that our money seems to last longer on video slots. So when we play together, a video slot is what we usually choose.

Use Time-Stretching Techniques—Because we play slots for entertainment, we've found some ways to budget our time so our entertainment seems to last longer. Here they are.

• Change machines frequently. We like to try the new bonusing games, but we often play just long enough to see what the bonus game is like on one machine, then move to a different one. Moving around creates downtime where we're not feeding coins to hungry slots.

• Choose games with long bonusing rounds. Scrabble, Word Jumble, and Monopoly have long bonus rounds, giving us entertainment for "free," since we're not risking money while we watch and play the bonus game.

• Just play slower. On reel slots, pull the handle instead of pushing the spin button. Cash out frequently and feed coins rather than using the bill acceptor or playing on credits. When your drinks come, stop playing to tip the waitress, then enjoy your drink for a while. This is the time Steve and I take to relax, people-watch, and make plans for later.

• Play on two machines if you have a partner, but

take turns playing while the other just watches. It's as fun to watch, especially on video slots that have bonus rounds, as it is to play. (This isn't so fun if you're playing reel machines, since watching reels spin can get pretty boring.)

• Look for small slot tournaments. Some casinos run inexpensive daily tournaments where risk is limited to the low $5 or $10 entry fee and you have a shot at a big payoff. Some tournaments are free. No skills are needed for these tournaments—just hit that spin button as fast as you can.

Choose Low-Denomination Games—It's a fact that regardless of the overall payback percentage of a machine, the less money you risk per hand, the less you'll lose. We usually play the lowest denominations—sometimes two- or three-coin quarter machines, but mostly nickels. When we're really low on bankroll, we look for penny slots. As Brad always says, "You can play one penny at a time and still order the best drinks in the house."

Make sure, when you sit down at a multi-denomination machine, that you're playing the denomination you want—your $20 won't last very long if you leave it on the $1 denomination the last person played instead of changing it to the nickel setting you planned on playing!

And be careful about the "just" temptation: It's "just a nickel" or "just a penny" slot. Pushing the max bet on multi-line multi-coin nickel, or even penny, machines can have you risking more per hand than dollar players. We like to play every line, but we stick to one coin per line to make our money and entertainment time last longer.

Set Firm Session Quit Times—Sometimes we're having so much fun that time gets away from us, especially if we're winning. But if we keep playing, often we lose all our winnings back very quickly and we regret not stopping while we were winners. So we set stringent rules for ourselves, *before we start,* as to when we'll quit playing a given session. Depending on our bankroll and day's schedule, these might be:

- when we earn a certain number of points, usually enough to get a certain comp, such as a buffet;
- when we lose an agreed-upon amount of money—usually only $10 or $20 at a time;
- when we've won a certain amount of money, perhaps doubling the amount we initially invested;
- when we reach a pre-set time;
- when we get hungry.

When we reach our "quit time," we find other fun activities to occupy us. We might go sightseeing, swimming, or window-shopping. People often don't get to enjoy their hotel rooms as much as they could, so we'll quit early for the evening and watch a movie, read a book, take a long bath, or just relax. And remember, Vegas is a very romantic city if you can forget about gambling for a while!

4

Video Poker—
Getting The Best of It

"Video poker is a gambling game where, for the most part, you get what you deserve."
—*Bob Dancer*

Video Poker Prelude

Do you want to explore a way to possibly win more on your machine play in a casino? Have you ever wanted to try video poker, but didn't know where to start? Here's a Question & Answer section for you.

Q: Why should I want to switch from slots to video poker?
A: Generally speaking, video poker players, even those who haven't learned how to choose the best

games or play using the proper strategies, lose less money per hour than gamblers who play slot machines of the same denomination.

Q: Why is that true?

A: Even the most uninformed video poker players will usually be playing at a *higher* overall payback percentage than they would be playing slots of the same denomination at the same casino. Need proof? Why do you think many slot clubs award fewer points for video poker play than for slot play? Think about it!

In addition, the thinking element in VP can slow down play; therefore, most people put less money at risk than they would playing a mindless slot machine over the same amount of time. (A possible side benefit: You might also feel smarter!)

Q: Okay, I'm interested. Still, I don't know anything about playing video poker. What do I do now?

A: I thought you'd never ask! How about a Video Poker Trial Run with me as your guide? Photocopy the next pages and take them to a casino. (This book was not written to be a decoration on a bookshelf or to collect dust on a coffee table. I would like to see it worn and dog-eared!)

If you have a gambling buddy, invite him or her along. If this buddy knows something about playing video poker, so much the better to help you. If he or she is also VP-clueless, two heads are still better than one. Make a copy of these pages for your buddy, then begin your Video Poker Trial Run together, using the bankroll you'd normally use for playing the slots.

CAUTION: I've given you some strategy suggestions in the Trial Run. If you decide to study video poker further, you'll learn that each VP pay schedule has its own unique computer-derived strategy that you must

play to achieve the best possible paybac
strategy chart I supply is only to be used
Trial Run; it is *not* suitable for subseque
I also suggest that you read *only* th
ing to do with the Trial Run. Please
further into the video poker section yet. Why not? Simply because there's so much information there that you'd put yourself in danger of giving up before you even start.

Finally, have faith. It isn't as hard as it looks, because you learn it gradually, one step at a time.

The More Frugal Gambling Guide for a Video Poker Trial Run

1. Instead of succumbing to your habit of heading straight for your favorite slot machine, look around the casino at various video poker machines. Choose one that fits the following requirements.

• It has only one play line. Multi-line machines, such as Triple Play, Five Play, or Fifty Play, are too complicated for beginners.

• It does not have wild cards, as in Deuces Wild or Joker Wild.

• It has a name like Jacks or Better, Draw Poker, or Bonus Poker.

• It's the lowest denomination you can find that has the preceding three characteristics. You don't want to risk too much money while you're learning.

Those with extremely small bankrolls can usually find a nickel game and bet just one nickel at a time. However, if you've been playing quarter slot machines, you might feel comfortable betting the full five coins on each hand (for a total bet of 25¢ per hand).

Sometimes the lowest denomination of video poker

. a casino is quarters. Unless you're used to playing dollar slot machines (with a very large bankroll), I suggest you play only one quarter at a time until you've studied more. (However, some people don't want to risk the potential anguish of hitting a royal flush and not getting the full-coin bonus!)

2. Once you've chosen a machine that fits the requirements above, sit down and study it. You'll notice that it has a paytable. It's usually printed on the glass, but sometimes on new machines you have to touch the screen on the word "Paytable" to bring it up on another screen.

If you've ever played live poker, even for matchsticks when you were a kid or for pennies with friends around your kitchen table, you're probably familiar with the ranking of poker hands—i.e., a flush beats a straight, a full house beats a flush, etc. Video poker games use these same hand names and pay a specified amount when you make them (usually paying more for the higher ranked hands). But not all VP schedules pay on the same winning hands, so you need to study the schedule to see which ones pay on the game you're playing.

Here's a list of hands in order of rank, from highest to lowest, for most video poker games. Note: Cards do not have to be dealt in any particular sequence; they can be mixed up in their order.

- Royal Flush: Ten, jack, queen, king, and ace of the same suit, in any order—K♦A♦Q♦T♦J♦.
- Straight Flush: Five consecutive cards of the same suit (need not be in order)—6♠7♠5♠4♠8♠.
- 4-of-a-kind (quads): Four like cards—A♦A♠A♣A♥X.
- Full House: 3-of-a-kind and a pair—3♥3♠3♦T♣T♥.

- Flush: Any five cards of the same suit— A♣3♣7♣J♣Q♣.
- Straight: Five consecutive cards, but not of the same suit (need not be in order)—9♥7♠5♣6♣8♦.
- 3-of-a-kind (trips): Three like cards—8♣8♦8♠XX.
- Two Pair: Two pairs of like cards—Q♥Q♣4♣4♦X.
- One pair of jacks or better: A pair of jacks, queens, kings, or aces—Q♠Q♣XXX.

Now you're ready to actually put money in the machine. (Of course, I don't have to tell you, do I, to first put in your player's card?) Simply feed coins or insert a bill using the bill acceptor to give you credits, the same as you do on a slot machine. Labeled buttons (usually) light up to show you what to do next: "Deal," "Draw," "Hold," or "Cancel." If you play one coin/ one credit at a time, you'll need to hit the Deal button to see your cards. The hand is automatically dealt when you play the maximum number of coins (usually 5) or hit the "Max Coin" button.

3. Next comes the strategy part, which is what differentiates video poker from the slot machines you're used to. In video poker you have a choice: You get to choose which cards to hold and which to discard, holding the cards you think will turn into the highest paying hand on the pay schedule by pressing the Hold button beneath each card you want to keep. Then you press the Draw button and the rest of your hand is discarded and replaced with new cards. Sometimes the five cards you end up with don't make a paying hand and you lose your bet. But almost half the time, you wind up with some kind of paying hand—anything from just getting your original bet back, usually with a pair of high cards (hey, a push is better than a loss!) to that rare but thrilling big-pay royal flush.

If you already know a little something about playing live poker, you might want to use your knowledge to help you decide what to hold. However, video poker is quite different from live poker, and I have to caution you against making two big mistakes. First, *never* hold a kicker (an unmatched card) when you have a pair, even a non-paying low pair. This rule includes even an ace kicker. High cards are valuable in video poker, but not in the same way as in live poker. And second, don't think you have to hold something from every dealt hand. You should throw away all five cards if there are no good possibilities to hold.

Here are some basic guidelines that will help if you have no idea what to hold.

• Always look first to see if you've been *dealt* a paying hand. Most machines light up the made hand on the paytable or note it above the hand on the screen; many also make some sort of sound to alert you. Hold only the cards (which can be from two to all five) in this paying hand. Now you're sure to at least get your money back. And if you can discard some cards for the redraw, you might end up with an even better hand.

The only exception to this rule is if the dealt hand also has four cards to that hoped-for royal flush. Here you can go ahead and take a chance: Throw away that sure pay—often a pair of jacks or better—and hold the four to the royal. Yes, most of the time you'll come up with a no-pay. Sometimes, you'll get back a small- or medium-pay hand, like a straight or a flush. But there's always the small chance—one in 47, to be precise—that you'll get lucky and pull that magic fifth card to the royal. That's VP heaven!

• If your first five cards don't include a paying hand or four to a royal, look for "good" non-paying starting hands. If you have two or more choices in one hand, choose them in the following order, starting at the top:

4 cards to a straight flush—10♣8♣9♣J♣X.
3 cards to a royal flush—J♥Q♥K♥XX.
4 cards to a flush—2♥4♥7♥9♥X.
non-paying pair (two 2s through two 10s)—
   2♣2♠XXX.
4 cards (consecutive, unsuited) to an open-ended
   straight—5♥3♣4♠6♠X.
3-card straight flush—2♣6♣4♣XX.
2 cards to a royal flush J♠Q♠XXX.

• If you don't have any of the above, you can look
for unsuited face cards (jack, queen, king, ace) and hold
as many as you find. (Remember an ace can be high or
low.)
• If you can't find any of the above, don't hold
anything and draw five new cards.

I can't guarantee that you'll win in this particular
first session of video poker, but win or lose, here are
the questions you need to ask yourself at the end of
the trial:
• Did I enjoy playing?
• Did I like the challenge of using my brain?
• Do I like the idea that I could study more about
video poker and have a better chance to lose less and
win more in a casino?
If you answered yes to all three questions, then you
can now start reading the rest of this video poker section. You've just become a student of video poker!

Choosing the Right Game

My first book, *The Frugal Gambler*, contains the true
"introduction" to video poker. In it, I explain the concept of positive- and negative-expectation games, how

to differentiate between the "good" and "bad" video poker machines by reading the paytables, the importance of learning the correct strategy for each game, how to pick your denomination, and how bankroll needs can be linked to the use of slot club benefits and promotions. If you're a beginning video poker player, there's still no better place to start your study than by reading that book.

But I wrote that stuff more than five years ago. Since then I've put in hundreds of hours of reading and practice, logged thousands of hours of VP play, and made the transition to higher-denomination machines. In addition, I've had to adjust to the constantly changing video poker inventories and policies in the constantly changing casinos. This section of the book is my attempt to share some of the things I've learned that can make it easier for you—whether an earnest beginner or an experienced student of the game—to become a better player in the brave new world of video poker.

Lenny Frome's Three-Legged Stool

The late Lenny Frome, truly the Grandfather of Knowledgeable Video Poker and my first video poker teacher (and close friend), left the world a large body of information about this casino game. Much of it consists of detailed charts and articles full of practical advice. Even though he was writing somewhat early in the development of the game, much of it is still useful to students of video poker today.

His most valuable legacy, in my opinion, was explaining video poker using the image of a three-legged stool. I heard him speak of this stool several times in public presentations. And every time I heard him, I was struck by how this simple object could describe such a complex subject so well.

I would like to keep his legacy alive by using this

image to explain the three main tenets that must be considered by everyone who plays video poker, from the casual recreationist to the serious pro. It's just as powerful today as it was years ago when Lenny first introduced it. The three legs to the stool are: choosing the right game, playing the right strategy, and knowing what to expect.

Cut off any leg and a three-legged stool would fall over, useless for any practical purpose. Similarly, ignore any of the three basics above and *you* will fall down when you play video poker.

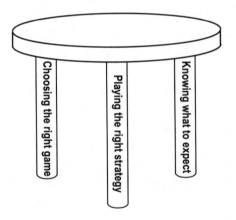

Definitions

The three legs are presented above in the order in which they need to be considered. But before we begin to choose games, I need to give you some basic definitions. These are just thumbnails that will help you understand some of the terms I use in describing specific VP games; later I discuss some of these terms in greater depth.

Expected Value (EV)—For comparison purposes, I put a percentage figure beside each game. This is commonly called the "expected value," or "EV" for short, of the game, although it would be more accurate to call it the "theoretical payback" or "average payback" of the game when you use a computer-derived perfect strategy for an infinite number of hands. We will discuss this more fully in the section of the chapter titled "Knowing What to Expect," so you'll understand what this EV figure really means when you actually get into a casino. For now, however, simply look at it as one way to compare games. (I've rounded *down* to two decimal places in most cases.)

Long Term—I use this phrase so often when I write about VP that I know my readers are probably sick of it. Simply stated, we refer to the "long term" as the length of time it will take to achieve the EV defined above. Theoretically, this would be after the play of a countless number of video poker hands. Later in this chapter, I'll talk about the practical considerations of long term as they apply to real-life players in real-life casinos, as opposed to never-ending play on a computer.

Negative and Positive Expectation—These are terms that describe any casino game, particularly video poker, depending on whether it has an EV, or theoretical return, above or below 100%. Any game with a theoretical payback above 100% is called a positive-expectation (or a "good") game and, using the correct strategy, provides a good chance to be a winner over the long term. A negative-expectation video poker game has an EV below 100% and by itself *cannot* be beaten in the long run. However, it's not necessarily a "bad" game; many times you can add enough slot club benefits and promotions to boost the overall EV to above 100%.

Volatility—Mathematicians talk about volatility by using the term "variance"—which describes how far your results can vary, good or bad, from the EV. I simply call volatility the "roller-coaster effect": How much you can go up when you're winning and, more important, how far down you might go when you're losing.

Low volatility means these ups and downs will not be so steep or frequent and therefore you can plan on needing a smaller bankroll to stay in the game. High volatility makes for a stomach-clutching ride up and down and demands a larger bankroll—as well as a continuing belief that the math *will* prevail, no matter how bad you're losing at any given time. This is one of the biggest problems faced by video poker players and this subject is discussed at length later in this chapter.

Strategy—Video poker strategy determines how you should play each hand, i.e., which cards should be held. Strategy charts are derived from computer calculations, using proven mathematical facts applied to innumerable trials. Deviating from these charts by playing "hunches" or "feelings" will reduce the game's EV and cost you money in the long run.

Drain—Drain refers to the amount of money you lose between jackpots. The whoosh of the money coming out of your billfold chasing the jackpots sounds just like water going down the drain!

Full-Pay, Short-Pay, and Super-Pay Games—"Full-pay" usually refers to a game with the best available pay schedule for that category; it can also refer to the pay schedule that is most common or was the original version. Note that it does *not* mean that it's a game with an EV of 100% or more; for example, 9/6 Jacks or Better (pays 9 coins for a full house and 6 for a flush) is a full-pay VP game, but the EV is only 99.54%.

"Short-pay" usually refers to a game with a paytable in which the house has decreased one or more of the payoffs from a full-pay schedule. Short-pay machines usually have EVs below 100%.

A "super-pay" game, usually limited in availability, is one that increases one or more payoffs to create a higher EV than the more common full-pay game.

Advantage Player—This is a person who plays only casino games that provide the player with a mathematical advantage, either on the game itself or when the game is coupled with extra benefits or promotions that put it over 100%.

Making A Good Game Choice

Lenny Frome always talked about how many different variations of video poker there were and how hard it was to keep up with the new ones. The last edition of his classic *Winning Strategies for Video Poker* listed 55 different pay schedules, but his head would be spinning if he were still alive today. New VP games are continually introduced to casino floors. Even though some of the games listed in his book no longer exist, there are still hundreds of VP pay schedules in casinos all over the country—and the number is growing rapidly, especially with the introduction of multi-game multi-denomination machines. Take a machine that contains 12 games, each with a different paytable. Add to that the fact that you can play each game in eight denominations, from a nickel to $25, with more changes to paytables. You now have 96 different games—in just this one spot!

There is real skill in choosing a good game. You can't just look at the name of the game (Jacks or Better, Double Bonus, etc.) to determine if it's "good"; there can be different names for the same schedule—and different schedules for machines that have the same name. You *must* learn to read the paytables themselves. And you will soon find out that you must look carefully at *every* line of the table. There can be differences anywhere, from the bottom payout to the top jackpot. Then, of course, you have to know (or know how to figure) the difference between the good schedules and the bad.

Another detail to look for is the ratio between the one-coin and five-coin payoffs on each machine. The payoff for five coins is *usually* five times the amount of the payoff for one coin on all payoffs except the royal, which traditionally gives a bonus for full-coin play. However, sometimes there's a bonus for five-coin play on other lines, particularly the straight flush. In this section of the book, I always refer to the payoff for *one* coin. Just remember that almost all of the max-coin payouts are multiplied by five. When there are royal and other full-coin bonuses, I list the payouts at one coin and five coins, separated by a slash: 250/4000. (Be careful; a few machines may require more than five coins to get the max-coin bonus on the royal.)

In this chapter, I discuss in detail just a tiny percentage of the VP games that you might see in a casino. I've chosen those that have the best paytables, or are the most commonly available, or are the most popular.

Jacks or Better (JoB)

"Plain-vanilla" Jacks or Better is the game that sparked the video poker craze. It's often called Draw Poker, but occasionally can have other names, such as Player's Edge. We often refer to the classic version as 9/6 JoB. Notice in the following chart that game #1 pays 9 for a full house and 6 for a flush (playing 1 coin)—this is where we get the 9/6 term that's bandied about so much. The reason we specify 9/6 is this: It so happens that, when a casino changes the paytable for its Jacks or Better machines, the place it most often makes changes is on the payoff for full houses and flushes.

This is a good "basic" game for a casual recreational player who wants to play a game with a strategy that's fairly easy to learn (JoB's strategy is more intuitive than

Jacks or Better-Type Games

	#1 JoB 9/6	#2 JoB 8/5	#3 Bonus 8/5	#4 Bonus 7/5
Royal flush	250/4K	250/4K	250/4K	250/4K
Straight flush	50	50	50	50
4-of-a-kind	25	25		
Aces			80	80
2s, 3s, 4s			40	40
5s-Kings			25	25
Full house	9	8	8	7
Flush	6	5	5	5
Straight	4	4	4	4
3-of-a-kind	3	3	3	3
Two pair	2	2	2	2
Jacks or better	1	1	1	1
Payback %	99.55%	97.30%	99.17%	98.01%

most other VP variations) and can be found in many of the casinos in Nevada, as well as in many other gambling locales. The JoB basic strategy can be used effectively on a few other games just as it is and on several others with a few modifications. Jacks or Better is a low-volatility game, which means money is likely to last longer in the short term than on many other games. It's the game Brad and I first learned.

Jacks or Better is also a good game for dollar (or higher) advantage players who want to get comps in luxury resorts. In many of the higher-end casinos, JoB is often the best game available on single-line, and sometimes even on multi-line, machines. Frequently, it's possible to get enough slot club benefits—cashback, promotions, upscale comps (or all three)—to reach an overall EV of 100% or higher.

The biggest problem with 9/6 JoB is that, although it's called "full-pay," it's still a negative-expectation game with its 99.55% return. (Though often quoted at 99.54% so it won't be rounded up to 99.6%, the actual return is 99.5493%.) It takes strong slot club benefits to bring it up to or over 100%. Played on its own, although less volatile in the short term, JoB is a definite loser in the long run. Another problem with JoB is that there are many versions, most of them extremely low-paying. The chart shows the effect on the EV when you cut the full house and flush payoffs, even by just one unit each (game #2).

Bonus Poker

Bonus poker is a popular variation of JoB, due to the bonuses for some quads. These give you more "jackpot" events that add to the enjoyment of the game and can bring you quickly out of a losing session. However, if quads elude you, you'll lose faster than on standard JoB, because the full-pay schedule takes away one unit each on the full house and flush—making it 8/5 instead of 9/6—to pay for those quad bonuses. And more bad news: These bonuses, even if you get the average number that the math dictates, will not fully make up for those cuts lower on the schedule, so you're paying for the "jackpot thrill" with a lower long-term EV of 99.17% (game #3).

As with JoB, lower-paying versions of Bonus Poker cut the full house or flush payouts even more, with the accompanying reduction in payback percentage—for example, the 7/5 version returns 98.01% (game #4).

Double Bonus (DB)

Although by the name it would seem that a double bonus game is an enhanced version of Bonus Poker—after all, wouldn't double bonus be better than just plain bonus?—I consider DB a different category, rather than an offshoot of JoB. Why? Because the return on two pair is now the same as it is for a pair of jacks or better: a return of your bet, rather than the 2-coin payoff on JoB games. Whenever the bottom part of a VP paytable is fiddled with, the game changes dramatically, because you get these lower-paying hands much more frequently than those at the top of the chart. When this occurs, there are two things to be aware of:

• The playing strategy usually has to be changed significantly.

• The farther down on the paytable a reduction is made, the greater the decrease in total EV—and it takes a lot of increase near the top of the schedule to make up for it.

The first Double Bonus game to show up (10/7/5)

Double Bonus-Type Games

	#5 10/7/5 DB	#6 9/7/5 DB	#7 9/7/4 DB	#8 10/7+80SF DB
Royal flush	250/4K	250/4K	250/4K	250/4K
Straight flush	50	50	50	80
4-of-a-kind				
Aces	160	160	160	160
2s, 3s, 4s	80	80	80	80
5s-Kings	50	50	50	50
Full house	10	9	9	10
Flush	7	7	7	7
Straight	5	5	4	5
3-of-a-kind	3	3	3	3
Two pair	1	1	1	1
Jacks or better	1	1	1	1
Payback %	100.17%	99.11%	97.74%	100.52%

intuitively became the choice of many Bonus Poker players, simply because the name implied a higher payback. However, it also became the preferred choice of many knowledgeable JoB players when they input the paytable on their computers and saw that the EV jumped into positive-expectation territory at 100.17% (game #5).

There are a couple of problems with DB, however. First, this expected long-term return is dependent on playing extremely accurate strategy, and the DB strategy chart is at least twice as complex as the chart for JoB. There's a long learning curve here—most players need long-term practice on computer software and continued reference to strategy cards during actual casino play.

Second, DB is extremely volatile, due to the decreased payout on two pair at the bottom of the schedule to make up for the increased payouts for the quads at the top. If you don't get your share of quads, you're dead. Most players agree with video poker authority Bob Dancer that this is an "ugly" game.

Still, many VP students have made the effort to learn DB:

• It's widely available in Nevada (except on the Vegas Strip), from quarters to dollars and sometimes higher.

• It's occasionally available outside of Nevada.

• It's sometimes found on multi-line games and with a progressive jackpot.

• It's challenging, and the assorted secondary jackpots on all quads keep your interest up and can bring you out of a losing spell quickly.

Double Bonus is often the basic game for knowledgeable dollar players, especially in Nevada where it's often the highest EV game available at that level. It can be played in many casinos that give cashback, and sharp-eyed and organized advantage players can combine it with slot club promotions, such as double points, to boost EV. Careful, however! The complex strategy and high volatility also combine to require a hefty bankroll.

Many machines labeled Double Bonus are low-pay versions. In the chart, I've given a couple of examples: 9/7/5 (99.10%—game #6) and 9/7/4 (97.74%—game #7), for example. DB is a game where you have to be especially careful to check the *whole* schedule. Casinos

Danger Alert!

	9/6 **Jacks or Better**	9/6 **Double Bonus**
Royal flush	250/4000	250/4000
Straight flush	50	50
4-of-a-kind	25	
Aces		160
2s, 3s, 4s		80
5s-Kings		50
Full house	9	9
Flush	6	6
Straight	4	5
3-of-a-kind	3	3
Two pair	(2)	(1)
Jacks or better	1	1
Payback %	99.55%	97.81%

Look at the two games here. Many beginners have heard that 9 and 6 are the numbers to look for in a video poker schedule. But these payouts must be accompanied by the 2-for-1 payout for two pair. This is the case in Jacks or Better, but not for a low-pay version of Double Bonus, which returns only a push for two pair. Notice the difference in EV!

are good at making cuts where you might not expect them, e.g., on the straight rather than (or in addition to) the usual full house and/or flush.

Conversely, sometimes you'll find schedule changes that surprise you with an *increase* in EV: 10/7 paying 80 coins for the straight flush is a super-pay version (100.51%—game #8) found on some Gamemaker multigame machines. It's often difficult to spot this version because the bonus on the straight flush is paid only if you play full-coin, and the whole schedule doesn't appear on the screen until 5 coins are actually inserted.

Double Double Bonus (DDB)

According to casino slot executives I've spoken to, DDB is the most popular video poker game in any casino. Is it because players win twice as often? Twice as much? Look at the low long-term payback listed in the chart on page 110 (98.98%—game #9) and you'll see that neither is the case. The reason this game is so popular is that players love the big jackpots that come with the addition of the "kicker hands" in the pay schedule. So they play their beloved Double Double Bonus even when the common 9/6 version is reduced to 9/5 (97.87%—game #10), 8/5 (96.79%—game #11), or lower.

But as usual in video poker, you pay a high price for the fun of an extra jackpot hand, in this case aces with a kicker, which appears on average only about every 16,000 hands. Most people who play at a medium speed of 500 hands per hour will see this hand about every 30 hours or so of play. And during the long time in between, that sucking sound is the money being pulled out of their wallets at a high rate of speed.

Who chooses this game? Plain and simple, players who want more thrills in their VP play—long-term EV be damned. I have to be truthful here. I simply don't

Double Double Bonus

	#9 9/6 DDB	#10 9/5 DDB	#11 8/5 DDB	#12 10/6 DDB
Royal flush	250/4K	250/4K	250/4K	250/4K
Straight flush	50	50	50	80
4-of-a-kind				
Aces w/ 2, 3, or 4	400	400	400	400
2s/3s/4s w/ A-4	160	160	160	160
Aces	160	160	160	160
2s, 3s, 4s	80	80	80	80
5s-Kings	50	50	50	50
Full house	9	9	8	10
Flush	6	5	5	6
Straight	4	4	4	4
3-of-a-kind	3	3	3	3
Two pair	1	1	1	1
Jacks or better	1	1	1	1
Payback %	98.98%	97.87%	96.79%	100.07%

understand how people can endure the long losing periods while waiting for these rare mini-jackpots. And most DDB players have never studied the proper strategy for the game, so they aren't playing anywhere near the computer-perfect EV. Double Double Bonus proponents are recreational players who hope to hit the mini-jackpot before their bankroll disappears. No jackpots? It'll definitely be a short session.

A few players I know have taken the time to learn the correct strategy for the 9/6 version in order to get close to the computer-perfect 98.98% EV, heavily using promotions and the slot club and comp systems to exceed 100% total. But this takes so much determination and study and practice that most players don't bother. Most DDB players not only end up losers in most short-term sessions, but they're doomed to lose in the long term.

Recently, a new super-pay version of DDB has appeared, with the full house increased from 9 to 10, yielding an EV of 100.06% (game #12). This is good news for those well-bankrolled kicker-loving players who can be patient between the mini-jackpots.

Deuces Wild (DW)

Classic Deuces Wild, with an EV of 100.76% (game #13 on page 112) is the best-paying quarter game commonly found in Las Vegas. Playing DW with very accurate strategy, you can be a long-term winner without cashback, promotions, or comps. Add those extra benefits and you have a big edge over the casino. Though these games are widely available in Vegas, they're found mostly in the locals casinos; don't waste your time searching for them on the Strip.

DW is a popular choice, not only for its high EV, but also because it has a good mini-jackpot (quad deuces), which can catapult you out of a losing spell without getting a royal. In addition, I believe Deuces Wild is the easiest VP game to learn (other contenders are JoB and Pick 'Em). The strategy chart is logically divided into four sections, according to the number of deuces in the dealt hand. That's all the organization I need to neatly compartmentalize the strategy in my mind.

Disadvantages? Full-pay Deuces Wild is rarely found outside Nevada. And even in Las Vegas, it's rare to stumble across this game in denominations higher than quarters, though some 50-centers (actually 10-coin quarter machines) pop up occasionally. The game is now practically extinct on multi-line machines. DW is also more volatile than Jacks or Better and therefore takes a larger bankroll to play within reasonable risk-tolerance levels.

Deuces Wild

	#13 Classic Deuces	#14 Really Ugly Ducks	#15 Still Ugly Ducks	#16 Fooler Deuces	#17 Not So Ugly Ducks
Natural royal	250/4K	250/4K	250/4K	250/4K	250/4K
Four deuces	200	200	200	200	200
Wild royal	25	25	25	20	25
5-of-a-kind	15	15	15	12	16
Straight flush	9	9	9	9	10
4-of-a-kind	5	4	4	5	4
Full house	3	3	4	3	4
Flush	2	2	3	2	3
Straight	2	2	2	2	2
3-of-a-kind	1	1	1	1	1
Payback %	100.76%	94.34%	98.91%	98.94%	99.73%

"Ducks" is the popular nickname for Deuces.

There have been many super-pay versions of DW in the past, but they're extremely rare these days. But watch out. Many DW games short the pay schedule for a much lower return. Many versions are known as Ugly Ducks ("Ducks" is a popular nickname for Deuces). Just one change—dropping the return for 4-of-a-kind from 5 down to 4—sends the payback plummeting by more than 6% to 94.34% (game #14)! Even if casinos sometimes assuage this pain by adding a unit each to the flush and full house, you're still up to just 98.91% (game #15) . And sometimes they'll try to fool you by keeping the bottom of the chart the same, including that all-important 5 for 4-of-a-kind that people have learned to look for. Many don't notice the drop on 5-of-a-kind from 15 to 12 and the drop on a wild royal from 25 to 20. These "Fooler Deuces," as I call them, pay back only 98.94% (game #16), still in the ugly category.

There is, however, a bit of good news in the Deuces department. A fairly new and already popular schedule is popping up in many casinos all over the country. VP expert Skip Hughes labeled it Not-So-Ugly Ducks (NSUD) and the name has stuck. This schedule has an average long-term return of only 99.73% (game #17)—not a positive-expectation game—but it's not hard to find it in a casino where slot club benefits push the total return over 100%. NSUD is often the best-paying dollar-and-up game in a casino and it's sometimes found in multi-line machines. Finding this opportunity to go back to the Deuces we loved in our quarter-VP days, albeit a different variation, is a real treat for Brad and me these days.

Joker Wild (JW, also called Joker Poker)

There are two main types of single-joker games. The easiest way to distinguish between the two is to look at the last paying combination on the paytable. If the lowest hand is kings or better, this is the game, sometimes called Vegas Joker Wild (although it's

---

The Battle Between Deuces Wild and Double Double Bonus

One reason you won't lose as fast on Deuces Wild as you do on Double Double Bonus is that you're playing DW at a theoretical EV of 98.99%, even if you *don't* hit a royal. That's higher than the EV of Double Double Bonus *with* the royal counted in. If you play DDB when classic DW is readily available, you're paying dearly for the thrill of those infrequent jackpot hands.

---

found in other places), which has a positive-EV full-pay version (100.65%—game #18). Occasionally, a super-pay version (101%—game #19) is found—these pay 4700 with five coins played for a natural royal flush. More frequently, though, you'll run into low-pay versions of Joker Wild that run in the 96%-98% return range. Once thought to be an endangered species, good Joker games have started to appear in multi-lines and multi-game machines.

These Joker Wild games have difficult strategies and are among the most volatile of VP variations, but good versions can pay the serious VP student well. Casual players tend to like the game because of the wild card, and it offers a couple of intermediate jackpot hands: the wild royal and 5-of-a-kind. In addition, the straight flush comes along fairly frequently and pays 250 for 5 coins just like in JoB, where it's much more rare. Some feel that JW is less boring than Deuces.

The second type of Joker Poker has 2 pair as the bottom-paying hand. It's often called Atlantic City Joker Wild, because it's one of the most common games in that city, although it's occasionally seen in other jurisdictions. On this game, a royal flush is counted as merely a straight flush and the top-pay jackpot is 5-of-a-kind. It's popular because you hit the top jackpot much more often than on other VP games, on average about every 11,000 hands versus the 40,000 for Jacks or Better. However, the severe drain between jackpots shows up in the low EV of 97.19% on the best pay schedule (game #20). Sometimes there's a progressive on these games, which raises the EV, but also raises the already high volatility. And, of course, there are decreased paybacks on many schedules, with much lower EVs.

There's also a Double Joker game in Atlantic City,

Joker Wild

	#18 Classic Joker Wild	#19 Super-Pay Joker Wild	#20 Atlantic City Joker Wild
Natural royal	250/4000	250/4700	100
5-of-a-kind	200	200	800/4000
Joker royal	100	100	100
Straight flush	50	50	100
4-of-a-kind	20	20	16
Full house	7	7	8
Flush	5	5	5
Straight	3	3	4
3-of-a-kind	2	2	2
Two pair	1	1	1
Kings or better	1	1	
Payback %	100.65%	101.00%	97.19%

with varying pay schedules. Those with EVs close to or over 100%, however, are becoming very difficult to find.

All American

This game offers a more "natural" payoff schedule than JoB, since in Jacks games you get about the same number of straights, flushes, and full houses. The strategy is difficult to learn, but some players like its challenge and its 100.72% return (game #21). All American has limited availability in Las Vegas and is found in a few other casino locations, some where it may be the best game in town. Watch out for a short-pay version that drops the quad payback to 30 and the EV to 98.48%.

Pick 'Em

Pick 'Em is a relatively new entry in the constantly expanding VP field. It's usually found in multi-game machines and is a great choice for both beginner and advanced players in many gambling locales where, with this schedule (99.95%—game #22), it's sometimes the best game available. Play it with good slot club benefits and promotions and you have a nice edge. However, be careful to read the paytables carefully—short-pay versions are beginning to show up.

Pick 'Em plays a little differently than regular VP, as you're dealt four cards instead of the usual five. Your finished hand will include the first two cards dealt (you can't discard them) and your choice of the third or fourth card (you can't keep both). After you throw away one of those cards, two more cards are dealt to form the familiar five-card hand.

Many find this game boring and frustrating, since

All American and Pick 'Em

	#21 All American	#22 Pick 'Em
Royal flush	250/4000	1000/6000
Straight flush	200	200/1199
4-of-a-kind	40	100/600
Full house	8	18
Flush	8	15
Straight	8	11
3-of-a-kind	3	5
Two pair	1	3
Jacks or better	1	
9s or Better		2
Payback %	100.72%	99.95%

a high 66% of the hands turn out to be non-winners. The big 6,000-coin royal (for 5-coin play) comes up very rarely and you can play long periods without getting a quad, making the short-term very volatile. However, the long-term volatility is lower than even JoB, because the royal and straight flush together contribute less than 1% to the total return, as opposed to most VP games where the royal alone usually contributes about 2%. In addition, the strategy is one of the easiest to learn, so you can speed along and rack up slot club points (and comps) at a fast pace.

Progressives

Any VP game can have a progressive jackpot. This added bonus is usually on the royal, but sometimes there will be multiple progressives, with meters on several of the other top hands. Occasionally, you'll find a progressive on a full-pay schedule, such as 9/6 JoB or 10/7 DB. In these cases, the progressive jackpot is always a true bonus. But more commonly, the progressive will be on a short-pay base game, such as 8/5 JoB or 9/7 DB, and you'll need to know how high the progressive jackpot has to rise before the game is as good as its full-pay counterpart. Playing VP progressives is a highly specialized skill and takes much study and a proportionately higher bankroll than playing non-progressive games.

Reel Deal

I hate to put this game in a chapter on VP, but I do so as a warning. It's a hybrid—the main game is ostensibly video poker, but when you hit certain hands, the machine goes into a "bonusing" mode where you spin the reels of a slot.

I ran across the following ad in a magazine for casino executives: "Reel Deal gives you more control of your floor by offering a wide variety of hold percentages with identical pay schedules."

Yikes! This is a video poker player's nightmare. After all, the reason we trust VP in most regulated jurisdictions is that its outcomes are random; the machine has to deal cards off the top of a freshly shuffled deck. This means that the pay schedule can be analyzed mathematically in order to determine the theoretical return of any game. But if you add a slot machine reel, there goes the math factor. I consider this kind of game (and any other VP machine with a bonus feature that cannot be analyzed mathematically) a cruel trick! I don't say you shouldn't play it, but don't imagine you're playing VP—you're really playing a slot machine that has a VP component. And the VP component usually has a very low-paying schedule that the occasional big bonus will not overcome long term.

A Good Play Versus a Good Game

By now, you may have the hang of identifying the best games—but that's only the beginning in deciding what to play. Knowledgeable VP players always take into consideration slot club benefits and promotions in addition to the EV of the game they choose. Locating a good play is often wiser than merely settling for a good game:

• There aren't as many 100%+ games as there used to be, so you often need the extra benefits to turn a negative-expectation game into a positive-expectation play.

• Even if you're playing a 100%+ game, in most cases the higher the total EV of the play, the lower the volatility and thus the lower the bankroll you'll need.

• A lower EV game with good benefits might be a wiser choice than a higher EV game with few or no additional benefits.

How Can I Keep Up?

With hundreds of different VP pay schedules in casinos all over the U.S., potentially more than 200 in one large casino alone, how can you tell where the good ones are? How can you pick the best one quickly without a time-consuming search? Tough questions. Even the most up-to-date book would quickly become outdated. You'll get some current information in *Strictly Slots* magazine, the *Las Vegas Advisor*, and other gambling resources, but there's really no printed source you can refer to when you find a new game and want to know its EV and an accurate strategy for playing it.

Lenny Frome's *Winning Strategies for Video Poker* did a good job for me up until 1997, but then I finally had to break down and buy a computer so I could use the available VP software. Several programs have been released over the years, each one improving on the last and adding new features. I'm proud to be closely associated with one of the latest, *Frugal Video Poker* by Jim Wolf. This video poker tutoring software is chock full of features that can help you become a better player. I'll talk about many of them later, but the basic features will help you mightily in your search for good games.

First, the program gives you the paytables and EVs for the vast majority of popular video poker games. However, if you find a game with a paytable not listed, you can simply input it into the program and, within seconds, get the game's EV. You know immediately whether it's a good game for you to learn or one to steer clear of. Furthermore, another valuable (and unique) function is that it can figure the value of the slot club cashback and add it to the returns from any paytable, so you can choose not just a good EV game, but the best EV *total play*.

The second advantage the computer gave me was

access to the Internet, where there's an abundance of information about the changing world of video poker. The best site, by far, is Skip Hughes' www.vphome page.com, a VP gold mine. It's not enough to know what the good games are; you also need to know where you can find them. Along with a ton of other useful information, this site has a full-pay VP chart listing casinos all over the U.S. that offer good games. It's a must resource for any serious player and a big time-saver for recreational players.

Bob Dancer, one of the foremost video poker experts today, says, "Surprisingly, choosing a machine with the right pay schedule is the most important element in winning video poker. Playing so-so on a good machine is much better than playing perfectly on a bad machine."

I, too, always emphasize the critical importance of game choice. However, you want to learn everything you can to play better. So, next we'll talk about learning how to play correct strategy, the second leg on our VP stool.

Playing the Right Strategy

Q: Why is that second leg of our video poker stool, correct strategy, so important?
A: Casinos win at least 2% more from uninformed video poker players than they do from those who play accurate strategies. The reason a casino can offer 100+% games is that most people play by the seat of their pants and go by feelings and hunches rather than mathematically correct strategies.

How does that 2% translate to dollars and cents? (Nerd Alert: Try to follow the math here; the money you'll save is worth a little wrinkling of the forehead!)

Let's say you play a slow 400 hands an hour on a quarter machine, playing full-coin, $1.25 per hand. Multiply those two numbers and you find that you're putting $500 an hour through the machine. Two percent of $500 is $10. This means that although sometimes you lose and sometimes you win in any one-hour session, over the long term you're *losing*, on average, about $10 more per hour than if you played accurate strategy. (You lose even more if you play faster.)

So how many hours do you play VP in a casino in one year? If only a couple, then this consideration is no big deal; I'm sure you don't miss that $20. But what if you go to a riverboat or Native American casino several times a month or take a few multiple-day vacations each year to a major casino area like Las Vegas, Atlantic City, or Biloxi? Many people put in a total of 50 hours a year on video poker machines. Is $500 a significant amount to you?

What if you play dollar machines instead of quarters? Multiply the above result by four. Now you're unnecessarily losing an average of 40 mind-boggling dollars per hour—$2,000 a year if you play just 50 hours!

Although these figures may vary some depending on the game you play, your natural mathematical bent, and your card sense, *everyone* who hasn't learned a computer-generated strategy will lose more money. And this holds true whether you're playing a negative or a positive game. In the long run, *everyone* would win more or lose less if they knew accurate strategy for the VP games they played.

Have I convinced you that strategy is important? If so, you now face several major issues.

First, video poker strategy is not intuitive (and having live-poker experience is not very helpful; in fact, it can be a hindrance at times). Second, each VP game has its own unique strategy; there is no easy one-fits-all version. Third, you have to study to learn correct strategy and this is not a task you can buzz through in just a few minutes. Fourth, most people, unless they're computer-savvy math whizzes, can't figure out for themselves the correct strategy for each game; and even if they can, it's a complicated time-consuming process.

Fortunately, all these issues can be resolved. It's simple. You determine that you're willing to put in some time studying in exchange for losing less money in a casino. You buy some inexpensive computer-derived strategy charts and some practice software that math experts have already developed. And you choose just one game at a time to master.

I've been playing video poker for 14 years, but Angela, a VP newbie, suggests that she take over at this point. She says I take too much for granted when it comes to VP strategy. "Mom, you've forgotten how complicated it can be when you first start."

Okay, kid, take it away.

The Frugal Princess Asks, "What in the Heck is '3Sf di noH'?"

The first time I looked at a video poker strategy chart, I thought I'd accidentally been given the one written in Greek. Of course, I knew it was in English, but the "codes," such as the one in the heading above, looked so complicated. (I later learned that this meant 3 cards to a double-inside straight flush containing no high cards.)

Video poker seemed simple to me when I first went to Vegas as a teenager and snuck in some play when Mom wasn't looking. I knew hand ranks from playing poker with my friends, so I'd hold whatever seemed logically best—pairs, 3- and 4-card flushes, 3 to a royal, etc. If I had two choices, I just went with my gut feeling.

When I turned 21 and Mom started teaching me correct strategy, I realized that VP was different from those clandestine high-school live-poker games. Old advice about the high value of aces and the inadvisability of drawing to an inside straight suddenly was no longer always valid. When I began to learn about expected value, I realized that if I wanted to get the most return for my money, I'd have to put in some study and learn the basics.

Here are some of the lessons Mom taught me.

Study Before You Enter the Casino

• Learn the strategy for one game at a time. Mom felt that classic full-pay Deuces Wild would be best for me, because I'd be playing mostly in Las Vegas and only for quarters. Quarter DW could be found in many casinos there, the strategy was fairly easy to learn, and with an expected return of 100.76%, it would give me the best chance to be a winner in the long term. This high EV would allow me to make some mistakes, as she assured me I would, and still be playing above 100%. She said that after I'd studied the strategy and practiced, I could probably be assured of playing at least at the 100.50% level. Being in the household of the Queen of Comps, I already knew that slot club benefits could be added to help me get to a higher overall return percentage.

• Study a strategy chart *before* you begin practicing with your VP computer software. Mom told me that it would be very time-consuming to learn strategy just by following the coaching on the practice software. You need a chart to teach you the basic strategy choices, *then* the software reinforces this learning and tests you as you play.

Be sure you have the right strategy chart for the right game. Always check the pay schedule on the machine to see that it's *entirely* the same as on the strategy card. Some charts can be used for more than one game, but most variations of a Deuces game require a different strategy than the one I'd be using. The chart for a classic Deuces schedule might allow someone to play another DW game a little better than by just guessing, but it wouldn't allow him to get the maximum EV.

Mom sat me down at the kitchen table and used a deck of cards to visually show me the various hands on the strategy card, going through the whole chart, explaining any abbreviations I couldn't figure out.

Taking My Training to the Casino

Fortunately, I had Mom sitting right beside me when I started playing VP with real money. She "translated" the strategy chart for me whenever I had a question; she stopped me when I was about to make a mistake, then showed me where I should look on the card to make a choice between two hands.

Before I get into specifics, I must say that you should be discreet about using your strategy card in a casino. They're not illegal and most casinos don't care if people use them openly; in fact, some sell them in their hotel gift shops. Recently, however, Mom has had a few reports of casinos being suspicious of players who were using them. So I usually keep mine down in the coin tray where it's easy to check, yet not as obvious as propping it up on the machine. Some players keep them in a shirt pocket or purse and take them out only when they need to check a puzzling hand.

Here are some of the many tricks Mom taught me

that she had learned, techniques that helped her play more accurately.

• *Never* try for speed. Always have accuracy as your goal. Speed will come naturally with experience. Mom says that speed causes more mistakes than anything else for serious VP players, both for beginners and for those who have been playing for years.

• Learn to pause and double-check your hold before you hit the draw button. Mom taught me this sing-song mantra: Deal—Hold—Pause—Draw. She stressed from the beginning that if I got into the habit of going through these four steps on *every* hand, I would always play more accurately, even after I picked up my playing speed; it would become just as routine as breathing. If you hold your cards and draw immediately without thinking briefly in between, then there's no chance to see a mistake and correct your hold. That slight pause to double-check the hand and see if there's a better hold has kept me from making a lot of mistakes.

• Pay attention when the machine identifies a winning hand by flashing the name of the made pay above the cards, or lighting up the made hand on the paytable. That doesn't mean that this is always the hold you will make, of course, but it sometimes shows a combination you didn't see right away. When I first started playing, I would study and study a hand before finally seeing a straight, for example, but then I'd feel pretty dumb when I noticed the machine had already told me what I was dealt. I think I'm like most beginners—I see a flush pretty quickly, but a straight, especially if the cards are mixed up, doesn't make an impression on my mind right away.

• Understand that just because you're using an accurate strategy, it doesn't mean that everything will come out the way you would like on every hand. One time I was playing Deuces Wild according to the strategy card and I correctly threw away two to a royal flush to keep a pair. The next three cards drawn were the other cards I needed to complete what would have been my first royal flush. Even though I knew I was playing correctly, I was almost physically ill for the rest of the day—thinking I'd thrown away $1,000. But Mom comforted me, telling me I had to have faith in the math, that I would get my share of royals in the long term, and that I wouldn't lose so much in between those royals if I played correctly. She said that I couldn't judge the right or wrong of a play by the results of one hand.

I'm lucky to have the Queen of Comps for a sympathetic teacher who will keep me from being derailed from the straight and narrow mathematical track! Back to you, Mom.

Strategy Help

Many kinds of strategy aids for video poker players are on the market today, in various formats and levels of complexity. There's VP strategy software for your

---

The Basics, Man, Just the Basics
A "dumb-VP" story from a Web bulletin board:

We were quite new to the game, but my friend Liz, who came out to Vegas with us for a few days, was a real VP virgin. She was dealt a straight and didn't know what to do—so she asked me, since I was the "pro."

"Wow!" I said. "A straight! Just hit the Deal/Draw button!"

She did, and the straight disappeared. I neglected to tell her to hold all the cards first.

---

computer. There are all kinds of strategy charts. But you must watch out for "help" that is not mathematically sound. Beware of generic strategy cards, often sold in casino gift shops; a strategy card must be tailored to a particular game. To help you make a decision about the strategy information you might see, here's a list of names of gambling experts that you can trust to give you mathematically sound VP help: Bob Dancer, Skip Hughes, Jeff Compton, Tomski, Dean Zamzow, Henry Tamburin, Dan Paymar, Michael Shackleford, and John Robison.

Here are my top recommendations for strategy help.

Frugal Video Poker (software)—Earlier in this chapter, I introduced this valuable new resource developed by Jim Wolf and explained how the software can help you choose good games. But it also has another basic function: generating accurate strategies for those games so you can squeeze out as much EV as possible when you play. This software combines the two elements you need—a tutor to guide you while you practice and strategy charts to study, which in the past has required the use of two separate software programs. When you make strategy errors in the casino, it costs you money and you may not even know you made them. But when you practice on the *Frugal Video Poker* program, it doesn't cost you when you make mistakes. The software points out the errors, allowing you to improve your strategy without pain in your billfold.

Frugal VP Strategy Cards—Although the above software provides the strategy for almost any game or paytable that you can print out (then laminate if you wish) and take to the casino while you're playing for real, many players prefer commercially produced strategy cards. There are several good sets on the market, but I recommend Skip Hughes' Frugal Strategy Cards.

Most strategy cards discourage the beginning player, because they look so complicated; due to the need for compactness, strategy cards must use some abbreviations. However, these cards are by far the easiest to understand, yet they're detailed enough that they can be used by the majority of players from the time they begin their study right through to the time they become experts.

How was Skip able to simplify his cards without significantly reducing the EV for using the strategy? He left out "penalty-card" entries. Penalty cards are cards in your initial five that will be discarded, but still have an effect in close decisions. This effect is usually very slight, so ignoring them causes almost no EV reduction. Hence, the return achieved by using these simplified strategies is so close to optimum that the difference is literally a matter of a few pennies a day for the quarter player, yet the tables are often as much as a third smaller than the complete strategy.

For anyone other than a professional who devotes full time to the game, these strategies will actually yield a higher accuracy than the much more complicated alternatives due to a lower error rate. Even highly skilled players usually agree that they earn more in cashback and other benefits by not stopping to look up every penalty-card situation than they would by slowing down to achieve absolutely perfect play.

Skip and Jim Wolf have used a similar style in setting down their strategies, so the cards and the *FVP* software work well together. Skip has cards for the following most common games: Jacks or Better, Deuces Wild, Double Bonus, Kings or Better Joker Poker, and Pick 'Em, with more in the planning stage. These are laminated cards using a soft yellow background that's easy on the eyes. Skip uses large print and the hands are color-coded according to type (flush draws, straight draws, etc.) The cards can be ordered from Huntington Press' www.greatstuff4gamblers.com or www.vp homepage.com.

Knowing What to Expect

Okay, so you now know the best games and how to learn accurate strategies for those you choose to play. Are you fully prepared to go out and play video poker? Definitely not! There's one more leg of the stool, and it's this leg that's the most difficult to understand and cope with. In this section I'll try to help you with the toughest concept of the game: knowing what to expect.

This is where many players fall right off the VP stool. They do everything right: They choose only games where the EV is over 100% and study the strategy until they have it down cold. Then they play … and lose. They're disillusioned, even shattered. "But Jean Scott told me that she wins at video poker and that I could, too. It must all be a cruel hoax!"

It's not a hoax. But video poker can definitely be cruel. That's why I need to explain to you what winning VP means.

Actually, it might help if I first tell you what winning video poker doesn't mean. It doesn't mean that you can go to the casino and win *tonight*. It doesn't mean you'll win every session you play. It doesn't mean that you'll win most of your sessions. It doesn't mean that you won't have long losing streaks. It's not even an absolute guarantee that you'll ever be an overall winner during your lifetime of play.

Well, then, what does winning video poker really mean?

Winning video poker means that *if* you play only

when you have the advantage and *if* you play only the correct strategy, then you're *very likely* to be a winner over the long term.

Yes, Virginia, there really is winning video poker. But I need to define a lot of difficult terms and explain a lot of complex concepts before that last short paragraph can be fully understood. Bear with me here— I'll make it as simple as I can.

What Does EV Really Mean?

Earlier in the section in which I talked about choosing the right game, I listed the EV for each game, expressed as a percentage, e.g., Jacks or Better (99.5%). EV is an abbreviation for "expected value" and it originally became familiar to video poker players as the measure used to evaluate playing decisions. Then, as now, strategy charts were made up to rank the best hold for any group of five cards depending on a comparison of EVs. However, players soon began referencing the EVs of return schedules as a whole, assuming perfect play.

The use of the word "expected" may be a little misleading. Tim, a math friend of mine, suggested that I could use "average return" as a more accurate description: "Using the term 'expected' can be misinterpreted, leading someone to think he should 'expect' to get that return every time, or at least most of the time. 'Average' addresses the time issue a little better, implying it's simply the midpoint of many possible outcomes. It implies a longer-term horizon and less of an exact expectation in the short term."

I agree with Tim wholeheartedly, but since EV is the common abbreviation accepted in VP circles, I continue to use it. Still, you have to understand clearly that it doesn't mean that you should "expect" to win every time you play. An Internet friend explained it this way: "The more hands you play on a machine with an over-100% EV, the greater the theoretical chance that you will be ahead than if you played machines with under-100% EVs. There is no absolute guarantee you'll be ahead, but the odds are more in your favor that you will be."

One other note about game EV, a fact that I cannot emphasize too much: These game EVs are theoretical, meaning that they're accurate only if a computer-perfect strategy is used. No human being can play perfectly for an extended length of time, certainly not forever. However, with study and practice, it's possible for most motivated players to play highly accurate strategies that will get them close enough to the theoretical EV to become winners.

Volatility

It's time to discuss the big bugaboo for every video poker player, the characteristic of this game that causes more grief than anything else: volatility. The math experts talk about "variance" when they discuss volatility—in other words, how far your winning and losing sessions will vary from the average return or the theoretical EV. I like my non-mathematical real-life definition, which I call "the roller-coaster effect." I don't have to explain this to anyone who's played VP for even a short period of time.

Why is video poker so volatile? One word. Jackpots. Whenever you have a "pyramid-pay" game (a range from lots of smaller payoffs to a few larger ones), where a large part of the long-term payback is dependent on jackpots that aren't hit very often, you have a recipe for high volatility.

Blackjack, for example, has much lower volatility; although you win more on blackjacks, doubles, and splits, it's not many times more than the usual hand—

as a royal flush is in video poker. Speaking in averages again, a royal comes up only about every 40,000 hands, depending on the game and strategy used. (We'll discuss this royal element later.) If you play 500 hands an hour and even if the royal comes up exactly at the average point (which it almost never does), that means you're playing 80 hours without that jackpot. A royal contributes, on average, about 2% to the EV in most games. That means that if you're playing a positive game with a high EV of 101%, you're actually playing at only a 99% rate of return for most of the 80 hours, even if you get the average number of smaller paying hands. So, you're losing for *many* more hours than you're winning, even if you end up a net winner when you finally hit the royal.

Bob Dancer, an expert video poker player, says that he loses, on average, two out of three sessions, but the money he makes in those fewer winning sessions more than makes up for what he lost in the losing ones. It's hard to endure losing two-thirds of the time, but you must take comfort in the fact that what's important is not *how often* you win, but *how much* you win in the long run.

So is volatility always bad? Actually, I don't think too many people would play video poker if there were no volatility. Let's say you find a positive $1 game in Predictable Casino located in Never-Never Land. Here you can play with a steady .2% edge, in which you get the same "win" on every hand. A .2% edge on each $5 hand played means you win one cent on every hand no matter what cards you hold and what resulting hand comes up. Wow, you think, I can play fast, maybe 1,000 hands per hour, with an hourly win of $10—not bad pay for just pushing buttons. But how long would you play before you got totally bored? Would you fly across the U.S. to play in that casino on your vacation?

I'm reminded of a tagline I read often on a friend's e-mail: "If you could win all the time, it wouldn't be gambling; it would only be a job."

Video poker expert Tomski wrote in *Video Poker Player*, "Variance is the component that provides the kick to the thrill of gambling." The jackpots—those higher-paying quads and especially the royals—are what make video poker exciting. The price you have

---

A Lesson on Volatility

The following comes courtesy of an Internet correspondent.

Let's say I have a deck of 53 cards—a regular deck, plus one joker. You have 20¢. In one game, you pay me one cent and you get to draw one card. If you draw the joker, I'll pay you 52¢. If you draw any other card, you lose. We continue to play this game as long as you desire, always starting with the 53 cards. As you can imagine, it's quite possible that you'll run out of money before you draw the joker. Of course, all you need is one win, and you'll be able to play many more games, and perhaps quit while you're ahead. However, because you need to win at least once in order to survive, this would be considered a game with very high volatility.

Now consider a game with the same 53-card deck. You still bet one cent, but this time you'll be paid four cents every time you draw any club. It's easy to see that you will win a lot more often, but only four cents at a time. Unless you have a very long run of bad luck, you should last quite a while in this game, though you may never be up or down very much at any time. This would be considered a game with low volatility.

Of course, if you want to play a machine in a casino with a 100% payback and zero volatility, look for the one called "CHANGE." Put in your dollar and out comes four quarters—every time.

---

to pay for this excitement is enduring many losing sessions between them.

The Royal Flush—the Guilty Party in Volatility

The royal flush is the most sought-after hand in all the VP kingdom—and the most elusive. When players hear that a royal appears about every 40,000 hands, they tend to believe that if they've played 40,000 hands, they're "due" for the royal. And I get more than a few notes from players complaining that they never get royals "on time."

Let me explain. First, this 40,000-hand figure is just a rounded average we use to talk about the royal cycle—the royal flush frequency—of most VP games. For example, the JoB royal hit frequency is 40,390; Deuces Wild is 45,281. (Why the difference? Because correct strategy has you hold more high cards and fewer deuces in JoB than you do in DW, so the odds of finishing with a royal after the draw are greater and the cycle shorter.)

Although these are exact figures, they represent an overall average, not a pattern. A VP machine deals the cards randomly; if there were a pattern of giving you a royal on JoB every 40,390 hands, it wouldn't be random.

Do a little experiment on your computer with VP software. On Frugal VP you can set the game to automatically play up to one million games (with perfect strategy). Maybe over the first 40,390 hands played, not one royal shows up. Or maybe there are two or three. During the next cycle of 40,390 hands, maybe there are none—or maybe there are a mind-boggling six. Maybe the machine goes five cycles without a royal.

"Hey," you might say, "that computer history of royals sounds just like mine!"

Don't give up; the longer you play, the more likely you are to get closer to that overall royal average. And remember: *It's just as possible to hit a streak of royals in a short period as it is to go long periods without them.* Volatility works both ways.

Brad and I have kept very detailed records of our play for the last seven years and we've enjoyed some amazing streaks of frequent royals. We've also been pleased when they came pretty close "on schedule." And we've suffered through some long and painful "royal droughts." But I'm always surprised that when we go back to our log and total all the hands we've played, we find that our number of royals is very close to that average of one for about every 40,000 or so hands.

A final warning: Many players are tempted to go for the royal every time they get the chance. And on the surface, this seems logical. Wouldn't it cut down on the volatility? If you got more royals, wouldn't you win more in the long run? Human logic is not as good as mathematical proof. Computers have played more VP than all the gamblers combined in casinos from Day 1—and they have proven that if you go for royals more than correct strategy dictates, yes, you will get more royals, but you will lose so much more money in between that the extra royals will not make up for it.

The phenomenon of selective memory is strong here. You remember well, for example, the once or twice you threw away a high pair in JoB to keep three cards to a royal and you got the royal. But you forget the hundreds of times you went against the rule and threw away a sure push and a possible improvement, only to end up with nothing. And the money from that push just might have provided the bankroll for the future bet that actually would, with correct strategy, win the royal!

Getting From the Short Term to the Long Term

Okay, there's that phrase I use all the time—the "long term"—the one that's been begging to be explained this whole chapter. I'm sure you're wondering: *Just how long will the long term be and when will you get there?*

I wish I had quick answers for these questions—the exact number of hours it will take you to reach this magical winning time—but I don't, and neither does anyone else. The best thing I can do is give you some math-based facts that might help you understand the concept of the long term.

First, the more volatile a game, the longer it usually takes to get to the long run. I discussed earlier that VP is much more volatile than blackjack, for example, because VP has big jackpot hands that are hit infrequently. And because of these infrequent hands, not only is the volatility increased, but you must expect the journey to the long term to be a longer trip.

Second, it's a mathematical fact that the longer you play VP with accurate strategy, the closer you'll come to the average return of the game—that misnamed EV percentage. This is true whether you play negative- or positive-expectation games. You may play a negative game and win at first, but as sure as the sun sets in the west, if you play long enough, you'll move closer and closer to that under-100% EV and long-term losing. Fortunately, if you always play positive games—even if you lose at first—continued play will move you closer and closer to long-term winning. People who play a lot are more likely to get closer to the EV. People who don't get to play much may never get as close as they would like.

There's a lot of misunderstanding where this concept is involved. For a long time I was guilty of believing that if you've been losing in the past, you'll win more in the future to "catch up." I had the right idea about the final result, but not the reason why.

Let me be more specific. In the past I might have said something like, "Brad and I have been on a super winning streak for six months; we're waiting for the other shoe to fall," meaning that we were afraid that we'd probably soon start losing. After writing this on a friendly Internet chat forum, Skip's VP List, I got some polite but stern lessons.

One person wrote, "It would be correct to say that your next few months probably won't be as good, not because you've done so well the last few months, but because of 'regression to the mean,' you're more likely to see typical, or average, returns."

Video poker expert Dan Paymar wrote, "If there was a tendency to 'catch up' by getting future wins that will offset your past losses, you could play on your home computer until you racked up a big loss, then go to the casino and be certain of winning real money."

Others emphasized that every VP hand you play is an independent event. The hand you're playing right now doesn't know whether you've been losing badly, winning big, or breaking even the last few hands or the last two hours or the past six years. While live poker is very different from video poker, the two games do have one thing in common: For both, it's true that the cards have no memory. Skip paraphrased another old adage: "This hand is the first hand of the rest of your life. You have the same edge on *every* hand in the same game; the odds are in your favor at all times when you're playing a positive game accurately."

Another consideration is how a long losing *or* winning streak affects your getting to the long term. When you have a long streak, losing or winning, at the beginning of your lifetime VP play, it *will* affect the length of time in which you might reasonably expect to get to your individual long term. Starting with a long winning streak probably cuts down the time and starting with a long losing streak usually increases the amount of play needed. However, *any* streak, good or bad, at *any* time during your lifetime play will have less impact on your long-term results as it gets "lost," or diluted, becoming a smaller percentage in a growing total of hands that will slowly but surely, although in no pattern that can be predicted, gravitate toward the long-term expected return.

Remember that this works both ways. If you have

Is the Short Term ...

Some players pooh-pooh the long term. "I'll never play long enough to get to that long term you're always talking about. So it really doesn't matter what game I play. It's all luck. I can get a royal on a machine with a bad pay schedule just as easily as I can on one of your 'good' machines."

It's true that royals are hit, in general, at about the same frequency on most types of VP machines—whether they have high-paying or low-paying schedules. However, it's not the payoff of the royal that has the most effect in the short term; it's the payoff of the hands in the rest of the schedule, those smaller hands that appear quite frequently.

Instead of trying to persuade you with words that your choice of a better schedule will improve your results in the short term, as well as the long term, allow me to suggest an experiment. Sometime when you're playing Jacks or Better, keep track of how many full houses and flushes you get in one hour. Then calculate what your win or loss would have been if you'd been playing on a JoB machine with a different schedule. If you're playing on a 9/6 schedule, how much less would you have in your pocket if you had been playing on an 8/5? If you're playing a 6/5, how much more would

---

a very long winning start to your VP playing time, you'll be gravitating *downward* toward the EV, not *upward* as will be the case for someone who starts with a losing streak. The end result, however, given enough play, will be the same: Both will be near the EV. This follows the math theorem known as the Law of Large Numbers, which in laymen's terms means, the longer you play, the closer your personal average return will move toward the expected theoretical return.

An Internet friend summed it up well: "Wins or losses that seem major in the short term are relatively

---

... Important?

you have had if you'd been playing a 9/6? And so on.

Your figures will depend, of course, on how fast you played and how close the frequencies of your flushes and full houses came to the average in that one short trial. However, on average, you get between five and six full houses per hour if you play at a medium speed of 500 hands per hour. During the same period, you would get about the same number of flushes. Let's say you're playing quarters at max coin on an 8/5 JoB machine. Every time you hit a full house you're getting paid $10 instead of the $11.25 that you'd get on a 9/6 machine. Every time you hit a flush you're getting paid $6.25 instead of $7.50. You're losing $1.25 every time you make either a full house or a flush. Multiply $1.25 times 11, the average number of both those hands you will make per hour, and you can see that it's costing close to $14 an hour.

What if you were playing a dollar machine? Now you'd average losing four times the amount you'd lose on the quarter machine—a whopping $55 an hour on a dollar 8/5 JoB machine vs. the better 9/6 JoB schedule.

As a friend of mine likes to say, the long term is just an accumulation of a whole bunch of short-term sessions.

insignificant over the long term. It's not that they mean any more or less to us *emotionally* at the time, but they're tiny blips in the long run, and our results will migrate closer and closer to that expected EV line the longer we play. The sheer volume of hands overwhelms the ups and downs and is always pulling us to that 'center,' the EV."

The math can really be a comfort at times. It's human nature to have doubts when you're losing in the short term, and these are the times when math is your friend. You can compare your long-term results to the math averages, and very often you'll see that you aren't very far from it. In fact, these days when we have a long losing streak, we merely go to our seven-year long-term figures where we see that our recent losses are small compared to our cumulative win over the years. That math makes it easier to keep the faith. An Internet friend posted this optimistic way to look at losing streaks: "This is when the long run truly comes to pass—when you've played so many hands that being terribly unlucky still leaves you with an overall profit."

The VP Bankroll Question

Talking about the long term often leads to another frequently asked question, "How big of a gambling bankroll should I have to play video poker?"

Why is it necessary to talk about bankroll when you're playing good games and using proper strategy? In one of his editorials in *Strictly Slots*, Adam Fine uses a graphic comparison that helps us explain the third leg of the VP stool.

"Think of yourself in a car (the right game), driving through the casino on your way to your destination (winning money). Strategy is merely the ability to steer the car correctly. Your bankroll is the gas that gets you to your destination. If you run out of gas, you

won't make it far enough to use yo'
you'll have to walk home."

Discussing VP bankroll requirer
best ways to explain and cope wj
ride on the volatility roller coaster. ı.
way to show what it might take to survive ̩
reach that elusive point called the long term. bʋ.
Dancer defined bankroll very well, in non-math terms,
in an article he wrote for *Casino Player*: "It refers to the
amount of assets you have that would allow you to
play the game over and over and over again with a
high chance of being able to play forever without going bankrupt."

The bankroll I'm talking about doesn't mean all
the money you take to Las Vegas on your yearly vacation—that's a trip bankroll. It also doesn't mean the
money you take to gamble with at your local riverboat
casino one evening—that's called a session bankroll.
Bankroll here refers to an amount of money you set
aside as a permanent "bank," money that will be used
only for positive-expectation VP play over the rest of
your playing lifetime. (You cannot expect to play negative-expectation games indefinitely without going
broke.) This money will not be used for any other purpose—not for playing negative-expectation VP or other
negative casino games, and not for other casino expenses, such as room, food, entertainment, or airfare.

As with all gambling funds, your VP bankroll
should be money that you're able to lose without negatively impacting your standard of living, without hurting anyone who is significant to you, and without causing you psychological problems. (Some people have a
smaller psychological bankroll than their actual financial bankroll, meaning that they could afford to lose
more, but it would make them ill to do so.) Your gambling funds to play VP come out of this bankroll and

f your winnings go back in. You won't spend any art of your bankroll until it's over the maximum amount needed to sustain the level at which you play.

In my first book, I talked about needing to have three times the amount of a royal as a minimum bankroll—$3,000 for playing quarter Deuces Wild. I said that we actually felt more secure if we had $5,000, because we didn't feel comfortable getting too close to the bottom of the barrel.

Since I wrote that, there has been more written on the subject of VP bankroll, with some new math formulas that are more precise. Many math experts have put out Risk of Ruin (ROR) charts showing bankroll amounts needed for various games, depending on how sure you wanted to be that you wouldn't go broke.

However, here are some general ideas that can help you decide your individual bankroll needs. I'm assuming quarter play.

• Although no general guidelines or precise math charts can *guarantee* that you will never go broke, if you play only 100%+ games, you will reduce your risk of ruin as you increase your bankroll. There is no bankroll that will protect you from going broke (eventually) if you're playing games that return less than 100%—you're forced to depend on luck.

• The higher a game's EV, usually the lower the bankroll needed (although volatility plays a small part here). A game's theoretical EV is based on the use of computer-perfect strategy, impossible for mere mortals to achieve. This is why I suggest beginners who play in Las Vegas choose full-pay Deuces Wild. The EV is high enough (100.76%) that you can make some mistakes and still be playing over 100%. But the more accurately you play, the smaller your bankroll will need to be.

• Although you'll be more secure if you have the

whole recommended bankroll before you start, you may have to start playing on a partial one. If you're fortunate, you'll have winning streaks near the beginning and be able to increase your bankroll with your VP profits. If you go broke on the smaller amount, you will need to re-group: Stop playing, find a way to replenish the bankroll, then continue.

• Adding cash benefits from slot clubs and promotions will increase the EV of a play and reduce the bankroll requirement. The reason that we never needed a bankroll of more than $3,000 when we played quarter Deuces Wild was that we chased promotions tirelessly and used slot club benefits to the max. We worked at it long and hard. If you don't want to work that hard, you'll need a larger bankroll: at least $5,000, assuming you usually play with some cashback or promotional benefits, and $8,000-$10,000 if you use extra benefits lightly or learn only a cursory playing strategy.

Most people don't have the assets to devote to a large gambling bankroll. Even those who have a large amount of discretionary funds often want to be as economical in their gambling as in other parts of their financial life. So I can't emphasize too often or too strongly to VP players who want to play on the smallest bankroll possible: *Play at the highest EV you possibly can and play as accurately as possible.*

Multi-Line Madness

I've saved the best for last in this chapter, a discussion of multi-line video poker, for many players the most fun you can have with your clothes on. The introduction of multi-line games has certainly given a powerful adrenaline boost to many video poker play-

---

The Frugal Princess On Bankroll

My husband Steve and I have experimented with different kinds of gambling bankrolls. We used to have a single sum that we brought to Vegas. It was all the money we could afford to spend or lose, and we called it simply our Vacation Bankroll. Our only goal was to have fun for the few days we'd be in town. Whether we were playing the games or seeing a show or eating at a restaurant, we paid for it out of our Vacation fund. After I learned about playing positive-expectation video poker, we began dividing our money into two bankrolls, one called PE (positive-expectation), which we used only for over 100% VP plays and couponing, and one called Fun, which we used for everything else.

If this sounds like playing VP wasn't fun for us, that's not the case at all. When we got home, our Fun bankroll was usually completely gone. But the first time we had some left in our PE bankroll, we realized that this was fun that *lasted*—and it inspired us to make playing good games well a bigger part of our future casino vacations.

---

ers. It started with just the three lines of Triple Play, then went to Five and Ten Play, then jumped to giving you a mind-boggling 50 and even *100* lines. I joked that they might just bring out Million Play—and you could save all that time in a casino by playing one hand and you would have a "lifetime" in at video poker.

Brad and I love playing multi-line video poker and we play it as often as we can find it where we have an advantage. I see many dangers in this new fun form of VP, however.

1. Overwhelmingly, the games offered in multi-line machines have less than 100% pay schedules, many of them extremely low-pay. If it's important to choose good plays on single-line machines, it's even more

important on multi-lines, because you're risking three times (and up) more money. Even if you compensate for this by dropping down in denomination (for example, from single-line quarters to five-line nickels), you face the fact that pay schedules often change for the worse as you drop to the lower levels.

It's becoming extremely rare to find a 100%+ schedule. Only slightly less rare is finding a schedule below 100% with slot club benefits and/or promotions juicy enough to produce a player edge—and that edge is usually smaller than we prefer, requiring a much larger bankroll than we like to put at risk.

2. Players are tempted to stray from the correct strategy they use for the same game on single-line machines. *Increasing the number of lines on a game doesn't alter the strategy.* I can't emphasize this too strongly: No matter what you feel you would like to do differently, you must use the same strategy or you risk losing much more long term, with the effect increasing as the number of lines increases. The same reasoning goes for making strategy mistakes. The loss of EV for each mistake is magnified correspondingly, according to how many lines are impacted. You definitely need to slow down and take extra care that you play accurately.

3. The volatility in the short term requires a larger *session* bankroll than many players think is necessary. Yes, you get to the long term quicker because you're putting more money per hour through the machine; hence, you don't have to calculate your *total* bankroll requirement by multiplying a single-line requirement times the number of lines. However, you're being dealt roughly the same number of hands per hour (on multi-lines you usually get in fewer dealt hands because of the time it takes to rack up the wins on each line), and your overall results are directly correlated to how good

or bad the dealt hand is. Therefore, you may have big wins or big losses in any one session, requiring a larger session bankroll. You get many more draws on the multi-liners, but they're dependent on the same number of deals as the single-liners. This becomes a bigger problem in the short term the more lines you play.

Experts disagree on the total bankroll needed for multi-line play, but from experience we feel that the general guideline is to have 1½ to 2 times the bankroll for Triple Play as for the same game in single-line, 2-3 times the bankroll for Five Play, 2-4 times the bankroll for Ten Play, 6-8 times for Fifty Play, and 8-12 times for Hundred Play. If you have the lower suggested bankroll, you need to prepare yourself psychologically for the likelihood that you'll have to go quite deep into that bankroll during one session or one stretch of losing sessions. The roller-coaster ups and downs will be much more extreme than you've ever experienced on single-line. That provides a big thrill when you're zooming to the heights during the winning periods, but many players can't take the plunging ride down so close to the bottom when losing. Therefore, conservative players might want to have the mental security of the larger bankroll recommendations.

4. Multi-line VP is so much fun that it can be addictive, leading players to take leave of their former good senses. They play inferior, or even bad, pay schedules they would have never played on a single-line machine—compounding the mistake by playing three or more times the coin-in per hand. The lure of big hands (like a dealt jackpot) keeps them chasing at machines with more and more lines. They play above their bankroll and get into financial trouble, some of them for the first time in their gambling years.

All multi-line machines should have a sign on them: Danger—Handle With Care!

The Big Question,
"Is Winning Video Poker for Me?"

By now, you might be ready to give up. Since you understand better what to expect, you might be thinking that it's too hard!

Actually, one of my goals in this section *was* to make it clear that learning to play winning VP is not easy. That takes a 25,000-word slog, not a 25-words-or-less magic bullet.

A few people took me to task over the discussion of video poker in *The Frugal Gambler*, saying that I made it all look too easy. I wanted to leave no unrealistic illusions in the mind of a single reader after finishing this book.

On the other hand, I don't want to be too negative, either. I don't want to leave you discouraged and ready to give up or never get started. True, some who read this section will decide that winning VP is not their cup of tea. Some don't plan to ever play hundreds of hours in their lifetime. They visit casinos only occasionally, much of their time there is spent on non-gambling activities, and they only dabble in the games. If your goal is purely to be entertained while you're in a casino—and there's nothing wrong with that—you can play whatever you want without worrying about studying how to choose the good games and play the proper strategies. I understand that many people go to a casino to relax and get away from work; they don't want to work while they're there.

However, there's a group of players who spend many hours in casinos every year, and although their goal is also entertainment, they're much more entertained if they lose less or win more. They're challenged by the idea that there are things they can study and practice that will make their entertainment bankroll last longer, thus allowing them to have what the Frugal Princess calls "lasting fun." They're willing to work to make their hobby more profitable so they can stretch out the enjoyment longer.

If you find that you're entertained more when you know you have a good chance of winning, then you'll welcome the advice in this section, instead of feeling that I'm trying to talk you out of learning.

III

TOOLS OF THE TRADE

5

Slot Clubs—
You Can't Afford Not to Join

"Are you getting your share of kickbacks?"
— casino sign advertising
the slot club benefits

A slot club representative once told me a story about an elderly white-haired woman playing a slot machine without a slot club card inserted. The rep approached the woman and asked if she (and her husband) would like to apply for a card so she could qualify for comps and cashback. The dignified little lady straightened up proudly and replied, politely but firmly, "No thank you; we brought enough cash with us for the trip."

Slot club benefits are not welfare, and they're not something players should clandestinely slink around to acquire without the casino "catching them." A slot club is the most powerful marketing tool casinos have to promote customer loyalty and they spend big chunks of their budgets trying to get people to join. You should never feel guilty or self-conscious about taking advantage of the benefits to the maximum degree.

Likewise, slot club benefits are one of the strongest armaments in any smart machine-player's arsenal. I emphasized this idea in *The Frugal Gambler* and I'll be pounding on it even harder here. Why? Back when I wrote the first book, Brad and I were mostly quarter video poker players and Deuces Wild was our cornerstone game. Sure, we used the slot club heavily to get comps and we liked the casinos that gave cashback, which smoothes out the game's ups and downs. But Deuces Wild could stand on its own as a profit-making activity. Slot club benefits were the gravy.

Slot Club or Players Club?

The trend is to have all casino players—at the tables and at the machines—in the same tracking system. Therefore, the more limited term "slot club" is slowly changing to "players club." I use "slot" card and "players" card interchangeably, referring to the same thing.

Fast-forward to the present. We're now mostly dollar players with no 100%+ Deuces Wild available in that denomination. So we mainly play Double Bonus, which we figure to be just about a breakeven game for most skilled players. Human error makes the computer-perfect 100.17% a pipe dream for all but the few select "masters." Therefore, to get to the 100%-plus side, dollar-and-up video poker players depend on good slot club benefits: upper-level comps and cashback. Those who play games that pay back less than 100%—and that includes all slot and many video poker machines, even that old video poker classic, Jacks or Better, at 99.5%—will have to be savvy slot club users in order to cut their losses. And they'll have to be slot club wizards to climb into positive territory.

Slot club membership is an integral, vital, critical part of your relationship with casinos. Its importance cannot be overemphasized.

To Join Or Not to Join— That's Not a Question

Before I tell you how to get the most out of your slot club membership, we need to discuss the join-or-not argument.

I can't tell you how many times I sit next to someone playing video poker who doesn't have a slot club card in his machine. If the person seems friendly, I often strike up a conversation and ask about his reasons for not belonging to the slot club. Over the years I've collected a list of them, ranging from superstitious or illogical to simply unobservant or lazy. Here are some of the usual responses.

• "I didn't know there was such a thing as a slot club."

Don't just sit down and start playing when you first go into a casino. Look around. Banners, signs, and brochures let patrons know of promotions available to them. Some casinos have signs on the machines or a scrolling message on the slot club reader encouraging you to join the slot club.

• "I thought it cost money."

No, it's *free* (my favorite word in the world).

• "I didn't know where to find the slot club desk."

As I say so often—*ask!* Don't waste time wandering around looking for it; ask the first employee you see. Many times the slot club is located at the rear of the casino, so you'll have to walk through the tempting gambling areas to reach it.

• "It takes too much time and I want to get right down to gambling."

Brad and I are as anxious as the next person to sit down at a video poker machine, but if we don't already have a slot club card from that casino, first we go straight to the slot club desk to sign up. We know we will often make more per hour in cashback or comps from our slot club points than we do on the machines, so we figure we're getting paid for the time it takes to join.

• "I have a slot club card, but I left it in my room (or at home)."

All you have to do is walk over to the slot club desk and ask for a replacement card. Sure, you may have to wait a few minutes in line, but investing those few minutes will give you much in return.

• "I can't be bothered; it's just too much trouble."

If making money is too much trouble for you, I have no comeback. Getting slot club benefits will definitely make up some of your losses—and can often mean the difference between winning and losing.

• "I thought I was going to play for only a few minutes."

You never know how long you may end up playing at one machine. I've seen many people sit down and say they're going to play "just until I lose this $20 bill" and still be sitting there three hours later.

• "The comps you earn don't really add up to much."

Which would you rather do: Wait in a long buffet line and pay cold hard cash to get in or stroll to the front of the line and hand the cashier a free meal ticket you got at the slot club booth? Whatever you save with comped meals or rooms or other slot club benefits leaves more money in your pocket for your gambling bankroll, extra money that allows you to play longer, extra time in which you might hit a big jackpot.

• "I don't want the casino to know who I am or have my address."

The most frugal thing you can do for yourself is to give the casino your name and address so it can send you special offers and promotions in the mail. Once you're "in the system," casino marketing departments will inundate you with information, special offers, promotions, invitations, and coupons. I say there's no such thing as junk mail from a casino. Open it all and read it—you'll almost always find some item of interest or some promotion that you can take advantage of to save money.

• "Casinos use the slot club card to gather information for devious IRS reporting purposes."

Casinos send routine information to the IRS only when you hit a machine jackpot of $1,200 or more, and you (and the IRS) get that W-2G *whether or not* a slot club card is inserted.

• "I don't want the casino to know how much I win or lose."

Actually, you do want the casino to know how much you're winning or losing or, more important, how much money you're putting through the machines, so you can get the rewards you've earned. Besides, you might be glad you can get an end-of-the-year win/loss record from the slot club if the IRS taps you for some supplementary proof of the gambling figures on your tax return.

• "Someone told me I won't hit as many jackpots if I have a slot club card in the machine."

This is probably the most frequent reason I hear. It's sad, because it's based on completely inaccurate information. The slot machine computer system that determines the payouts and the slot club computer system work *completely independent* of one another. No human or all-knowing computer chip determines that you've put in a slot club card, then pushes some button that keeps you from hitting jackpots. Besides, why would a casino want to punish a regular player? Even if this capability existed, wouldn't the casino want to encourage its good customers? Take my word on this: You have the same chance of winning every session whether you do or don't play with a slot card. The only thing playing without your card will do is make you miss the benefits of comps and cashback.

When Should You Join a Slot Club?

Although there's almost no good reason not to use a slot club card when you play, there is some difference of opinion about whether you should join every slot club you can, even if you don't plan to play in that casino soon or ever.

The main reason, and a compelling one, for not joining as many slot clubs as you can as fast as you can (without plans for playing in every casino where you get a card) is to wait for a good sign-up bonus. From time to time, casinos offer juicy new-member incentives. This could be bonus points during your first 24 hours of play, or a good food comp for a small amount of action, or a free-room deal on your first visit. You might get cash or gifts or free points just for signing up, even before you play. Lately, a popular sign-up bonus is to return a portion of losses, often $100-$200, incurred during a period of play—usually the first 30 minutes or an hour. This is an extremely strong money-saving program for new slot club members.

A correspondent weighed in with the following: "Over two years in Atlantic City [2000-2002], four casinos offered new-member promotions providing a bonus of $100 to $1,000 (or more). Three of these featured cashback-multipliers for one or more visits (3x,

5x, and 10x), while the other provided a 110% loss-refund guarantee on a first-visit loss up to $1,000."

Had a person already run through the A.C. casinos joining every players club, he would have severely limited (or eliminated altogether) his eligibility for these promotions. This would suggest that in a locale where a person expects to be a repeat player (even if infrequently), he should generally avoid new-member promotions of limited value, unless the quality of play itself at a casino attracts him for extended play.

However, through the years we've found that, although we've lost out on a few good signing bonuses, we've profited more by joining as many slot clubs as we can, whether or not we plan to play in that casino at that time. Here are a few reasons for making the accumulation of a slot card collection your new hobby.

1. Even if you aren't planning to play at all in a particular casino, you might unexpectedly stumble on a must-play machine (for example, a high progressive) that you want to grab and pound immediately. Or you might have an unexpected wait—at a restaurant, to see a show, etc.—and you can spend this short time going to the booth to get a card rather than playing without one.

2. Often by just showing your card, whether you've actually played on it or not, you get discounts all over a casino property: on shows tickets, in restaurants, at gift shops and health clubs, at child-care centers, on activities like bowling and movies and golf, on parking charges, and on room rates.

3. Sometimes there's a special (usually shorter) show or restaurant line for cardholders.

4. Some casinos send out free or discounted offers (rooms, shows, food) to everyone in their databases, regardless of the level of play—or lack thereof. Brad and I have received great offers (like a room for three

nights) from casinos where we've never dropped a nickel into a machine, but had signed up for the slot club at one time.

5. Consolidations of casino ownership bring cross-marketing goodies. You may not plan to go back to Caesars in Atlantic City, but you might appreciate the offer from Caesars in Las Vegas or Tahoe, a benefit from the Atlantic City casino sharing its customer database with sister casinos.

6. Some casinos have a special room-reservation phone line for slot club members. You won't get a free room if you show little or no play, but you might get the casino rate, which could save you a significant amount of money over inflated rack rates for the general public. Or you might snare a room when the regular reservation agent claims the hotel is full—the slot club often has a block of rooms set aside for its exclusive booking.

7. Finally, you won't miss out on every signing bonus. Some casinos give unadvertised sign-up bonuses routinely, varying them each month or so. Over the years, Brad and I have gotten such signing bonuses as T-shirts, valuable gifts, little trinkets, and many keychains to add to our extensive collection. We recently joined a slot club at a small Las Vegas off-Strip locals casino. In a few days, before we'd had time to go back and actually play, the casino sent us each a welcome letter and a coupon for $10 redeemable on our next visit.

So there are several advantages to joining clubs rather than holding out for a good bonus. Still, I don't recommend that you do so at the expense of choosing one core casino to put in your major amount of play. If your casino time is limited, you should usually pick one casino that you like (whether for its comps, good machines, or whatever) and make it a priority to play there until you achieve a level where you can get the benefits you want. Only then should you begin to concentrate on joining slot clubs at numerous casinos.

Single Account or Joint Account?

Whether to open one or two accounts is a decision faced by couples every time they sign up for a new slot club. Casinos used to allow only couples with the same last name to have a joint account, but many have now joined the 21st century and allow non-traditional (same-sex) or unmarried (opposite-sex) couples to have joint accounts, particularly if they have the same address. Some slot clubs, however, still don't offer joint accounts—and everyone, regardless of marital status, is automatically signed up separately.

In almost all cases, it pays for each member of a couple to have a separate account. Usually, both can play on just one card if you're trying to get to a higher comp level (see the next section for a caution here). And at most casinos you can each play on your own card and ask your host to check both accounts and combine the playing action when determining comps.

The advantage of having separate accounts comes primarily from casino-marketing practices. Casinos often send promos to everyone in their databases—not only to the regular players, but sometimes to those with little or even no play—for free nights or meal comps. If you and your partner each get these invitations, you can combine them for longer stays and double the food. A few casinos might set their computer to kick out mailings for different members with the same address and some offers stipulate one per household. However, this is usually for high-level offers, such as big-money invitational tournaments and VIP events. In most cases, two people, even with the same last name and same address, will receive all the offers they've earned on each of their accounts, double what they would have gotten with one joint account.

Another advantage of separate accounts is that they allow you to get around the frustrating policy in force at some casinos that base comp benefits on a daily gambling-dollar average. An organized couple can use one card when they plan to put in heavy play on one day, then play on the other when they plan to put in minimum time—such as on the day they arrive or depart, or when they've scheduled non-gambling activities, or are visiting other casinos. This protects the higher daily average on the main card.

What if two of you set up a joint account in one casino in the past, but now want to have separate accounts? I wish I could tell you this is always an easy fix. Sometimes it is; you merely go to the slot club booth and the primary cardholder keeps the old number, while the secondary name gets a new one. However, I've known players who've found it almost impossible to get this simple transaction done. Many booth personnel will argue that there's no reason not to have a joint account; each player has his or her own name on the card, after all. Then they'll just stand there looking helpless when you point out that both cards have the same number, thus it's the same account.

I've found that it's easiest for a woman to get her own card after having a joint account. All she has to do is march up to the slot club and declare her independence—by demanding her own account. I'm not saying that you should lie and tell them that you're divorcing the bum. Be nice first. Then firm. But if you have to, cause a scene! This is the 21st century, for heavens sake!

One woman took desperate measures: She stormed up to the slot club desk, announced that she was divorcing her deadbeat husband, and demanded that she be given an account of her own with a new number, using her maiden name and her parents' address. In most cases, this probably won't be necessary, though it often takes going higher than the front-line slot club clerks. Sometimes a supervisor will be more understanding. If not, some have had success writing to the casino manager.

To avoid this type of problem, I suggest that couples do not go to the slot club desk to join at the same time; some casinos will still insist on a joint account if you're there together. Go at different times, even different days. Just leave blank the space for spouse when each applies. In fact, Brad often joins a slot club, then we wait awhile before I join. Occasionally, we can snag some bonus points for Brad, who "recommends" me for membership.

Playing on Someone Else's Card

Most slot clubs have rules stating that everyone must use his or her own slot card at all times. However, for married or other couples who have the same last name and same address, casinos don't usually make an issue of playing on the same card. Brad and I switch machines a lot and often don't bother switching cards. In 14 years of playing video poker, we've never had a casino employee question this practice. However, when we're playing a coupon or promotion that specifically states a bonus will be paid only if you have your slot card inserted, we make sure we're always playing on our own card.

You have to be careful here. This is an area that's ripe for abuse and you can't blame the casinos if they strictly enforce this rule. Some players give duplicate cards to their friends to help them qualify for a lucrative promotion. Others routinely wander the casino looking for people playing without a slot card. They

A Death in the Family

What happens when a slot club member dies and there's a balance in his account? Each casino has its own policy here. Most clubs state in writing that cards and benefits are "nontransferable," which means that *legally*, the membership would be terminated and the balance lost, because it can't be transferred to another person.

However, in most circumstances, clubs take a more compassionate stance. If a survivor is a spouse, close relative, someone with the same address, and (especially) a regular player, a club supervisor or a host will most likely see that the balance in the account is transferred to the survivor's card, with no hassles.

The only time a casino will enforce the nontransferable clause, according to leading slot club authority Jeffrey Compton, is when there's a sticky divorce case that the casino doesn't want to become involved in or when card privileges are used for some definite violation of club regulations, i.e., the selling of comps or circumventing of promotion rules.

then try to sneak their cards into the machine without the player noticing; others try to sweet talk the player into using their card.

I know one woman who tries to push her card on anyone not using one by saying that it will bring luck. This way she gets extra club points for no play or risk on her part. And I've heard of another woman who must have been a master persuader. She never played at all at one top-level casino, yet still accumulated enough points to get invitations to all the VIP parties and receive gifts as nice as a Gucci watch, in addition to all the attending cashback.

A gray-area technique I've heard of is to play exclusively on one person's card for months at a time, while the other card "plays hard to get," waiting for the casinos' we-miss-you letters that often include special offers and coupons for cash. When those offers come, that card gets all the play, while the first card "rests." The process is repeated over and over.

This is an area where your ethical standards can be tested. I like to ask myself this question, "Am I breaking only the technical letter of the policy, or is my motivation to get something from the casino that I don't deserve or haven't earned?" As in all of life, it boils down to letting your conscience be your guide.

To Each His Own

A few general comments apply to all slot clubs: The casinos offer them; players earn benefits by putting slot club cards into machines while they play; and players are throwing money out the window if they don't join. I can't overstress, however, how important it is to learn the slot club system details for *each* casino. There are so many different systems, variations, special considerations, nuances, and individual characteristics of slot clubs that entire books have been written about them.

Just joining the club will not automatically cause benefits to come flooding your way. True, simply joining may get you a gift and a spot on the mailing list with, perhaps, some basic offers occasionally arriving in your mailbox. But you'll miss out on a lot of the major benefits if you don't become a student of the systems in the casinos in which you play.

In the sections that follow, I'll discuss some slot club variables and details to watch for.

How Much Will They Tell You?

Secretive and spell-it-all-out systems represent the two extremes with regard to how much detail about their slot clubs casino executives are willing to reveal.

Some bosses feel that as long as a customer is happy coming to his casino and paying for his room and food, there's no reason to let him know that he can earn extra benefits. They run systems that don't spell out what players are entitled to. There are no specific details in the club's brochure, assuming there even is a club brochure. The card readers usually say no more than "Accepted" when you put in your card and point balances are not displayed. If you want to find out what benefits you might be earning, you have to stop playing and stand in line at the slot club desk. And when you finally talk to a human being, he or she either isn't very knowledgeable about the system or makes you feel like you're begging for something you don't deserve.

There might be one benefit to systems where details aren't written down in black and white: A player who goes to the trouble to educate himself and isn't afraid to be a little assertive might be able to get more from the system, since there aren't as many participants as there might be in a more open slot club. Don't-ask won't-tell clubs (as Jeffrey Compton refers to them), however, are becoming rare, especially in Las Vegas, where competition is fierce. In fact, even a handful of casinos in little Reno, one of the last bastions of secretive slot clubs, are upgrading their systems to be more open.

On the other hand, Atlantic City remains the king of don't-ask won't-tell slot clubs. According to an e-mail buddy, 12 of the 13 Atlantic City casinos will not tell you how much play it takes to earn a point or what comp value a point has. My friend submits the following: "I have politely asked very clear and precise questions and I get well-practiced non-answers. Here's an example.

"Me: 'How much play does it take to earn a point and how many points do I need for a comped buffet?'

"Slot club clerk: 'They don't tell us that. The computer determines your comps based on how long you play.'

"Me: 'OK, how long do I have to play, and at what denomination, to earn a buffet?'

"Clerk: 'I don't know. The computer figures it out.'

"Me: 'Well, I'm very familiar with computers. Computers are mathematical. The computer knows how much value to assign my play based on a mathematical formula, but no one who works here knows what that formula is?'

"Clerk: 'It's based on what you play and for how long. The computer figures it out.' Ad nauseum."

Spell-it-all-out slot clubs are much more user-friendly for the customers, and most slot club managers are coming, albeit some slowly, to the conclusion that they're more effective in the long run. Prospective members simply sign up for the club and are handed a brochure, which specifically delineates the available benefits. A lot of people are shy about asking for anything, so if the system isn't spelled out, they may decide to go to a casino where it's easy to find out what the benefits are and how to get them.

But whichever system a slot club has, if you learn its ins and outs and are politely assertive, you'll do much better than the average member. There are almost always methods for getting more comps and benefits beyond just what's printed in the brochures and literature. You can depend on what's usually done and get what everyone else gets, or you can watch for exceptions and get extra benefits with no extra play or risk.

Which is Better—Cashback or Comps?

Another way to categorize slot clubs concerns the general type of benefits they offer—cashback and comps—for the points you earn. There are three basic combinations.

Perhaps the most common is the "cash-and-comp" system. The points you earn collect in a "bank" and determine how much cashback you can redeem according to a set published schedule, i.e., 400 points equals $1. Then there's usually some kind of parallel bank in which comp points or credits accrue. How you earn and collect these comp benefits varies greatly from casino to casino.

In a "comp-only" system, you have only one bank of points, which can be redeemed only for "amenities," as opposed to cash: rooms, food, gift-shop purchases, movies, shows, etc.

In a "comp-or-cash" system, your points also build in only one bank. However, you choose how you want to use them, either for comps or cash, though not both. Usually, but not always, points are a little more valuable if you use them for comps. If you choose to take them in cashback, the percentage is often set slightly lower.

Many variations and exceptions are found within these three basic types, so there's no way to say which system is best. In comp-only systems, casinos sometimes run promotions for limited-time cashback. Or they may mail bounce-back-cash coupons based on the number of points earned in a certain period, making this as good or better than the cash-and-comp system. I know one comp-or-cash system that also has a hidden comp bank that's not publicized; you can ask for comps from this bank and save your points for cash—kind of like having your cake and eating it too.

Rich Get Richer

In some casinos, mostly on the Vegas Strip, if you're a high-roller slot machine player (usually not a video poker player and especially not if you're known as a skilled one), you can sometimes negotiate a higher rate of cashback than the standard that applies for the general public. Jeff Compton says, "If your daily slot action *exceeds* $25,000, you could bring up the subject with your slot host."

It's imperative to study the slot club systems where you play to get used to their idiosyncrasies. I agree with one wag who said that most slot clubs have "let's confuse the hell out of them" policies. I knew of one casino where you had to redeem cash and comps at the same time—redeem only the cashback and you lose the corresponding comps. At another casino, the card readers displayed comp points, although it also gave cashback—just the opposite of every other casino paying both cashback and comps at the time.

No single book can cover every slot club tactic, much less any one chapter. Sometimes I think casino executives stay up all night, trying to find some new little slot club trick for their customers to stumble over. I've purposely not given many specific examples in this chapter. Slot clubs change so frequently, specific information would probably have been out of date before this book came back from the printer.

When it comes to the comps-versus-cash debate, asking which I prefer is like asking me which of my grandchildren I love most. How you choose a slot club, whether one with cash or comps, is a matter of personal likes and goals and there's no one right answer. Someone who flies to Vegas once a year for a vacation away from a stressful job may not care about cash rebates. He makes good money at his job and wants to be pampered, so he's probably more interested in earning comps at a luxurious resort casino. Before you judge him too negatively, it's possible that he'll actually earn more value with the high-level comps than he'd make with cashback at another casino.

Furthermore, Jeffrey Compton makes a good case for the superiority of comps. He says that no one goes back to the Midwest after a trip to Vegas and brags about the $20 or $30 cashback he earned. But you'll certainly hear him talk in glowing terms about the comped meals he ate, even if they were just buffets. I see Jeff's point. For the once-in-awhile recreational gambler, getting a comp makes him feel special, like a VIP, something simple cashback doesn't do.

On the other hand, to a frequent player who isn't staying overnight, such as a Vegas local or someone who goes on daytrips to a nearby riverboat casino, comps are not as important. Comped meals are appreciated, but the frequent player often earns more of those than he can use. He gets enough comps that they no longer make him feel that special. He's more interested in cashback, which allows him to choose how he wants to spend his slot club benefits.

A few casinos that have offered cashback in the past have changed to all-comp systems. Other casino executives are watching these conversions with interest, since most casinos would love to cut out cashback completely. Doing this, however, is always a publicity nightmare. Customers don't like to have benefits cut, whether by a one-time major change in the system or by smaller roundabout changes over a period of time. I'll admit it out loud, in print, right here and now: Cashback is our most cherished slot club benefit. Some trivialize it, saying, "When I lose three hundred dollars in an hour, earning a few dollars in cashback isn't going to make me feel better."

That's the wrong way to look at it. First of all, slot club cashback is real money you're entitled to whether you win or lose. It's a bonus for doing something you were doing anyway, playing the machines. (Of course, you should never play more than you ordinarily would and never play above your bankroll just to collect cashback—or comps.) Secondly, most casino visitors play more than one hour in their lifetime. You need to look at this long term; over time, the dollar amount turns into a substantial sum, money you can save or spend or add to your gambling bankroll.

Thirdly, the amount you earn in one play won't always be trivial. You can increase your cashback dramatically by playing on bonus-point days. During one four-month period in Las Vegas when we were able to play on a lot of triple-point days, Brad and I logged 633 hours, mostly at dollar machines, and collected $6,501 in slot club cash. Ten dollars-plus an hour is not bad "pay" for sticking a card in a machine. Even when we were quarter players, we averaged about $3 extra per hour in cashback by playing mostly during bonus-point periods.

Lastly, and perhaps most importantly, cashback is *always* a plus number. Can you say that for any other casino activity? Your gambling results on slots or video poker will have plus and minus numbers over the long term—probably with many more minuses. Cashback figures may look small for one session or even for several casino vacations, but it's always a plus number, no matter whether you win or lose on the actual machine. Gambling winnings are iffy; cashback is the surest thing in the casino!

Slot Club Hints from the Frugal Princess

• Join slot clubs before you leave home. Many casinos have Web sites where you can do this, or you can call the casino's toll-free number to see if they offer this convenience. Sign up early and you might get some free offers in the mail before you ever step into the casino.

• Carry as many club cards as is practical. If you find yourself in a casino unexpectedly, it's nice to sit down to play and not have to waste time going to the booth for a duplicate card. Mom and Brad have so many cards in Vegas that they only carry those for the specific area where they'll be—but the others are filed in a box in the car where they can be retrieved quickly if travel plans change.

• Study up on each slot club you join by reading all the literature and asking questions at the booth. Find out all you can about how to earn points and how to use them. (I was pleasantly surprised at one casino when I learned that I could use our points for on-site child-care facilities.) Look for the club policy on the expiration of points (often one year) and be sure to use before you lose.

• If you constantly forget your slot club card in the machine when you leave, get a bungee cord that most clubs hand out free. Attach one end to a hole in the card and the other end to your wrist.

• Don't forget to put your card back in when an employee has taken it out to insert his own, a procedure usually required for a hand-pay or machine fill. I wonder how many points have been lost because players' slot cards are lying on top of the machine where the employee left them.

• Watch out for slot club systems that stop recording points when there hasn't been play for a certain number of minutes. For example, if you take a bathroom break or stop playing to talk to a friend or a slot host, you cease to be logged into the system. This is done to prevent players from leaving their cards in machines after they leave the casino, hoping someone else will come by and play that machine, unwittingly racking up valuable points for them. Some of the card readers start flashing when you've "timed-out," but often that's not enough to catch your attention. I've lost a lot of points this way!

Loving the Bounce-Back Wars

If you've always loved cashback, as I have, then you'll be thrilled, as I am, with the new bounce-back wars. My introduction to this state of affairs occured a couple years ago after Brad and I had already moved to Las Vegas, but had to return to our previous home in Indianapolis to sell our condominium there. When we returned to Las Vegas after being away for nearly two months, I had the sad task of throwing away hundreds of dollars worth of expired bounce-back-cash coupons. Seeing the offers all together like that, I realized that the casinos were at war with each other in terms of their efforts to entice customers to return via cash coupons in the mail.

The History of Bounce-Back

Bounce-back casino cash is a promotion in which the casino gives you some kind of cash incentive to get you to come back through the doors.

There used to be a fairly obvious distinction between "earned cashback" and "bonus bounce-back cash." For many years, if a casino offered cashback (not all did), as a general rule it could be redeemed anytime, even on the same day you earned it if you wished. In fact, it was sometimes referred to as "same-day cashback." And the amount you earned was directly correlated with the number of slot club points you racked up. For example, if you put 1,000 points on your card, you could go to the slot club booth and redeem them for X amount of dollars. Bounce-back cash, on the other hand, was something extra that came in the mail. Sometime after you'd visited and played in a casino, you'd receive a cash coupon or voucher that you had to take back to redeem. It was a carrot that the casino dangled in front of you to encourage a return visit. You usually couldn't easily discern the criteria for qualifying for this bounce-back cash reward.

Then casinos began changing their slot club policies and marketing techniques, at which point the terms began changing meanings. Many casinos, especially in Atlantic City, talked about giving cashback, but you couldn't get it the same day you earned it. A coupon or voucher would show up a few days after you returned home. It could be redeemed for your cashback only if you came back to the casino within a certain length of time. At most casinos, you knew how much you would get, because it, too, was directly correlated with the number of slot club points you earned on that last visit. It was earned cashback, but distributed in a bounce-back fashion. That was not a welcome change, but at least players could count on getting exactly what they knew they'd earned if they could get back to the casino to collect within the required time period.

Then came the great casino innovation of target marketing. This led to drastic changes in slot club systems, which really muddied the waters for a casino visitor who wanted his gambling to result in the most lucrative cash bonuses possible. Almost all casinos in the

U.S. had slot clubs and at many of them, you could still determine how much cashback or comps you could get for those points. But many casinos, i.e., Harrah's, decided that not all machines' points were equal for earned cashback or bounce-back bonuses. You couldn't earn 1,000 points and be sure of what you were entitled to as your reward. You had to go home and wait by the mailbox to see what coupons arrived.

Some casinos, such as the Coast properties in Las Vegas, feature both earned cashback, redeemable the same day, and bonus bounce-back cash, which comes on a monthly coupon sheet. There are varying levels of these coupon sheets, although you have to be a persistent detective to find out what the criteria are for each level, since it's not in any published casino literature. Others, such as Station Casinos in Las Vegas, have an elaborate bounce-back system to make up for not giving earned cashback, with published tiered levels, although the amount of play needed to get different bounce-back cash amounts is not specified and seems to change often at the whims of marketing.

So, yes, bounce-back cash can be defined as an incentive sent by mail to get you to return to a casino. It can be in lieu of or in addition to same-day cashback. However, it's often not directly correlated to the exact number of points earned. Oh, sometimes you can figure out the formula in order to keep these bounce-back checks coming; occasionally, a casino has a regular schedule or even publishes the tiered levels so you know what it takes to get the cash on each level.

However, often the criteria for the levels of bounce-back-cash coupons are a deep dark secret kept somewhere in that mysterious realm of a casino called the marketing department. Any number of factors can be fed into the computer to figure how to best attract the kind of gamblers that will contribute the most to the casino's bottom line: what games you play, how long you play, how much coin you put through a machine, what denomination you play, your skill level, your frequency of visits, how far you live from the casino, whether you've won or lost, or the color of your hair. Okay, I made that last one up, but you can see that the method for awarding bounce-back cash is exceedingly complex and often frustrating. It's no longer possible to know exactly what you can do to get the most cashback for your play in a casino, whatever the terms you use or the type of cashback the casino offers.

Not all casinos send out bounce-back cash, but I've noticed that it's one of the fastest-growing casino promotions around. Atlantic City is probably the grand-daddy in this field, because it was the first gambling venue that depended primarily on day-trippers who can be easily lured by this technique, since they're able to return frequently. For many years, the customers coming in by bus have not only been given coins or cash vouchers they could use that day, but a bounce-back coupon for use on their next trip. Then came the riverboat and Native American casinos, which could use bounce-back enticements, because much of their business came from locals who, like players in the New Jersey market, could also visit frequently.

The Las Vegas Welfare State

Las Vegas, on the other hand, has embraced this marketing ploy only recently. For a long time, the Strip attracted mostly occasional tourists who were more interested in free-room promotions. But with the exploding population came the steady rise of casinos in the outlying areas, and these "locals casinos" had to find ways to compete for the locals' gambling dollars. The result? A bounce-back war is now in progress in Las Vegas that would have been inconceivable only a few years ago. Brad and I together regularly get at least $1,500 a month in bounce-back, with hundreds more some months depending on the irregular mailings of some casinos.

We local Las Vegas gamblers call bounce-back mailings our "welfare checks." The first of every month I spend a good chunk of time scheduling them (I keep needing bigger and bigger calendars to write them all into!), since they always have a specified pickup time, ranging from one day only to a usual period of three-to-four days and occasionally all month. Most of the best and most regular bounce-back checks come from the locals casinos and you can get many of them only if you have a local address. (This is why a lot of players from nearby states, or who visit Vegas several times a month, get a mailbox here.) Some locals casinos do send these cash coupons to out-of-towners, usually with a much longer period for picking up the cash, but on a more irregular schedule. Many Strip hotels have jumped on the bounce-back bandwagon, only they mail vouchers mainly to their out-of-town customers and only occasionally to the locals as well.

This bounce-back-cash war is not limited to Las Vegas. Internet bulletin boards and e-mail lists are filled with happy reports from players from all over. Those who can visit a casino during the week are picking up big cash as Atlantic City tries to overcome the "weekend-destination" syndrome. Many Mississippi casinos are giving earned cashback and bounce-back cash. One riverboat in the Chicago area sends its high-rolling players $200-$500 every *week* as long as they continue to play heavily and regularly. However, there are many players, even those playing no higher than quarters, getting frequent smaller bounce-back checks every week from riverboats all over the Midwest.

Of course, the casino's purpose for its bounce-back-cash program is to get you to come back to play, rather than going next door or spending your entertainment money on a non-casino activity. To continue getting bounce-back cash, you must continue playing. Bounce-back cash is not only a reward for your past play, it's also an incentive to attract your future gambling. Even if the specific reward levels are not published, there's the general perception, and a correct one, that the more you play, the more bounce-back rewards you'll receive. Therefore, I must warn you that casino bounce-back programs can be a danger area for a player who cannot control his gambling. Simply throwing away bounce-back coupons may be the best choice for some gamblers. However, for the majority of casino visitors, bounce-back cash is just another way to get more value for the entertainment dollars they spend in a casino.

Maximizing Your Bounce-Back Cash

Here are some tips I've gleaned from my bounce-back-cash experiences that will help you get the most out of these programs.

• Learn as much as you can about the bounce-back policies at the casinos where you play. This is not an easy task, since every casino has its own criteria and most of them do not publish information about it.

How do I get my information? I talk to the hosts, who sometimes (but not always) are privy to the marketing department's secrets. Sometimes I get valuable information at the slot club desk, especially if I ask to talk to the slot club manager. Often the fastest way to get this information is to join an Internet bulletin board that discusses casinos and gambling. And sometimes I learn through our own experiences: Brad and I will play differing amounts for a period of time at one casino and see how our bounce-back cash differs.

• Many casinos have a sliding scale, depending on

your level of play. Remember that, although the requirements may not be exact, a general rule is that the more you play (in time and/or in denomination), the larger your bounce-back-cash amount. However, all casinos have a ceiling and it's valuable to know what it is. Instead of overplaying, you can stop when you reach that level and start playing at another casino to build up your bounce-back there.

• You must keep playing at a casino on a fairly regular basis to keep the bounce-back bonuses coming, but it varies from casino to casino just how often this must be. Some casinos base their bounce-back rewards on weekly play, but in many casinos, we manage to stay at the maximum level by playing big just once a month. A few have quarterly requirements that we can knock off in one longer session every three months. We feel no obligation to play at a casino on the same day we redeem a bounce-back coupon, and this is almost never a requirement to keep the coupons coming. Rather, we play on a day that fits into our busy schedule and at the most advantageous time. For example, we may have to pick up a bounce-back coupon at Casino A on a Monday or Tuesday, but if there are no promotions we might wait to play on the weekend when they're giving triple points.

• Remember that each casino has its own bounce-back schedule (or lack thereof). Sometimes bounce-back cash is one coupon sent monthly; other times your monthly or irregular mailing will have four to six coupons to use at specific periods over an entire month's time.

• Look for extras. Many bounce-back-cash coupons come with additional coupons for meal comps and many casinos include coupons for free or reduced-rate show tickets and other casino activities and benefits, including free room nights.

• Again, as I've mentioned earlier, in the vast majority of cases it's better to join a slot club with an individual rather than a joint account, as individual accounts are good for getting duplicate mailings for free-room offers and other benefits. It really does hurt to have a joint account that reduces the number of promotions you can take advantage of, especially the number of bounce-back-cash coupons. Most of the time you don't know in advance whether it will matter or not; therefore, my recommendation still stands. When you join a new club, keep separate accounts. If you have a joint account now and see that you're missing out, *separate!* (Your accounts, not your relationship!) Brad and I *each* play enough to stay near the bounce-back ceiling in most of the casinos in which we regularly play in Vegas. It would cost us hundreds of dollars a month if we had a joint account and got only one set of bounce-back coupons.

• There's usually no way to bend the rules of the bounce-back-cash program, since the coupons are generated by a computer program in the back of the house. If it requires that you have a certain number of points to qualify during the last three-month period, there's usually no one you can explain to that you were in the hospital during that period and weren't able to visit the casino and play like you usually do.

However, sometimes talking to someone at the slot club booth or to your host can fix bounce-back problems. Since these cash coupons come by mail, there's always the possibility that they've gotten lost. If I know I've fulfilled the specific requirements for one casino's coupon mailings, i.e., earned X number of points, I'll be very aggressive in finding out why I didn't get one. I've never been unsuccessful in getting a replacement and this has happened to us quite a few times.

I've also asked hosts (nicely, of course) if there's

anything they can do about bounce-back coupons that expired while we were out of town. Although some casino policies don't give the host any authority here, I've been surprised at the number of times she can extend the date for us, knowing that we're good customers and will play often in that casino with or without bounce-back-cash enticements. Remember my mantra: "Just ask."

• Never be surprised if bounce-back cash doesn't follow the usual rules of rewarding you for your play. Recently, Brad and I each got a bounce-back-cash coupon from the same casino—mine was a large one and Brad's was a smaller one. You might assume that I played a lot more at that casino than Brad did. Wrong! I hadn't played at that casino for many months. Explanation: Brad's coupon was a reward for his recent play—mine was a "we-missed-you-and-want-you-to-come-back" coupon. It's times like these that Brad and I give up trying to figure out every casino's criteria. We just enjoy the windfall when it comes.

• Accept the fact that casino bounce-back programs change often. It seems that marketing is constantly tweaking its systems, always seeking that perfect bounce-back formula that will bring in the most gamblers who will contribute to the casino's bottom line. These changes are usually made with no advance notice to customers. One month you play just as you have each prior month for the last six, and instead of getting your usual $200 in bounce-back coupons, you get $50. The letter introducing "a new and exciting" reward program is never followed up with one of explanation when the program is suddenly scrapped just two months later.

• Take into consideration your time, effort, and life goals when you decide what casino bounce-back programs you want to try to qualify for. Some are so limited in their pick-up time frame that the whole thing becomes frustrating rather than enjoyable. In some locales with many casinos, there may be more than is humanly possible to take advantage of. In Las Vegas, we've had to start limiting ourselves to those casinos with the best programs (and those that are most convenient for us). I've had more than one Las Vegan tell me that they've had to cut back on the number of casinos where they play, because running all over town qualifying for, and collecting, bounce-back cash had made gambling seem more like a job than entertainment, which was their original goal. I know one high-roller couple in the Midwest who live three hours from a riverboat casino that regularly sends them valuable bounce-back coupons. They sometimes have to make the difficult decision to pitch them, because they can't make the time for a six-hour round trip to redeem them on the specified day without neglecting family responsibilities.

• Bounce-back cash can take several forms. It can be a coupon or a voucher or a check that you take back to the casino to exchange for good old American dollars. You don't have to put it into a slot or video poker machine or buy chips with it to use at table games. The casino hopes you give them a shot at the extra cash by gambling, but you can take it shopping or stuff it in your pocket to save for a rainy day—whatever is your pleasure.

Growing in popularity is the issuance of coupons for "free credit play," which requires that you play bonus credits through a machine at least once in order to cash what's left. Sometimes casinos will send out, especially to table players, a bounce-back bonus in the form of matchplay coupons or promotional chips. With matchplay coupons, you have to put up your own money in the amount of the coupon for each bet, and

---

BURPing at Barley's

My favorite slot club name is the one they used to have at Barley's, a microbrewery-casino in Henderson, Nevada. The full name was Barley's Ultimate Reward Program—the acronym worked out to be BURP!

---

they're good for one bet only. Therefore, the value of a matchplay coupon is a little less than half its face value, depending on the house edge of the game you use it on. If they're "full-value chips," they can be played alone without any of your own money at risk and are worth face value. These have to be played until you lose them; they cannot be redeemed for cash, but you can pocket all the real chips you get on winning bets.

To sum up, bounce-back programs are complicated, time-consuming, unpredictable, frustrating, even heart-breaking on occasion. But a good bounce-back coupon has the effect of getting Brad and me into a casino faster than you can say "free money."

Maximizing Bonus-Point Promotions

Earning points for cashback and/or comps is the basic slot club benefit. And the easiest way to earn extra benefits is to look for bonus-point promotions. Many casinos award double, triple, and even higher multiple points at various times, often on holidays or graveyard shift. A casino that gives points at a base rate of .25% often becomes a must-play for us when point-accumulation rates double to .5% or triple to .75%.

You need to learn the details of each casino's bonus-point days. A lot of casinos have separate systems for comps and cashback, which work independently of each other. So it's possible that a slot club will double or triple your points for cashback, but comps continue to accumulate at the base rate. Other casinos use the same count for both comps and cash. Some casinos have tiered levels of awards and benefits and only base points count in assigning you to a particular tier.

You also need to know how the doubling or tripling of points is recorded. A master computer might be switched on when the double-points period starts; then the card reader automatically gives you the doubled or tripled amount. If it usually takes $100 to get a point, on a double-point day it takes only $50. Some systems do it another way: After putting through the $100, the computer adjusts your account so you get two points instead of one.

At some casinos, points are accumulated on the reader at the base rate, but when you pull out your card, the points are doubled or tripled immediately. We've played at casinos where the card reader doesn't calculate or show the point bonuses at all—you have to go to the slot club and tell them to sign you up for double or triple points. They write down your name and card number and at the end of the day, someone goes through and credits those double or triple points manually.

Another question concerns what a given casino calls a "day." Often, it's a logical designation, like from midnight to midnight. If they advertise bonus points on Tuesday, you can actually start Monday night at midnight and go to 11:59 Tuesday night. But you can't always count on this. I know some casinos where the day begins and ends at 2 a.m. So if there's bonus points on Tuesday, they start at 2 a.m. Tuesday morning and last until 2 a.m. Wednesday morning.

On some riverboats, it's an entirely different system. Double points on Tuesday means that you can earn the double points from the time the boat opens on Tuesday morning at 8:30 a.m. until it closes, as late as 5:30 a.m. Wednesday morning.

For a casino that's open 24/7, you know its day is 24 hours, but you should check on when it begins and ends.

How to Get the Maximum
Point Credit for All Your Play

You must learn the details of a slot club system to be sure your play is generating the maximum number of slot club points possible. In some casinos, the card readers do a "countdown" and you don't get a point until the countdown hits zero. At that point, the countdown starts over again.

In some cases, the card readers keep track of the countdown from machine to machine. In other words, if you start a countdown on one machine, then switch to another machine in mid-countdown, the second machine begins where the first left off. However, most slot club readers don't "remember" the countdown from a previous machine. So you have to be careful about switching. For example, on a machine that requires 50 coins to earn one point, if you play 45 coins through and change machines, you'll lose credit for the 45 coins you've just played.

I once saw a man in Atlantic City screaming at the slot club booth employees. He argued that he'd played all day, but there were no points on his slot club card. What had happened was he kept moving around and never played long enough to get to the end of a single countdown!

New York-New York in Las Vegas has a good system that addresses this problem. It's called the "Follow Me Countdown Program" and it allows you to move from machine to machine without losing credits.

Another thing you must stay alert for is seeing that your points are accumulating correctly. You have to be especially wary of some of the new multi-denomination machines (the ones where by touching the screen, you can play nickels, quarters, dollars, etc,). In most cases, these machines are wired so that you're credited the proper number of points for your play. However, we've heard of, and personally experienced, a few instances where they weren't; every game was giving points as if you were playing the lowest denomination. Players who were feeding in dollars were receiving points as if they were playing nickels. What a terrible thing to happen—these players were getting only one-twentieth of the points they'd earned. This is a particular danger at casinos where the slot club system awards a different number of points for higher and lower denomination play.

To make keeping track of your points even harder, when you insert your slot club card in some casinos the reader simply says "Welcome" and doesn't show you the countdown or the number of points you are accumulating. In these cases it's very difficult to trust that the casino is giving you the accurate amount of points for your action. There are ways to do it by tracking how many coins you put into the machine for a short time, then checking at the slot club desk to see how many points were earned, but it's complicated and involves a lot of time-consuming record-keeping.

What to Do When People or Computers Make an Error

You can never just assume that a slot club system is working the way it's supposed to. Some systems are so old that, although your points are counted by the individual machines, they're not transferred to and credited by the main computer for hours, or even days.

Even a new system can have bugs that keep it from working correctly—for example, it gets overloaded in recording when casino play is heavy on double- or triple-point days. And remember, computers are programmed by people, so no system is exempt from the possibility of human error.

Because mistakes are very common in this area, many experienced players keep detailed records—such as how long they play and how many points the machine indicates they've earned—and check their balances frequently. They also check the first few minutes of play to make sure that they're accumulating points at the proper rate. These observant players are the ones who often have to bring it to the attention of casino personnel that someone forgot to activate the double points on the main slot club computers at the advertised start time.

I find that it pays to check any time points are recorded manually. Some older systems don't give points on hand-pays. They're supposed to be put on later from the paperwork, but this often gets neglected. I recently signed up at the slot club desk for a senior-citizens double-points day, then discovered the next day that my points hadn't been doubled. I don't know if the data processor got mixed up or just missed my name, but it would have cost me $50 if I hadn't checked.

Even if everything is taken care of by computers, it still pays to keep track of your points yourself. If you see a mistake in your point balance, bring it to someone's attention ASAP, the same day if possible. The longer you wait, the harder it is for someone to rectify a mistake. You usually have to talk to a floor supervisor, but sometimes it can be taken care of with a supervisor at the slot club desk. I've even enlisted hosts to take care of these kinds of problems.

Most casinos will make a special effort to make

adjustments in the cases of casino errors, but I've heard of people who've been cheated out of their points. That's bad for business, because often that player never returns and the casino loses a valuable customer over a very small amount. This is a perfect place to remember that magic word *ask*—and ask nicely. You'll find that most places will fix mistakes in this area cheerfully.

Recently, a machine I was playing at a Midwest riverboat casino needed a fill. A floorperson came, took out my card, and put it on top of the machine while he inserted his card to record the transaction—routine in many casinos. Then he took a slot club card from the top of the machine and put it back into my machine. The only problem was, it wasn't my card! At this casino, your name doesn't appear on the card reader during play, so I played for 45 minutes on a $1 Five Play, racking up points quickly before taking the card out to check my point balance. In many casinos, slot club personnel can tell from the computer how long a card has been in a machine, but in this casino they couldn't. I knew approximately how many points I was earning per hour, so the supervisor took my word for it and manually added the proper number of points.

Staying alert and being familiar with the nuances of the system you're playing will enhance your chances of catching and correcting the errors of both man and machine.

Points for All Seasons

Add-ons are always a welcome bonus wherever we find them, whether in a fast-food restaurant that gives away a little toy with a child's meal or on an airplane that awards frequent-flier miles. In the same vein, there are many extra ways to accrue slot club points other than just playing a slot or video poker machine. Not all casinos offer these extras and some of the examples given may be gone by the time you read this, but this discussion should encourage you to keep your eyes open for chances to snag extra slot club points.

Some slot club systems have the capability to track your gambling action in other casino games besides the machines. Take your card to the keno lounge and perhaps you'll get points for your play there. Many bingo rooms give slot club points, with bonus-point days the same as on the machines. You can earn points in some race and sports books, particularly in Vegas locals casinos. Likewise, you can get slot club points when you play live poker at some casinos, such as Foxwoods and Mohegan Sun in Connecticut.

There's been a long-term need to combine machine and table play into one integrated system, but this has progressed slowly, with some casinos using it just informally in awarding comps; it hasn't really been a true marriage. For a long time, Circus Circus in Las Vegas was the only casino that awarded points for table play, and only at blackjack tables. At one time you could get cashback for those points, but today the slot club points you earn at the blackjack table can be used only for comps. Recently, the Las Vegas locals casino Terrible's opened with an integrated system that included table games. It's a start—and I hope that casinos will soon see the value of having a real "player's club" to reward customers no matter what game they play.

Casinos often give bonus points to their slot club members. Sometimes this happens when you join or refer someone else to join, or perhaps as a birthday gift. Sometimes you'll come across coupons for bonus points, often in a casino funbook. And watch for special-promo coupons. The Orleans in Vegas gave out free-point coupons at its pool parties one summer. And I've heard of a casino giving a coupon for bonus points for cashing a paycheck at the cage. Occasionally, casinos give points as prizes in drawings or contests or tournaments. We've gotten them for filling out casino opinion questionnaires.

We've accumulated slot club points for making purchases on a casino-branded credit card. We've seen programs that allowed you to earn points by flying on an airline that partnered with a casino.

Probably the most unusual way I've ever heard of to earn slot club points was a one-day promotion at the Gold Coast in Las Vegas: Donate blood and earn 2,500 free slot club points. One cynic on an Internet board said: "What next? Not only do they want every dollar out of your wallet and nickel from your pocket, now they also want your blood."

Slot Club Cards As Discount Cards

Be sure to carry one slot club card—from any casino, it doesn't matter which—in your wallet at all times. Brad and I learned this lesson on a visit to New Orleans some years ago. We went to board one of the riverboat casinos and had to pay a hefty entrance fee, which would have been waived if we could have shown a slot card from *any* other casino. We had more than 100 at home, but didn't have one on us.

More recently, an online acquaintance reported that his party of four saved $75 on a gambling day cruise out of a Florida port by flashing a slot club card from a Las Vegas casino.

New Slot Club Trends

I used to say that the word I feared most in casino-speak was "change." In fact, if a casino mentioned "exciting slot club changes," my face got longer immediately. In a casino, "exciting changes" usually means that the bean counters have found a way to increase the bottom line. And where does this increase come from? From reducing slot club benefits! The majority of slot club changes are not exciting for the player.

However, I'm seeing some trends in slot clubs these days that I like.

1. Multi-level divisions within slot clubs. Levels, ranging from two to four tiers, are usually named after a precious metal or gemstone—silver, gold, platinum, diamond. A multi-level system, especially if the requirements for each level are clearly spelled out, allows players to be informed and more in control of their slot club benefits, rather than tossed about in uncertainty at the whims of changing marketing schemes.

You don't have to be a "whale" to get to the highest levels. Most programs give you a long time limit to qualify for a tier—usually at least three months and sometimes a whole year. Therefore, regular dollar players can usually qualify for the top tier quickly and quarter players who play heavily are able to qualify over time.

These programs reward ongoing loyalty, so they require that you re-qualify, usually quarterly or yearly, in order to maintain your level. Many of these programs cover a number of casinos in the same company, so you have lots of playing choices both for qualifying and redeeming benefits. This type of system is yet another reason for my frequent reminders to concentrate play at just one or two casinos (or within multi-casino systems), building up points rather than scattering action all over and never earning enough for top-tier benefits in any one casino.

Something you always need to check in multi-level systems is whether bonus points (such as double- or triple-point days) count toward the level requirements—often only base points are used for determining your ranking.

Most of the upper-level divisions accord plenty of extra benefits—some previously enjoyed only by big-time table-game high rollers. Slot club members in the top level are often invited to golf tournaments, cigar parties, yacht cruises, sporting events, and other off-property VIP activities. At some casinos, premium players can walk into any non-gourmet restaurant and eat on the house; instead of a written comp, you just show your specially colored players card. Preferred parking, property-wide discounts, lavish party invitations, free slot tournaments, line passes, automatic room upgrades, extra bonus-point days, and private VIP club lounges are being offered to the highest levels of players at casinos across the nation.

We liked the "Inner Circle" program at the Empress in Joliet when we used to play there frequently while living in Indiana. Our top-level silver cards had our pictures on them, which functioned as our casino ID and prevented abuse of the better privileges. The cards gave us access to the concierge lounge with a buffet, bar, snacks (including my favorite, chocolate-covered strawberries), and off-track race betting. It was an island of tranquillity amidst the crowded madness of riverboat tables and machines. At the Venetian in Las Vegas, the premium-level Gold Club gives the valuable benefit of 50% more cashback than at the base level.

And the multi-tiered slot clubs are not just on the

Vegas Strip. Station Casinos, catering to locals all over Las Vegas, provides its top-level players with deep buffet discounts and line passes (a great perk at these busy casinos), special comp lines at other restaurants, discounts in the gift shops, invitations to special promotions and VIP parties, and bonuses on travel. And wherever in the country you find a Harrah's casino, you can work your way up the ladder of increasing perks and benefits, from Gold to Platinum to Diamond level.

Some negatives are associated with tiered slot clubs. The biggest problems come from casinos that don't spell out the details of the program. Then it becomes a searching game for the players who want to be well-informed. Sometimes you can ask at the slot club booth, but these employees aren't always given complete information either. You may have better luck talking with a host, but amazingly, not even all of them know all the ins and outs. Sometimes you have to depend on your own trial-and-error experiences and compare your information with that of other knowledgeable players.

Another potential problem with tiered programs is that they may tempt some to gamble beyond their bankroll. You have to be careful here. Trying to reach higher tiers by concentrating your play in one casino makes good sense. But playing and losing more than you can afford will negate any benefits you get by reaching a higher level.

2. Slot club consolidation. Consolidation within the casino industry has made it possible to issue a single players card for many different casinos owned by the same company, not only in a single gambling venue such as Las Vegas, but all over the country. Leaders in this trend include the Harrah's Total Rewards program, where your players card is good at nearly two

dozen properties around the United States, and the Las Vegas locals chain of Station Casinos, consisting of more than a half-dozen casinos.

As I write this, many company-wide player-tracking systems are in the works or already in place, although full implementation might not be complete for some time:

• Mandalay Resort Group: Casinos (Mandalay Bay, Circus Circus, etc.) in Las Vegas, Reno, Laughlin, Tunica, and Detroit.

• MGM Mirage: Casinos (MGM Grand, Bellagio, etc.) in Las Vegas, Atlantic City, Mississippi, and Detroit (Primm currently not part of the system).

• Park Place Entertainment: Casinos (Caesars Palace, Bally's, etc.) in Las Vegas, Reno, Lake Tahoe, Laughlin, Atlantic City, Mississippi, and Indiana.

• Harrah's: More than two dozen properties across the country.

• Station Casinos: Casinos in Las Vegas and Thunder Valley in California.

• Fiesta Casinos: Fiesta Rancho and Fiesta Henderson in Las Vegas and Thunder Valley in California.

• Coast Casinos: Casinos throughout Las Vegas (with the current exception of Barbary Coast).

• Carl Icahn Properties: Two Arizona Charlie's and Stratosphere in Las Vegas and the Sands in Atlantic City.

Don't assume too much in this area; not all companies have linked slot clubs or even plans to create one. Although it's sometimes possible, with fairly heavy play and by going through a host, to get comps at a sister property in unlinked casinos, the usual procedure is to use your comps at the casino where you earned them.

I expect this trend to continue, although, as usual with casinos, not all systems will have the same elements and, sad to say, some won't use this innovation to make their club easier for a player to figure out. The best clubs from a player point of view are those where you can earn points at the same rate in any of the individual casinos and redeem them in any other casino in the system without complicated restrictions.

One big advantage of all of them is that this consolidation is a timesaver—you won't have to fill out umpteen club applications and stand in umpteen lines waiting to get umpteen different cards that you have to carry around. Brad applauds any innovation that keeps him from standing in line and I appreciate anything that makes my purse lighter.

3. High-tech advances. I like new technological systems already in place that give faster access to comps, cashback, and other slot club benefits. At some casinos, the slot club system allows you to comp yourself right at the machine; the paper comp waits for you at your chosen restaurant. Other casinos have kiosks where you can redeem your points and the comp slips are printed out for you, thus avoiding long slot club lines. And some now have point-of-purchase (POP) systems that conveniently let you swipe your card when you want to spend your points and your account is automatically debited right then and there.

As usual, there can be a downside to technology. Many of these systems require pin numbers to protect your points from being used by unauthorized people, but others depend on employees checking IDs. Since this may not be done consistently, it behooves you to guard your slot cards as you would cash.

Other technical innovations you might see, either now or in the near future, include casino-wide systems that not only track your play on machines, but for any other type of gambling you might do in the casino—whether on the tables, in the race and sports book, or in the bingo room. Realizing that money you spend anywhere on property—on hotel rooms, in restaurants, for entertainment, and in shops—can be as important to the bottom line as what you spend on gambling, the new integrated systems can issue points for all your non-gambling expenditures, as well.

Taking it a step further, this system can allow you to spend your points in the places that you earn them. Technology already exists that would let you deposit money in the cage and download any part of it as credits directly into the machine you're playing. Some systems allow you to collect your cashback right at the machine as credits you can play or cash out. (The casinos like this one, figuring you're more likely to play it, and most likely to lose it, rather than carry it out the door to spend on frivolous things like gas or groceries!) Cash coupons with barcodes will be redeemable at kiosks or any machine, again doing away with those long lines we hate.

And, of course, computer technology is charging ahead. You can already go online to some casino Web sites and join the slot club or check the status of your point balance.

Coming Up

This is the end of the chapter on slot clubs, but it's not the end of the subject. The next chapter examines promotions, and most promotions are slot club promotions. In fact, the next chapter follows right on the heels of this one, and the break is simply to give you time to catch your breath before I throw more frugal hints your way.

6

So Many Promotions, So Little Time

"Hurrah for competition!"
—the closing words of the Promotions
chapter in The Frugal Gambler *and still*
my rallying cry six years later

In *The Frugal Gambler*, I called promotions "casino gravy," implying that they were something that added a little flavor and texture, but weren't an important part of the casino "meal." The longer I play, however, the more I realize that the best gambling feast isn't one with several individual items arranged tastefully on a plate, but a hearty stew in a big bowl. Good games and slot club benefits are the meat and potatoes, but promotions are the vegetables, the colorful and flavorful carrots, celery, and onions, which make this a winning one-dish casino dinner.

The Why of Promotions and How They Benefit Players

All casinos are for-profit enterprises and they run promotions designed to add to their bottom line. If that's the case, however, you may be wondering how a promotion can ever be good for the customer.

The purpose of most casino advertising is not to persuade people to gamble. Rather, it's to persuade people to come through the advertiser's, rather than its competitor's, doors. Promotions are an incentive for the gambler who's planning to play somewhere anyway. This gambler might have an opportunity to play the same games at several different casinos, so if he plays them at a casino where he can take advantage of a good promotion, this is an added value that can positively affect *his* bottom line.

So how do casinos benefit from promotions? Occasionally, they don't. Atlantic City, for example, is famous for its bus wars. The casinos there get locked in battles for the business of the day-trippers who come in by bus from surrounding cities. Bus-fare rebates and other benefits escalate till the whole thing gets out of hand and all the casinos lose money. In fact, newspaper financial pages occasionally report that a bus war is responsible for a drop in quarterly revenues citywide. But no casino wants to be the first to cut back, afraid to lose a big share of its customer base.

Well-run promotions, however, are usually long-run moneymakers for casinos, which is why they're so prevalent. Good promotions bring in customers, new and old, who hope to benefit financially from the promotion itself, but will usually have a losing bottom line. Perhaps they don't fully understand the promotion or how to maximize its worth. Perhaps they're not knowledgeable about the games or haven't learned accurate strategies. Or maybe they're unaware of all the benefits of the slot club and comp systems. The purpose of this chapter is to help you avoid fattening up the casinos' profits by getting sucked into a promotion—then not knowing what to do with it.

How to Find Promotions

As I discussed in detail in *The Frugal Gambler*, I'm always on the lookout for a good promotion. When I fly to a casino destination, I look for promotional material at the airport-information and car-rental desks. I scour the racks of flyers in every tourist-information bureau I pass and check them in motel offices. I read billboards and casino marquees while driving to a casino.

When I walk into a casino, I look for banners, posters, and signs. I make a pass by the bell desk to look for freebie magazines that often tell about good current promotions. I read all the informational literature and magazines in my hotel room.

I always buy a daily local newspaper and pick up any newsweeklies in any casino town I'm in, to check for casino advertisements of promotions. In Las Vegas, in the "Neon" section of the Friday *Las Vegas Review-Journal*, Jeffrey Compton and Bob Dancer write an excellent column called "Player's Edge," which focuses on promotions and lists the whens and wheres of current slot club point bonuses. Also in Vegas, *Gaming Today*, a sports-oriented weekly tabloid with a lot of casino promotional information, can be picked up free on Tuesdays in many casino race and sports books and on Wednesdays in some grocery stores.

And the slot club is a must-stop. I look for posters, or brochures and flyers I can pick up, to learn about promotions and events I might not have heard about elsewhere. And I always check with the slot club clerk, especially if I'm a new member or haven't received mailings from them, asking if there are any promotions going on.

I remember inquiring about promotions once at a riverboat casino that we hadn't visited before. I found out that it was double-points day for seniors. The clerk told me that the double-points schedule was always included on a monthly calendar sent to regular customers. However, since no sign about this bonus appeared anywhere in the casino, we never would've known to sign up for it if I hadn't asked.

Although all the above are good sources, if you're connected to the Internet, you have oceans of additional information on your computer. In fact, that's a good description—I sometimes feel like I'm drowning in it! But here are some Web sites that will get you to valuable promotional information quickly.

For information on Las Vegas, go to www.review journal.com/columnists/edge.html and read the "Player's Edge" column I mentioned above. Click on www.americancasinoguide.com/Promotions/VE-GAS-VALUES.shtml and you'll find promotional gold in Scot Krause's long Vegas Values list. And although I've always strongly recommended the *Las Vegas Advisor* newsletter (even before Huntington Press was my publisher), you can now enjoy their accurate and unbiased reporting online, with up-to-the-minute updates you can't get in weekly or monthly publications, at www.lasvegasadvisor.com. Check the "What's News" box for daily updates that often include promotion notices, and sign up for the free weekly e-letter, *Las Vegas Advisor Lite.* I help maintain a list of current bonus-point opportunities on this Web site—click on Bonus Slot Club Points—that will let you know where to play in Las Vegas to earn extra cashback and other benefits.

Many Web sites specialize in casino information; you can search for those that cover specific locations or limit themselves to particular casino games. Most casinos now have their own Web sites, which can be good places to find out about individual promotions, especially tournaments. For video poker players in all parts of the country, there is no better place to go than Skip Hughes' site (subscribe at www.vphomepage .com), where you get advance notice or current news about changes in schedules, machine placement, and the like, along with reviews of promotions, saving you miles of travel and hours of legwork to check out each promo yourself.

Internet bulletin boards are a rich source of information about promotions. I really don't know how I kept up before I bought a computer and jumped on the information highway in cyberspace.

Once Found, How to Participate

If you find out about a promotion from another player and you haven't received your own invitation, use the magic word and *ask*. I know many people who frequent Internet bulletin boards, find out about a promotion, and do this.

Say there's an invitational tournament in a casino where you play regularly. Talk to your host about how you love tournaments and you were wondering if he could check your play to see how close you are to getting invitations to them in the future. You'll be surprised, especially if you're fairly close to the playing requirements, how many times the host will put you into the current tournament right on the spot. Even if this doesn't happen, you haven't wasted your effort—you'll at least know how much more you need to play to score those valuable invites.

A word of caution here: The ways of casino marketing are strange indeed—often unfathomable, in fact. So don't be disappointed if this technique doesn't always work. You may hear of a good promotional offer sent out to customers who haven't been to the casino for a while—an offer that regular players can't

get no matter whom they ask. Invitations for a promotion that includes cash coupons usually can't be
snagged without an individual mailing to you directly—even if you ask nicely all over the casino—unless yours was lost in the mail. And many times, marketing offers come from a decision-making source that
even hosts can't influence, so they can't help you.

The Frugal Princess' Promotion Hints for the Casual Low Roller

• Read the details of all promotions carefully, especially the fine print. If it's a drawing, do you have to
be present to win? If you can't be there, you may want
to give your tickets to someone who can. If it's a video
poker promotion, what are the rules for multi-line
machines? Sometimes they allow only one bonus per
hand, and sometimes only on the bottom line. If the
promotion is a pool party, don't go out and buy a new
swimsuit, as I almost did once. Luckily, I checked at
the slot club desk and learned that these events are
usually *around,* not *in,* the pool, and are often dressy,
even upscale.

• Check to make sure that a promotion you've
heard about hasn't been discontinued or changed. You
can avoid making a wasted trip, or worse, being disappointed after participating, by calling ahead and
verifying details with the slot club.

• Choose promotions that fit into your schedule
and accommodate your goals. If you have to start out
a gambling vacation with a small bankroll or you're in
the middle of a long losing streak, a time-stretching
low-risk promotion can help maximize your gambling
dollar. For example, entering tournaments with several rounds, looking for free spins, or using coupons

for free souvenirs are good time-gobblers. On the other hand, if you're short on time, you might choose to skip all those that require a long wait in line or afford a low probability of winning anything of value, such as a scratch-card promotion with only one million-dollar prize.

• Be sure the promotion fits into your bankroll constraints. Try to avoid the temptation to play longer and lose more than you wanted just to get a promotional bonus. Even though earning double or triple points is great, your bankroll may dictate that you should quit playing before the bonus period ends.

• Remember that not all promotions are good values. I once saw an ad in a magazine that sounded great: Play four hours of blackjack and this casino would give you an airline voucher for a free companion ticket. I couldn't wait to call Mom about my frugal find! I was surprised—and disappointed—when she didn't sound very enthusiastic. I found out why after I took her suggestion to call the 800 number for further information. I learned, as Mom had already guessed, that you had to use a specific travel agency that sold you the first ticket at a price that was higher than two fares at a discount price elsewhere.

• Look to piggyback two or more promotions to make a play more valuable. On one occasion we found a casino that allowed Steve and me to use WinCard non-negotiable chips *with* funbook matchplay coupons for blackjack, roulette, and craps—something that's usually not allowed. We each played a $5 funny chip, backed by a $5 matchplay coupon. When we won, we were paid $10 in real chips and forfeited the coupon, but not the chip, which we could play again. Only when we lost did they take the coupon *and* the chip. For only the $20 buy-in for the chips in the two WinCard packages, we played a long time and cashed out a nice $50 profit when our funny money was finally gone.

Still Stalking the Wild Promotion

I covered many different kinds of promotions in *The Frugal Gambler* and most of that general information remains valid today. Bonus slot club points are still one of the strongest promotions for drawing us into a casino. Brad still loves promotions in which he can win casino logo jackets, and his closets are still jammed with them (although I did finally persuade him to get rid of the oldest ones during our huge garage sale in Indy before we moved permanently to Vegas).

However, many of the examples I gave of specific promotions no longer exist. Even some of the casinos I mentioned are no longer around. And in these last six years I've learned even more valuable lessons about many kinds of promotions; hopefully, they will be helpful to you in getting more bang for your buck.

Senior-Citizen Promotions

In the first book, I stated that there weren't too many special deals for senior citizens, because casinos preferred promotions that targeted a broader range of customers. In addition, they thought that their prices, especially for food, were so low, seniors didn't need additional discounts. Well, casinos have recently awakened to Gray Power. It seems that they're now finding it's to their bottom-line advantage to cater to the older player, who's usually retired, has lots of free time, and, often, has a good amount of disposable income after a lifetime of frugality.

Las Vegas casinos, especially those off the Strip in the neighborhoods, are now setting up more special programs and promotions for seniors, including early-bird meal specials, morning exercise events, monthly entertainment with music and dancing, seminars on subjects that interest seniors (such as estate planning), and free bingo giveaways. This has also caught on in Mississippi, where there are numerous food specials and an occasional free seniors-only slot tournament or drawing. Midwestern riverboat casinos have offered special senior bonus-point days. Casinos on some Native American reservations have offered free health testing to seniors.

In Atlantic City, the Sands opened the luxurious Senior Class private lounge and Caesars redesigned a whole area called Temple Tower to cater to the special needs and wants of seniors, with additional handrails in guest bathrooms, brighter lighting in the halls, and shorter walks to the lobby and parking garage.

So, all you seniors, wherever you are, ask at the slot club desk if there are any promotions for you. They might even give you a special player's card that you'll be happy to carry, because it will put extra money in your pocket.

New-Customer Promotions

New-customer programs that promise to rebate some or all of your losses for your first play at a casino are among the strongest promotions around, but you need to take many things into consideration before you decide to take advantage of one.

First, read the details carefully. Determine when you can collect this rebate; most times you have to wait for the casino to mail you a time-sensitive voucher that can be redeemed only at the casino. Be sure you'll be able to return in the allotted time. Also be sure you can afford to do without the money you lose until you can get back to collect the rebate.

The specifics of each promotion vary, but a typical one might go something like this: The first hour you play after joining the slot club, the casino rebates up to $200 of losses. You must play the whole hour; you can't stop sooner, like as soon as you've lost the $200.

One good way to optimize the value of this promotion might be to take 75% of the rebate amount, in this example $150, and start playing on a $1 or even a $5 machine, hoping for some big hits before your $150 is gone. Set an amount, maybe $100 or $200, whereby if you're lucky and get ahead, you'll quit—happy that you made a nice profit and, like fire insurance, you didn't need the rebate. However, if you lose the $150, take the remaining $50 of your stake and play slowly at a much lower denomination, even one nickel at a time if necessary, to stretch it right to the end of the required hour. Multi-denomination machines are a great choice for a promo like this: You can adjust your level of play up or down, depending on the time.

A hint: Don't automatically assume that you won't qualify for a casino's new-member promotion because you joined the slot club several years before—even though you haven't played there for a while. Some casinos clear players from their computer systems if they haven't used their cards for a certain period of time. Check at the slot club to see whether or not you are indeed a member.

Holiday Shopping Points

At some large casinos, slot club benefits include accumulating holiday shopping points in a separate account. For example, for every point you earn toward cashback at the Venetian in Las Vegas, you also earn a Grazie Gift point; some months, the Venetian awards double Grazie points. During a specified few-day period in November or December, you can come to the casino and redeem your points. At the Venetian, they set up a mini-mall in one of the ballrooms, with various companies and stores represented. You use your points to buy products and services. You can pick up your gifts right then, get gift certificates to spend (or give as gifts) in stores later, or order items to be shipped to your home. You can choose anything from a Sony clock radio for 500 Grazie points up to a BMW X5 luxury ride for 858,000 points. (And some of the high rollers have enough to get two or three of them!)

As with all casino promotions, you need to check out all the details. Some holiday-gift programs use only a catalog. The choice and type of merchandise in these programs can vary greatly; you may not find things you really need or even want. You almost always have to go to the casino in person to do the shopping. This is a definite minus for people who live out of town and might not be able to get to the casino on the exact five or six days usually allotted. I know many people who've had to let hundreds of dollars in gift points expire unused. But for those who can plan ahead, this can be a lucrative slot club benefit for any player. For video poker players looking for opportunities to play with an edge, this holiday shopping spree can sometimes turn an unplayable casino into one that offers a positive opportunity.

Brad especially loves these shopping programs. Since he was raised in the Depression and didn't have many toys while he was little, he's in heaven in the mini-malls and catalogs. One year he passed by all the practical items and got two Razor scooters "for when the kids come to visit us." Never mind that the grandchildren or other kids might come to our house only once or twice a year. Yes, he does love to ride with the neighborhood children and once in a while he gets me to ride along, too.

We played enough one year to take the grandchildren (and their parents) on a cruise. The kids already thought Santa Claus lived in a casino; now they know this for sure.

WinCards

WinCards is a trademarked promotion, used by casinos to encourage people to play table games. They're usually advertised by a brochure at the slot club or casino cashier. Although WinCards are most common in Nevada, I've seen them in casinos on cruise ships, Native American reservations, riverboats, and in the Caribbean. You can find a complete list of casinos that offer WinCards at www.wincards.com/GamingLinks.html.

One part of the WinCard package is instructional, with basic information about three games: blackjack, craps, and roulette. This instruction comes in the form of small plastic cards with wheels that you turn to find out what to do in various table-game situations. The information is simplified, especially for blackjack, but the wheels do a good job of teaching beginning crap and roulette players the various bets and payoffs.

The other part of the package, and the one that interests us, is gambling chips. How much you have to pay for the cards and how many chips you get vary from casino to casino and jurisdiction to jurisdiction. Typically, you pay $10 and receive $15 in non-cashable chips, which can usually be played on even-money bets on any table game. The chips might be in $1 or $5 denominations; we like the smaller denominations because you play longer and have a better chance to even out the ups and downs. When you win your bet, you're paid in real chips that you set aside to be cashed in (or played) later.

Keep in mind that the WinCard chips are *not* matchplays, which must be accompanied by your own money along with a chip. They're special chips (we call it "funny money") that can be bet by themselves over and over. The dealer takes them only when you lose. I've heard of some instances where an unknowledgeable dealer takes the funny chip even after a win—this is the time to ask the dealer to check with the pit boss!

If you have a long winning streak, you can make a lot of money—with no more risk than your original investment for the package. Of course, you can also lose your whole original investment quickly. If you play this promotion often enough, though, you'll find that the average long-term expected return on your $10 cost is very close to $15.

A good and simple way to look at this chip program is to think of it as the casino giving you $5 to add to your gambling bankroll. Here's the math (thanks to AJ, a savvy Internet friend) for "action chips" like those used in the WinCard program. These are much more valuable than matchplay chips. On average, you'll bet about $30 before $15 in action chips is gone; $15 in action chips is worth about $15 minus $30x (x being the house advantage). If the house advantage is 1%, they're worth about $14.70 ($15 - ($30 x .01).

A neat added feature in the package is a pink "tip slip." This coupon, which you put down with one of your bets, is a $1 wager for the dealer that requires no money from your pocket.

How often you can buy WinCards and chips varies from casino to casino. On one cruise ship, we could buy a set each day of the cruise. Some casinos allow you to buy one set every calendar month. Many just say one per person without specifying whether that's a lifetime limit. At casinos where we don't know the time restrictions, we usually try buying sets a month or two apart. If they check the computer and turn us down the second time, we then ask when can buy them again. Most casinos clear their computers of this information at the end of the calendar year or a year after your first buy, so you can usually buy at least one per year.

Drawings

We have a love/hate relationship with drawings. They're hard to win and the hassle factor is high, so most of the time they end up being disappointing and time-consuming. Occasionally, we score some little prize—even hearing our name called for a T-shirt or a couple of free buffets makes us feel a little better. And every so often, one of us wins something worthwhile, like money—maybe $1,000—or a video poker machine (see "A Textbook Case on Drawings," page 213) and we go home with big smiles on our faces. And there's nothing like winning "the big one"—like the time I won a car at the Stardust—to make you believe you always have a chance and motivate you to enter as many as possible.

Still, qualifying for and entering drawings *is* time-consuming, so we follow some guidelines to help us choose the best opportunities and maximize our chances of winning any drawing we enter.

• We look for drawings where we can have a large percentage of the tickets in the drum. Some megacasino might give you a drawing ticket for every $1,000 you put through a machine and when you go to the drawing, you see well-heeled high rollers who've been feeding $5 Ten Plays or $25 single liners and have garbage bags full of tickets. We don't even enter those drawings—our dollar play for just a few hours a day doesn't generate enough tickets to give us much of a chance of winning. In Las Vegas especially, some video poker pros play such long hours and at such a high denomination that we lesser beings barely have a chance.

On the other hand, if we're playing dollars at a smaller casino where most everyone else is playing nickels or quarters, we might go for this drawing, because we'll be able to collect more entries than most players. Of course, you must remember that there's no sure thing. I know one VP pro who once had almost two-thirds of the tickets in a drawing drum to win a car—and didn't. The winner had just two tickets in the drum!

We like drawings where there are relatively few tickets or everyone has the same chance. We've been invited to some VIP parties where each of the 100 attendees had just one ticket in the drawing for a luxury car—we wouldn't think of missing one like that!

• We try to choose a time to put our tickets into the drawing drum when there won't be as many entries. You can usually do better on weekdays than on weekends, especially in the casinos that have lots more tourists than locals. A locals casino will have more entries in the evening after work hours than during the day. I've heard of some drawings that were held every few hours around the clock. If you've ever been in a casino at 4 a.m., you know why some night owls score big at these.

• For a series of drawings that last a long time, i.e., all month, it might be best to divide your entries equally among all the drawings, so you might win more than once. However, it's often too time-consuming to attend every one, so you might want to divide your tickets among a few drawings or even hoard them for one grand effort.

However, I suggest you never choose the final drawing for the bulk of your tickets, since final drawings often have the largest number of entrants and your odds of winning can drop precipitously. In fact, some players concentrate on earning entries during the first part of a promotion, attempting to snag some nice prizes while the drum holds fewer tickets.

• Many drawings have a rule stipulating that you must be present to win. Try to use this to your advantage. For example, this rule might give you a better chance in a drawing that runs all month at a casino that caters to tourists. While there might be lots of entries, there's a good chance the entrants won't be there on the day of the giveaway. Whereas at a locals casino, a mob of people is almost always milling around the drawing area. Locals love to participate in drawings and you have to get there early just to get a space in the parking lot.

• Never play beyond your bankroll just to get drawing tickets. Recreational players should look at drawings as gravy. If you have the time to show up at the drawing and if you didn't bet when you wouldn't have ordinarily just to get tickets, then it's a good play.

• Some advantage seekers crease or crumple their tickets, believing that this makes them more conducive to being drawn. Some soak tickets in water to make them thicker. Don't do what Brad did one time, though, and decide to soak them after you've filled them out; the ink ran, the information became unreadable, and he had to spend another three hours filling them all out again. Also, be sure the casino allows the entries to be folded, spindled, or otherwise mutilated; some casinos disqualify such entries.

We've also used name stickers and bought stamp kits to avoid having to write our names on hundreds of tickets (see "A Textbook Case on Drawings," page 213); again, make sure this is permitted by the rules.

• Watch for blank entries that have been thrown away. Many people just leave their drawing tickets at the machines or in the trash near the spot that they're given out. Many times people tell us that they can't be at the drawing and ask if we want their tickets. Of course, we're always neighborly and accept them.

• Always keep your ticket stubs. I heard of one woman who had her name called in a drawing, but the winning ticket stub was in the car. Fortunately, they gave her some extra time to get it. But I've also heard of people not getting a prize when they didn't have the stub to turn in within the designated few-minute time limit. Talk about good-news bad-news!

• Have identification with you. You *always* have to show photo ID. In almost all cases, no ID, no prize, no matter the reason.

• Some casinos require a mug shot of each winner in addition to photo ID, in case there are any problems later (there have been instances of counterfeit entries, for example). Other casinos don't require a photo, but ask if they can take one for possible use in advertising. Many drawing rules stipulate that by entering, you give permission for your photo to be used for promotional purposes. Even so, most casinos will honor a request that your picture not appear in public, e.g., in the newspaper.

People might not want their name or photograph associated with a drawing prize for many reasons, mostly having to do with privacy. Someone may not want a spouse to know that he or she was out gambling. Or if the prize is a large sum of money, a winner might not want friends and relatives to come out of the woodwork begging. Many people just prefer to remain anonymous.

• If entries are based on obtaining some specific hand on a machine (e.g., quads in video poker), you'll have to decide if it's worth your time to stop playing and wait around for a change girl to bring you the ticket. This is a good thing for someone playing a negative-expectation game, since he'll play—hence, lose—less. But when we play positive-expectation video poker, the delay cuts down on play time and we could be, theoretically speaking, losing more money than the entry is worth.

For example, if you're playing a game where your expected return is $12 per hour, you're theoretically losing 20¢ every minute you wait for the ticket. Is the expected value of the ticket worth it?

Also, too much downtime is simply boring. Many casinos plan drawings that are labor intensive for the change people, but then don't increase the staff. That's often a reason to skip a particular promotion.

• If I anticipate long wait times (between several drawings in one day), I participate only when it's at a casino where I can play with an advantage while I wait. It would negate the drawing advantage by playing inferior games and in Las Vegas, there are too many good plays in other casinos to waste time waiting. I look for special bonuses after a drawing, like double points the rest of the evening. I always like to have more than one reason to make a special trip to a casino.

• I like drawings where the entries are collected electronically through the slot club system. No filling out hundreds of tickets. No crowding into tiny spaces around drawing drums. No endless waits for winners to show up when you want to be back gambling at your machine or you want to go home.

Sometimes the winners are chosen by the computer and announced over the PA system. Sometimes the winners don't even have to be present to win and are notified by mail or phone.

The only problem here is one of trust: Only casino employees are around when the computer picks the winners. Can casino personnel pick favored customers? I have no proof that this is done, but I've been in casino drawings where the winners were too often suspiciously well-known to the casino employee in charge. Frequently, big players are chosen. This is normal, of course, if the more money you put through on a game, the more entries you get. However, I've seen people grumble about a fix when the same name was called more than once. Maybe the good old drum is the best way after all, so everyone feels they're getting a fair shake.

A Textbook Case on Drawings

Here's how we won a casino drawing for a video poker machine Brad really wanted for the Casino Comp Museum in our garage. (We already had an antique slot machine in the condo and, thank goodness, there was no more room to turn our house into a mini-casino.)

We probably had more than half the tickets in the drum. Why? A lot of players weren't interested in the prize, so there were fewer entries that night than usual for this casino. Also, many players gave us their tickets. Either they didn't live in a state that permitted ownership of gambling devices, or they didn't have room for a machine, or they'd already won one in a previous drawing and were prohibited from winning again. In this case, waiting until later in the promotion and dumping all our entries into the drum at one time was a good tactic.

We earned a lot of tickets ourselves, thanks to a loophole that hadn't been recognized by casinos at the time: They hadn't adjusted their contest rules to take into consideration multi-line video poker games. The casino was giving one entry for every 100 points earned. Back in the old days when there was only single-line video poker, this might have been a good and fair system. Now casinos have Ten Play, Fifty Play, and Hundred Play machines. Even Triple Play, which we were playing at the time, allows far too many entries to be earned on multi-line machines. (These days, most casinos have taken these new machines into consideration and introduced rules that don't give the multi-line player an unfair advantage over the single-line player.)

Our abundance of entries forced us to develop a new casino tool—a make-your-own-stamp kit—and now we won't leave home without it. We had so many tickets that we never would've had time to fill them all out by hand, especially those earned in the hour right before the drawing. In addition, we would have wasted valuable playing time—the drawing was in conjunction with quadruple bonus points, so we were playing at a good expected hourly rate. We bought the kit at Office Max for about $20. It includes an ink pad, two sizes of stamps (a one-liner and a four-liner), umpteen tiny letters and numbers, and small tweezers to put them into the stamps. We already had name and address stickers and stamps we could use on drawing entries, but often other information is needed. In this case, they asked for our slot club number.

I have to admit that we weren't too surprised when Brad's name was the first one called to win one of the three machines they gave away each night. However, it became a little embarrassing when it was also the third and fourth name called. You could hear the slightly skeptical murmur of the crowd around the drum, even though those entries were discarded because of the one-machine-per-person rule.

So now we have a Double Acey-Deucy video poker

machine sitting in the place of honor in our garage, with coin cups full of nickels for anyone who wants to play just for fun. Yes, it's a negative-expectation game—gasp! But Brad had a choice and believe it or not, that's what he wanted. We play positive machines in the casinos when our hard-earned money is on the line. So at home we wanted a chance to play a fun kicker game. And our grandchildren aren't old enough to know or care about pay schedules!

Tournaments

Slot, video poker, blackjack, crap, and keno tournaments are common casino promotions. They range from free or small-entry-fee ($10) daily events to big blowout affairs that last several days, cost anywhere between $500 and $10,000 to enter, and include room, food, parties, and gifts. How do you choose the best ones? This is a personal decision determined by your goals, the games you regularly play, and your bankroll. But the more you know about how tournaments work, the better able you'll be to make good choices.

One of the primary draws of tournaments is that they provide entertainment. The free ones, especially, are an attractive no-risk gambling activity. Even the low-cost (usually slot) tournaments can be a frugal option. First, your risk is limited; you know up front that the most you can lose is the entry fee. Second, you have the exciting chance of hitting the jackpot—the top prizes are large in proportion to what you're risking. And perhaps most importantly, participating in tournaments with a small set cost takes up time that you might ordinarily be spending at other casino games where you could be losing more than you wish. If you have a small gambling bankroll or you're just tired of losing so fast, a tournament might be just what the frugal doctor ordered. (You'll find a good list of Las Vegas tournaments on the *Las Vegas Advisor* Web site, www.lasvegasadvisor.com.)

Tournament Equity

If a tournament has a substantial entry fee, then figuring your "equity" is an important skill. Equity merely means how much, on average, the tournament is worth to you, both in cash and non-cash benefits. Cash equity is easy to figure if you know how many entrants the tournament will have and what the total prize package is.

Here's an example. Your local riverboat casino is giving away a total of $60,000 based on 400 tournament entrants. By dividing $60,000 by 400, you find you have equity of $150.

But should you expect to win $150 in every such tournament? No. You must consider the $150 as an average expectation *over the long term*. That last phrase is important to understand. Most tournament prize structures are top-heavy, with only a small percentage of the entrants cashing for large amounts. That means you'd have to play in a lot more tournaments than is normally possible for any one person, even over a period of many years, in order for the equity to average out.

I've started using what I call a "real-life" equity figure. Using the example above, I subtract the top five cash prizes from the total prize package, which removes $20,000. I have a more likely shot at that remaining $40,000. I divide that by 400 entrants and come up with a more realistic equity of $100. If we ever cash big, that'll be gravy.

A few problems can arise in trying to figure out cash equity. Sometimes it's not clear whether the total-prize-package amount includes non-cash benefits (i.e., the tournament gifts), which may have little value to you. Sometimes the tournament brochure doesn't state how many entrants will be allowed. This can work in your favor if the total prize money is guaranteed. In a few cases, judging by past experience and knowing what dates are less busy, we've been able to enter when we expected fewer people to be participating in the tournament, making our equity higher.

A more likely scenario is when the casino specifies the number of entrants, then adjusts the total prize package downward if fewer show up. That doesn't change your equity if it's done proportionately. However, I was in one tournament where it was decreased radically below what would have been fair—in fact, so many of us complained that they revised it upward more proportionately. On the other hand, I've been in tournaments where the casino permitted more entrants than stated in its invitations, but didn't increase the prize money, thereby decreasing the equity. This is poor public relations and has led to some customers, including myself, crossing that casino off their play list.

Sometimes non-cash benefits can figure into the equity. Tangible items, such as free rooms and meals, parties, and gifts, can be counted as part of your overall value. (But be careful here. If you get your rooms and food comped anyway because of your level of play, you shouldn't add it in.)

Then there's the fun factor, an intangible consideration that's important to many people—the party atmosphere, the thrill of competing for big-money prizes, the pleasure of making new friends or seeing old ones, the honor of being treated like a VIP.

So if you have to pay an entry fee for the tournament, you need to add up all the cash and tangible benefits and compare the total to your cost to enter. Many times the value of the tangibles makes a tournament a positive-equity proposition, albeit over the very long term. If the tangibles are worth less than your cost, you need to decide whether the intangibles are enough to make playing in this tournament a good value for you.

Here are a couple of hints from Steve Bourie, author of the *American Casino Guide*. Steve points out that many tournaments with large entry fees give early-bird discounts. This might turn a negative-equity play into a positive opportunity. Also, if you need a casino room during a high-demand time, especially holiday weekends or convention periods, and find the rates are very high, check out tournaments. You'll sometimes find that a normally negative-equity tournament that includes a free room becomes a strong play.

Invitational Tournaments

Even if you don't have to pay an entry fee—for example, it's a tournament you've been invited to participate in at no charge—you still need to make a decision on whether it's a good deal for you. Invitations to free tournaments are based on your past play and the casino expects you to give them a certain level of play during the tournament period. If for some reason you don't do so, don't expect an invitation to future tournaments until the level of your non-tournament play gets you on the invitation list again. So the other side of the coin here is to be careful that you don't overplay your bankroll just to get these invitations. If you lose more than you can afford to, these tournaments won't seem free at all and the whole fun factor might disappear.

For the video poker enthusiast who plays only when he has the edge, an invitational-tournament offer in the mail becomes an exercise in arithmetic. Figuring equity starts out the same way—calculating the prize package's average cash value and the value of other tangibles. But then it's necessary to know what video poker games are available in that casino. If machines are available that, with proper-strategy play, have an expected return of 100% or more, you've hit the jackpot—all the tangibles and intangibles of the tournament will be gravy.

Unfortunately, the best invitational tournaments are often in casinos that don't have over-100% video poker, particularly in the higher denominations that are often necessary to achieve the heavy play requirements. In this case, the savvy VP player has to consider the return of the machine he will play—let's say 9/6 Jacks or Better with only a 99.5% return. Then he adds in the slot club cashback and other benefits (perhaps a holiday shopping program or bounce-back cash), the comps that are of real value, and the tournament equity. If this total is less than 100%, then it's a "free" tournament that he can't afford to accept. If it's more than 100%, whether he accepts or not will depend on what he personally requires as a minimum edge for a good play.

We don't play in as many invitational tournaments as we used to. The long-term aspects I've discussed and the trend of casinos cutting tournament benefits make the play too volatile to be fun. And fun is one of the important intangibles for us.

That's us. If tournaments interest you, how do you get on these invitational lists and how do you find out how much play is required to keep you qualified? Unfortunately, this is sometimes a deep dark secret hidden in the computer of a casino marketing executive. I've rarely seen it spelled out in black and white in casino printed material. (I suspect that, because the requirements change so frequently, casinos simply opt to save on the printing costs.) You can still ask. Hosts are usually glad to give you the playing requirements if they know them, although in some cases don't be surprised if they're a bit nebulous or evasive. Some casinos seem to run on the premise that if their customers don't know the details of their comp system—and an invite to a tournament is an upper-level comp—they'll play more, hoping to reach this mysterious higher comp level.

The Skill Factor

There's another consideration when deciding whether a tournament is a good deal for you. Your equity can be increased or decreased if skill is a factor in the tournament. Luck is always the biggest factor in any short-term gambling activity and tournaments are short-term events. In any one tournament, even one where good strategy and experience are helpful, the results can depend as much as 90%-95% on luck. Anyone can win any one tournament. However, knowledgeable tournament players find that even a 5%-10% skill factor eventually translates into winning more than the average player who depends completely on luck. I don't want to be unskilled in a tournament with these players! If they win more often, that means my chances decrease.

A good book to improve your results is *Casino Tournament Strategy* by Stanford Wong. He covers many kinds of tournaments where skill is a factor: blackjack, craps, baccarat, keno, and horse-race handicapping.

If you're serious about playing in skill tournaments, I suggest you first enter some of the small ones with low entry fees before you put up big money. Many casinos run weekly tournaments known as "minis," especially in slots and blackjack, that cost only $10-$25 to enter. These are often fun tournaments, mainly for recreational players; however, they're a great place to gain the experience you need to have a better chance in the bigger tournaments.

The importance of the skill factor varies, of course, depending on the game:

• **Slot** tournaments are for people who don't want to think. Here, skill is a factor only when speed of play matters; if you have unlimited credits during the playing time, then the more hands you get in, the more chances you have to hit more payoffs. Don't choose this format if you think you can't pound on a Spin button for 10-15 minutes without getting tired.

Luck is the only factor in the more common non-speed slot tournaments. In these, everyone gets the same number of credits and ample time to play them off. And something to remember: Slot machines used in tournament play are set to hit jackpots more frequently in order to make the action more exciting. Don't be fooled into thinking you're hot or that these machines will be just as loose when the tournament chip is changed and they're put back into regular operation on the casino floor.

• **Keno** tournaments take special skills, usually requiring a large bankroll and sharp math skills to figure out the advantage. Amateurs shouldn't try to tackle these, unless the entry fees are small or the non-cash benefits are extremely valuable.

• **Blackjack** tournaments are a different animal than regular play at the casino tables. Card-counting or even basic-strategy skills aren't nearly as important here as knowledge of special and complex tournament strategy. You need to know the format of the tournament—that is, how many rounds there are and what it takes to advance—and whether you'll be using non-negotiable tournament chips or real money.

Betting strategy is pivotal—you aren't trying to beat the house, you're trying to beat the other players. I've been in blackjack tournaments where participants played like they did at a regular blackjack table, the same small bet every hand, trying so hard to beat the dealer, getting so happy with a small win, even though it was with tournament chips that had no cash value. They didn't even notice that others were hundreds of dollars ahead of them and that they had no chance to get in the money or advance to the next round.

There are many possible strategies, depending primarily on the betting patterns of the other people at your table. You might come out betting big in the first hands, hoping for wins that will put you far in the lead. Then, once ahead, you might drop down and let everyone else chase you. This is a charging technique and when it doesn't work, you're out of the tournament fast. I use this technique—and often snag the first-out prize! But it can win big for you some of the time. Or you might bet small for the first couple of hands to see how the others are betting, then make big bets only when you see that there are aggressive bettors you must not let get too far ahead. The important thing in a blackjack tournament is to watch the piles of chips in front of your tablemates and bet accordingly.

• **Crap** tournaments incorporate no skill factors in the game itself; the skill is in the betting strategy alone and it's even more complicated than in blackjack. You not only have to size your bets carefully, but you have a myriad of different bets from which to choose.

• **Roulette** tournament strategy is the same as craps. There are no skill factors in the actual game. The betting strategy is all of it and again you have many different kinds of bets available.

• **Video poker** tournaments fall into two categories—speed and non-speed. If speed is a factor, the more hands you play, the more chances you have to accumulate credits. If you're slow, you'll be at a definite disadvantage in a tournament with a lot of experienced speed demons. I don't play in video poker speed tournaments if I have to pay an entry fee, since I'm not a fast player.

Strategy skill is important in both speed and non-speed video poker tournaments. Knowing how and when to modify basic strategy for the game schedule you're playing maximizes your chances of winning. Sometimes, especially for the first few minutes, just using optimal strategy is the best decision. However, often it's necessary, especially in the last minutes, to go more aggressively for the big hands (quads, aces, a royal) because a big hit is the only thing that'll give you a chance to get into the money or advance to the next round. I love it when I can switch to the aggressive mode, which allows me to do some of the wild things I have to resist the temptation to do in a regular game: things like throwing away good hands to go for a royal or playing just for bonus quads.

The player who knows when and how to change his strategy always has a little edge on the player who doesn't. But the fact that anything can happen in a tournament—the luck factor—is always alive and well. This was certainly the case in a story a woman told me about a tournament she and her mother played. She'd been playing VP for years, knew the strategies cold, and could play very fast, while her mother had never played VP before and was very slow. The daughter bombed out in the tournament, while the mother ended up in first place. Everyone went away shaking their heads. The mother was about 400 coins ahead of the next highest score—and she still had almost 200 credits left on her machine when the time ran out!

Thorny Promotion Issues

Taking Advantage of
Casino Errors or Misjudgments

In most states, it's illegal to knowingly take advantage of machine errors or malfunctions in casinos. Usually, specific regulations on the books cover this. However, I've known of many instances in which players have found and taken advantage of a flaw in a machine. It might give out too many slot club points. It might award credits at the wrong denomination. A machine might even pay out more coins than it should. Some players have gotten away scot-free before the casino discovered and fixed the error. Other times a casino has caught them in the act and taken away any cash or benefits they'd accumulated. It's rare for casinos to press charges. If it's a blatant and clear-cut case, they usually just 86 the player, meaning that if he ever comes into that casino again, he can be arrested for trespassing.

However, the casino often makes mistakes that a player can take advantage of and not be technically guilty of breaking regulations. It's quite common, for example, for casino employees to forget to reset the master computer to return to the regular point schedule after bonus periods. This usually gives the players somewhere between a few more minutes and a few extra hours for the bonus, but I've heard of some instances where this went on for days on some individual machines.

Once a friend called me to say that machines at the casino where he was playing were registering five-times points instead of the advertised triple points. Should a player notify the casino of this type of error? It's in that gray area of ethics. Most won't. They're too busy playing as fast as they can to think about it.

Many casino errors, however, do not fall within an

224

illegal or even a gray area. If a casino puts in video poker machines with a rogue pay schedule that gives the player an unheard-of high advantage—in one case I know of, good enough for as much as a $200-per-hour expectation—you can't blame those who flock to them and play until their eyeballs fall out.

And if a casino runs a too-good promotion that isn't well thought out, it's not unethical to do everything you can to benefit from it. In fact, the savvy player is constantly on the lookout for these opportunities, hoping to strike gold by finding one that has an unexpectedly high return, usually created by a marketing employee who doesn't have a strong background in math.

I've found that with many good promotions, it's best to use the early-bird-gets-the-worm tactic. Sometimes the promotion is so lucrative that the only way to get in on it is to arrive early, before the casino changes the rules or discontinues it entirely. This is something a casino can legally do—and it happens quite frequently.

For example, one casino announced that comp points could be used for gift certificates at a local mall. Some casino executive didn't think about this very carefully; he should have checked to see how many points were outstanding in the slot club accounts, especially those of the big players. At that point, he would've realized that they'd run out of gift certificates quickly, which is exactly what happened. Three or four big players with tons of comp points showed up and asked for 10, 20, 30, or more $25 gift certificates at a time and in less than an hour the slot club's whole stock of certificates was gone.

Of course, there was an outcry from players who came in later that morning, thinking they were being prompt, but weren't able to get the advertised certificates. The casino eventually got more certificates and changed the rules, setting a limit on the number each member could get. And this was one time I actually thought that changing the promotion procedure was a good thing. I'm all for rules that make it fair for everyone to get an equal shot. However, I certainly have my eyes and ears open at all times for extra good promotions and you'll often see Brad and me at a casino when one first begins.

A prime time to look for casino errors or high-value promotions you can take advantage of is when a new casino opens. Smart video poker players look for extra-good pay tables that might have inadvertently been chosen by overworked slot techs in the pre-opening rush, especially on multi-denomination multi-play machines. At one Vegas casino opening, the early birds found a nice unadvertised surprise—some credits already waiting to be used on every machine. Of course, the next time that company opened a casino, many of us waited in line for a long time to be one of the first in when the doors opened. Our long wait was in vain; not surprisingly, the company didn't repeat that promotion.

I heard of another opening promotion that turned out to be a dud for the casino. They advertised that they'd hidden a single million-dollar coin in one of the hoppers. Did that get a lot of people playing? No. But the pros had a ball, running from machine to machine stuffing $100 bills into the bill acceptors and immediately cashing out in coins!

Abusing and Killing Promos

I've been talking about the proper and ethical use of promotions in order to increase chances in a casino, even if the promotion is the result of casino error or misjudgment by casino executives. But there's another side of the coin—outright player abuse of promotions. And there are plenty of opportunities for this.

Take new-member promotions that offer big bonuses. A player rounds up all his non-playing friends and relatives and has them get slot club cards, but he puts in the play on all of them himself, a definite violation of slot club rules. He then has his friends collect their big joining bonus, keeping a small percentage and giving the rest to him. The purpose of the promotion, to attract new players to the casino, is completely negated. Players who want a bigger piece of an equity-heavy invitational tournament have used this same tactic; they qualify out-of-town friends and relatives by playing on their cards and making agreements to retain most of their winnings when they come in to play the tournament.

The most brazen abuse I've ever heard about was by a player who was participating in a particularly generous new-member promotion that rebated losses over the first few days as a slot club member. He pulled his slot card out of the machine after *every* hand was dealt and his coin-in had been credited, then played out the hand with *no* wins ever being recorded, because his slot club card wasn't in. Now, I'm sure other players realized the weakness in this promotion and perhaps did some card pulling when they were dealt high-paying hands. But this joker did it every time, then pranced up to the slot club to collect his rebate. His card registered that he'd put $10,000 through the machines and hadn't won a *single* hand. A definite candidate for a "Dumb Crook" show, this guy didn't get a penny of the rebate after some higher-ups reviewed his account.

As with illegal actions, a casino will take various measures when it sees abuse. The player who qualified others for the new-member bonus had his slot club membership revoked and the players caught qualifying others for invitational tournaments were no longer invited themselves. And the brazen card-puller, I'm certain, could never again earn slot club benefits in that casino, even if he wasn't completely 86d. In the last case, one person's abuse led, as it so often does, to the whole promotion being scrapped—thus hurting honest players.

Ethical Standards?

A casino will run a promotion only as long as it's profitable. This subject always stimulates a lively discussion among players, often with strong disagreement. Does a player have an individual responsibility with regard to preserving promotions? Are there ethical standards to consider when deciding to hit a promotion hard, especially when you know that by doing so you may cause it to be yanked?

This whole issue is a hot one. One side argues: "Let's not overdo it with our playing time and maybe the promotion will last longer." On the other side are those who say, "If I don't take advantage of it, someone else will and the promotion will be canceled anyway." Many have suggested that common courtesy and an ability to look at the long-term benefits of moderation would be the answer, but it's impossible to find a situation where everyone embraces these concepts.

I liked the attitude of this poster on the Internet: "I was with someone at Vacation Village who won the airfare reimbursement in their Wheel Spin promotion for visitors just arriving in Las Vegas, then was going to leave without playing at all in the casino. After forcing this person to gamble a little (I was driving), we left. I told him if you hit the big prize and run, the promotion will die." (This promo is dead now, but not because of abuse—the casino was sold and then closed.)

There will always be the hit-and-run promotional player. And sometimes promotions do end after attracting too many of them. However, the majority of gamblers continue to play after a promotion—and that keeps casinos using promotions as one of their top drawing tools.

I promote legal and ethical behavior by casino customers: Follow the rules. But there's no rule that says you must continue playing in a casino for an indefinite period of time; it's okay to leave a casino after a promotion is over. The casino hopes you will stay, or return at a future non-promotion time. We sometimes do, because a promotion brings us into a casino where we find good gambling or dining or entertainment opportunities. But we can leave with a clear conscience if we find no reason to stay or return.

The Future of Promotions

In *The Frugal Gambler,* I posed the question, "Is the promotion train slowing down?" And I predicted that competition would keep it chugging away. Today, six years later, I see no reason to change my mind on this. Rapidly expanding Native American casinos in California will keep Las Vegas and Reno casinos hopping to find promotions that will lure the California drive-in visitor. New casino projects in Atlantic City will likely heat up the incentive bus wars. Riverboats will always try to come up with ways to increase the visits of local patrons.

Now that Brad and I live permanently in Las Vegas, we're inundated with at least 10 times more promotions than we have time to take advantage of. I think continued casino competition will ensure that the Golden Age of Promotions will last a long time.

7

Joining the Court of KuPon

"The question is not whether or not to use coupons, but how many!"
— *a coupon hound writes on the Internet*

Although these days I'm known mostly as the Queen of Comps, I haven't forsaken the activities that originally earned me the nickname the Queen of KuPon. It's true that we don't coupon as much as we used to. Because we play mostly at the dollar-and-higher level rather than quarters, we're a little choosier about which gambling coupons we use.

If Brad and I are playing video poker in a situation where our combined expected theoretical win is $50 an hour, it doesn't make financial sense—although I'll explain later why there might be other than purely financial reasons to consider—for us to spend an hour to walk or drive to another casino to play four $5 matchplays for a theoretical win of less than $10. And we rarely use 2-for-1 or discounted food, show, or room coupons any more, because we routinely get most of these 100% comped. Since we now live in Vegas, we rarely need a hotel room except for occasional out-of-town company. We get more food comps through our regular play than our waistlines can stand. And we can get more free shows than we have the time or energy to attend.

Still, we do use gambling coupons frequently. When?

• When the coupon value is high enough to make a special effort. Some of the coupons in the *Las Vegas Advisor's* Pocketbook of Values (POV) package fall into this category, such as coupons for a 3-to-1 payout on your first blackjack that have been included in recent books. Another example: When the Las Vegas locals casino Terrible's opened in late 2000, they put out a coupon booklet that brought tears of joy to my eyes. Not only were there loads of video poker bonus coupons, there were also weekly $25 blackjack matchplays. With an expected value of almost $100 a month for the two of us, we made the extra effort to use them.

• When it doesn't take too much extra time or energy and fits into our schedule. We call this the "senior factor." In the Terrible's above example, we would usually be in the vicinity of the casino at least once a week anyway, so it was convenient. However, we did skip one week when we didn't get to that side of town and decided that we were just too tired to make a special trip across the traffic-choked Strip. We don't like coupons with time restrictions, and I've never seen a coupon valuable enough to get me to a casino on the graveyard shift! To make couponing easier and more convenient, we keep a plastic file in our car, with coupons organized by casino and location. That way we avoid the problem of "Oops, I don't have that coupon," when we have a change of plans on the road and end up in an unexpected part of town.

• When the coupon can be used for a game we're playing anyway. Since video poker is our core game, we look for video poker coupons that will enhance our profit expectation. Frequently, a marginal play becomes a must-play with a coupon for bonus slot club points or bonuses on specific hands.

• When coupons cluster in one area. At one time there were coupons or promotions at Ellis Island, Tuscany, Key Largo, Terrible's, and the Hard Rock, all conveniently located in the same vicinity of Las Vegas. We constructed a nice walking tour, allowing us to use a number of lower-value coupons that would not have merited a special trip on their own. When we wanted to play at the Fiesta Rancho in the northwest part of Las Vegas, we'd check to see if we had any coupons for the nearby Texas and Santa Fe Stations. We would do the same for the Fiesta Henderson, Green Valley Ranch, and Sunset Station in the far southeastern part of town.

• When we want to be "paid" for exercising or taking a break. Now that we're locals and primarily play in the neighborhood casinos, we miss the long walks up and down the Strip that we used to take as tourists. So even low-value coupons from two Strip casinos, preferably an ample distance from each other, give us an excuse to exercise in this nostalgic way. And we love to have a coupon, even a little one, for a table game in the casino where we're playing or one nearby, so we can take a physical and mental break from the glare of the video poker screen and the concentration on proper strategy.

• When out-of-town friends and relatives (or a TV crew) come to town and we want to show them the best way to achieve a short-term gambling win. We pool all our individual coupons or I dip into my "Coupons to Share" file and we're almost certain to end up winners, while also having a good time together.

Couponing—The Best Gambling Payoff for Most Players

Although couponing comes second for us, after skillful dollar video poker play, for most casino visitors who want to get the most for their vacation dollar, couponing should be the first priority.

Why? The overwhelming majority of gamblers in a casino are playing negative-expectation games, meaning the house has the mathematical edge, and they will usually lose money. Remember, you can only win in the long run if you're not giving the casino that little admission fee, its edge, on every bet. That's not to say it isn't possible to win on a negative-expectation game one day or one trip or even for several trips in a row. But in the long run, if you play negative-expectation games, the house edge will see to it that you're an ultimate loser.

Couponing affords you the opportunity to turn things around and get the edge in your favor. For example, if you're lucky enough to have a blackjack coupon that makes your first card an automatic ace, you're playing with a whopping 55% edge (assuming you get to play it again after a push, which you almost always do). No, you won't win on every coupon, no matter how big the edge, but you will get to the winning long-term much faster.

Since couponing takes the edge away from the casino and gives it to you, it's possible to gamble with a much smaller bankroll. Because you always have the edge, and sometimes quite a large one, you'll become an overall winner more quickly than playing a regular casino game without a coupon. Of course, you must make coupon bets that are compatible with your bankroll. If you have only a couple hundred dollars, you'd better stick with $5-$10 or one-bet coupons. It takes a larger bankroll to play some large-bet or extended-time-play coupons, e.g., $25 matchplays or double-pay for blackjacks for the first hour of play. If you make an effort to track down a lot of those smaller coupon plays, you'll be surprised how soon you can build your bankroll for the bigger plays that yield even greater profits.

Couponing is an extremely important tool, even for casino visitors who are playing positive-expectation games. For the skillful video poker player at the quarter level or the blackjack card counter who makes only low-money bets, couponing may be the first line of defense against the casino edge. Brad and I played quarter video poker for many years and all during that time, our per-hour profit rate in couponing far exceeded what we made in video poker and became an important contributor to building our gambling bankroll so we could progress to higher-denomination play.

Coupons for free or reduced-price food, drinks, hotel rooms, or shows are found money if you're not getting these things comped. I've known couples that paid full-price for a show when there was a 2-for-1 coupon in the unopened freebie magazine sitting in their hotel room. People are given a coupon book when they check into a casino hotel and the maid finds it on the dresser after they check out—a coupon for $5 in free coin, with no playing requirement, still intact. (And guess who the maid would sometimes meet who took those leftover coupons off her hands!)

Almost all casinos used to offer bargain-priced meals, rooms, and show tickets, but this is changing quickly; Las Vegas, especially, is going upscale. If you're are on a limited budget, you'll find that the time and effort you spend looking for the non-gambling coupons will allow you to afford some of the higher-priced splurges. Even though we play often enough to get all the free drinks we usually want in a casino, I always carry a few drink coupons in my purse in case we want to meet friends in the lounge and not face a big bar bill.

Know Your Coupons

There are many different types of gambling coupons. Some are more valuable than others. Some can be played for less risk. Some are so strong that casinos eventually discover they can't afford to offer them. You need to be able to tell them apart.

There are also many different ways to play most coupons, with some games or bets yielding better returns than others. It can get very complicated, mathematically—though, in the examples that follow, I attempt to keep it as simple as possible. Credit for calculating many of the returns listed below is due James Grosjean, the author of the book *Beyond Counting*, who also penned a brilliant article titled "Beyond Coupons" that was published in the Spring 2003 edition of Arnold Snyder's *Blackjack Forum*. I'm grateful to James for allowing much of his work to be used here.

Matchplay

Whether it says "$5 matchplay" or "Bet $5 and We Will Pay You $10 If You Win," it means the same thing: The casino is giving you money. However, you can't just take this money and stick it in your pocket. The free money must be used for a bet and comes with a condition. You must risk some of your own money at the same time. Here's how it works.

We'll use the most common gambling coupon—a $5 matchplay for blackjack. Take the coupon to a blackjack table and place it on an empty betting circle with a $5 bill on top of it. You don't have to sit down. And if you plan to leave after playing the matchplay, it's often better to remain standing. Some casinos let the bill play; some exchange it for a $5 chip. In either case, you now have a $10 bet riding—your own $5 plus an extra unseen bet of $5 that the casino has given you by matching your bet. If you win, the casino pays $10. If you lose, the casino merely takes away the coupon and the $5 that you put up. You risk $5 to win $10.

This is how it works in general for all table games and all denominations of matchplay coupons. If you have a $25 matchplay, the casino matches that amount and you have a $50 bet. You're paid off at $50 if you win, while giving up only your own $25 (and the coupon) if you lose.

You will win about half the time on matchplay bets, depending on the game and the type of bets you make. A rule of thumb to figure out the value of a matchplay coupon is to cut the matched amount in half and sub-

---

Non-Even-Money Coupons

Almost all matchplays can be used only on even-money bets. However, if you get one that can be wagered on non-even-money bets, the optimal use is to bet it on the longest long shot available—like straight-up on a number at roulette.

Example: If you're betting a $25 matchplay (use it once and lose it whether you win or lose) at single-zero roulette, betting on an even-money bet—black/red, odd/even, etc.—yields an expected return of $11.48. But taking a shot straight-up on a number jumps the EV to $22.98. The problem is that you pay for your extra EV with extreme variance. But if you're well-capitalized and you're allowed to bet your matchplays on non-even-money propositions, it makes sense to maximize the EV in this way.

tract the effect of the house edge, which averages around 2% (of what you bet of your own money), depending on the game, the bet, and your skill level. I usually just subtract 10¢ on a $5 matchplay as a round figure. This renders a $5 matchplay worth about $2.40. A $25 matchplay is worth about $12 ($25 divided by 2 minus 50¢).

Lucky Bucks

This type of coupon generally adds a dollar or two extra to an even-money payout. For example, with a 7-5 lucky buck, you play the coupon with a $5 chip or bill and if you win, you're paid $7. Like matchplays, you win, on average, about half the time, so the coupon is worth just a few cents less than half the bonus, about 97¢.

There are also occasional 3-2 and 2-1 lucky bucks, but you often can't find a table with minimums that allow you to bet that low and sometimes you're not permitted to use them with a larger bet, even if you explain that you still only expect the same dollar bonus. For example, if you have a 3-2 lucky buck and the lowest minimum is $3, you should be (and often are) allowed to bet $3, making it an effective 4-3 lucky buck. But some places just won't have it. In these cases, I've given up trying to educate dealers (and even pit bosses) that this is actually better for them than a 3-2, since

---

Super Bucks

Almost all matchplay and lucky buck coupons are good for one play only. Occasionally, however, you'll find "play until you lose 'em" versions. These provide the potential for a big score and have an EV close to their face value.

I'm putting more money at risk for the same measly bonus. (I guess I'm getting too old to argue over small change. Brad says it's about time!)

First Card is an Ace

Put this coupon in the betting spot on a blackjack table with the amount listed on the coupon—usually $5—and it becomes your first card, a valuable ace. The dealer skips you on the first card of the deal, then gives you a second card. You play out the hand the same as if you were dealt a first-card ace, getting paid immediately if you make a blackjack. Otherwise you hit, stand, split, or double as usual.

This coupon gives you an enormous 55% edge, assuming the free ace can be kept (and replayed) on pushes, which it almost always can be (even when it can't, the player edge is 50.5%). It doesn't take playing too many of these aces to become an overall winner and have it become your favorite coupon, as it is mine.

Free Play

This coupon is usually distributed as a bonus for past play at a casino and an incentive to come back; it's sometimes referred to as bounce-back cash (see Chapter Five). If the coupon is for slot play, you usually have to go to the slot club to have credits activated on a slot or video poker machine, then you have to play them through once before you can cash out the winnings.

If the coupon is for chips, you usually get special non-negotiable chips at the cage. These chips cannot be exchanged for cash, like regular chips, but must be played. These are usually not matchplay, but can be bet alone, with no money of your own at risk. When you win a bet with these chips, you're paid in regular chips that you can cash in. In most cases, you continue to bet with these special non-negotiable chips until you lose them; therefore their worth is close to the face value of the chip.

Read the rules for all free-play coupons carefully and note any special instructions or restrictions. They're often valid only on or until a specified date. The table-game chips might be "for one play only," and the slot credits might specify or exclude certain machines.

Blackjack Bonus Coupons

There are two versions of these coupons, both very valuable, but the risk level for both is high. They usually allow you to bet anywhere from $5 to $25 a hand.

The first type, and the most common, gives you a bonus on your first blackjack, usually by paying either 2-1 or 3-1 instead of the usual 3-2. Since you'll average an untied natural about every 22 hands, the value of a 2-1 coupon is between about $2 and $10 (the range encompasses flat $5 bets to flat $25 bets). A 3-1 coupon has an EV between about $7 and $35. Unfortunately, blackjacks, like most things in gambling, usually don't come exactly on schedule. You could get one on the first hand you play. Or you could wait a long time for one to appear, which means it's possible to lose an amount equal to many bets in the process of cashing this coupon.

The other variation of these coupons, which is more rare but potentially more valuable, pays a bonus for every blackjack you get over a certain period of time, i.e., an hour. With these you should try to find a table where you can get in as many hands as possible, perhaps playing heads up with the dealer in the middle of the night. But again, the risk of losing is great, so you need a large bankroll.

Personally, since we no longer play much blackjack, we don't use this type of coupon unless we have the time to play a lot of them, making us a strong favorite to pull out an overall profit. However, if you plan to play blackjack anyway, using these coupons is a great way to add value to your game.

Table-Game Coupons

Many beginning gamblers, and even experienced machine players, don't take advantage of table-game coupons, because they've never learned to play the tables. The majority of gambling coupons are for table games, so machine players are losing valuable money-making opportunities if they pitch them in the trash.

How can you learn to play the table games? One way is to have a friend teach you. Another is to read a book explaining how the games are played—the rules, etiquette, and nuances. Or you can buy a teaching video or computer program. Or if you only need to know enough to play a coupon and aren't shy, you can just walk up to the game and ask a dealer or pit boss how to play. More often than not, they'll happily walk you through and even celebrate with you if you win.

Once you have a general idea of how the game is played, a good second step for learning more about a table game is to take one of the free classes that many casinos themselves offer. These are usually given on weekday mornings and early afternoons (the least busy times) with set schedules for each game. Some freebie magazines publish these schedules or you can call a casino and ask. Although the choices of classes vary from one casino to another, most offer blackjack, craps, roulette, and baccarat. Some also teach the Asian games, e.g., pai gow poker.

A few not only offer instruction by experts, but follow the class with a beginner's game: slow-paced, using real money, but at low stakes. This provides the novice player with an opportunity to practice with real play without being hurried or embarrassed by more experienced players.

A warning about these casino-sponsored classes: Don't expect to get an advanced lesson in smart table-game strategy or to learn complicated best- or worst-bet percentages; you need to go to a book for this study. However, casino table-game classes are very good at teaching you the basics of the games, enough so you'll be able to feel comfortable using some of those valuable coupons you've been throwing away.

Often a coupon will give you a choice of table games to play it on. With these, you can just choose the game you're most comfortable playing or the one you enjoy the most. You don't have to worry about which game is the absolute best to play; you usually have a healthy advantage over the house regardless which one you choose. We sometimes play our coupons on craps or roulette to have fun at a game we like, but wouldn't ever play without coupons because of its negative expectation. Some coupons are game-specific, so let's compare the various table games and bet options, assuming that you have a $5 matchplay coupon.

Baccarat

Baccarat is a good choice for beginner couponers, because it's simple and there are no strategy decisions to be made by the player. Due to table minimums, you'll usually have to use your coupon at a mini-baccarat game in the main casino, not in the hoity-toity high-roller room with the tuxedoed staff. Put your coupon and $5 on either the "bank" or "player" spot on the layout and the dealer will deal a hand for each;

you never touch the cards. He takes your money if you lose and he pays you if you win; you don't even have to understand why. It's that simple.

For the reasons mentioned earlier (see "Non-Even-Money Coupons," page 237), the best place to use a matchplay coupon is on the long-shot tie bet, where the expected return for a $5 matchplay is $3.09. But assuming that's not allowed, you'll have to play banker or player. Winning bank bets require that you pay a commission, which is usually charged on the entire win, including the bonus. For this reason, the player bet is not only less complicated, but also yields a slightly higher EV: $2.40 to $2.35.

Craps

Craps is a good second choice for using coupons. Ignoring every other wager on the table (again, the non-even-money wagers are usually not matchplay eligible) you have to understand only one bet: the pass line. You win about 49% of pass line bets, with an average overall win for your $5 matchplay of about $2.40. Note that the don't pass has the same EV. But since most of the table will be betting the pass, it's usually beneficial to the overall experience to play with, rather than against, them.

Many people shun the crap table—it's so noisy and looks so complicated, while everyone else seems to know what they're doing. The Frugal Princess has a suggestion for the timid who have a crap coupon to use: Stand near one of the dealers at an uncrowded table and tell him that you're just a beginner and need some help placing a pass line bet with your coupon. The dealer is usually happy to tell you when and where to place the bet.

Other Frugal Princess crap hints include the following: Don't make your pass line bet until the start of a new roll, known as the "come-out." You can tell when that is by watching the large round "puck" that the dealers use to mark the "point" when it's established. When the puck's black side is up and it's positioned in the box marked "don't come," it's a come-out roll. When the white side is up and the puck is on a number, you know the table is in the middle of a roll and you need to wait to place your bet until the dealer flips it back over with the black side showing. And be sure not to dangle your arms over the table. Crap players are very superstitious and think it's bad luck for the dice to hit someone's hand.

Roulette

Roulette's main advantage for couponing is that it's easy to play. Place the coupon on any of the outside areas—red or black, little (1-18) or big (19-36), odd or even. You'll average winning about $2.20 for your $5 matchplay on a double-zero roulette game and about $2.30 on a single zero.

Here's a Frugal Princess roulette hint: Remember one basic rule that it's all too easy and embarrassing to forget: Don't place your coupon and bet down on the table until all bets from the last spin have been paid off and the dealer removes the marker from the winning space. Breaking this rule can get you a no-no wave-off from the dealer and a look of disdain from the experienced players around the table.

Pai Gow Poker

Pai gow poker is a table game I've only recently learned, the result of having some good coupons that could be used only on this particular game. The first thing I found out is that it often provides a good way to sit awhile and relax, since ties make coupon replays frequent, adding to an already slow game.

For coupon play, I suggest you stick to being the "player." You sometimes have the option to be the "bank," but it's complicated and doesn't make sense if you're just sitting down to play off a coupon. Playing this game can be confusing, so taking a casino-sponsored class might be helpful. But most dealers will assist you, setting your hand for you in accordance with the "house way." In addition, the other players often chime in with their friendly assistance for on-the-table training.

The EV of a $5 pai gow poker matchplay is about $2.11 (this includes the accounting for the 5% commission charged on winning bets—like baccarat, usually charged for the total winning bet). The casino edge on pai gow poker (as played in Nevada casinos), according to Stanford Wong's *Optimal Strategy for Pai Gow Poker*, is 2.84%. But we like this game so much that we sometimes decide to stay and play a little longer after our coupons are gone, just for fun.

Frugal Princess pai gow poker hint: If you win one or more bets, don't forget you have to pay the 5% commission—not after every bet, the dealer keeps track of it for you—but before you leave the table.

Blackjack

Blackjack is the most popular and familiar of the table games, therefore it's the game of choice for many coupon aficionados. Ironically, it's one of the worst games on which to use coupons. A typical $5 matchplay for blackjack is worth a profit of $2.35. I say typical, because this can vary greatly according to available rules and the degree to which you alter strategy to squeeze the most out of a blackjack coupon (see "Yes, Insurance" on the next page). Diehard math heads can apply an adjusted coupon-play basic strategy that will extract the optimum EV by having you double down and split less than normal basic strategy dictates (for the last word on this subject, I refer you again to James Grosjean's article, "Beyond Coupons"). However, most casual gamblers will do fine playing their normal blackjack strategy.

Frugal Princess blackjack couponing hints: If it's a game where the players hold the cards, put one hand behind your back if you can't remember the one-hand-on-the-cards rule. And here's some advice I learned from the Queen: When doubling down, always put out enough money to double the "phantom" part of the bet too, without asking in advance what the casino policy is on this. That is, if it's a $5 matchplay and you have out a $5 bet, place $10 more out when you want to double. Most dealers won't tell you in advance that you can do this, but casinos sometimes allow you to double both parts of the bet. If, after you put out the doubled amount, the dealer says you can't, quietly

---

Yes, Insurance

For a look at how basic strategy is altered due to a matchplay or lucky buck, take a look at insurance. The first rule of blackjack basic strategy is never take insurance. But throw a coupon into the equation and the advice is reversed. If you're playing a matchplay, lucky buck, or first-card-ace coupon and the dealer has an ace up, the correct play is to always take insurance unless you have a natural of your own. The reason is that the $2.50 insurance on a $5 bet insures both the original bet and the coupon. That is, if the dealer has a ten underneath the ace for a natural, you save both your $5 and the coupon, but you didn't have to put up half of the coupon's value to insure it. That makes it a positive bet. The reason you don't insure when you have a natural of your own is because the worst you can do is tie, and the coupon will be saved anyway.

---

remove the doubled part without question, unless you think the dealer is just not informed about this option being available—and many dealers aren't. In that case, politely request that the dealer check with the pit boss for a final decision.

The Frugal Princess Primer for the Beginning Couponer

• Look everywhere for coupons: on the Internet before you leave home (www.billhere.com/coupons-lists.htm is my favorite for Vegas coupons); in every local newspaper or freebie magazine and brochure you find in racks at the airport, hotel and motel lobbies, rental-car agencies, bus lobbies, and at bell desks; on casino floors; handed out on the street in front of casinos; even on the top of trash cans (though you don't need to feel obliged to rummage inside the dumpsters, contrary to how my mom used to misbehave!). Funbooks are a good resource for getting multiple coupons; they're often given out by the casino-hotel when you check in or join the slot club, and by travel agents when you book a package deal with them.

• Read everything you can about how coupons work. You need to understand the difference between coupons that carry risk and coupons that are risk-free. Of course, that's what you're doing right now, and there's a good section on this in Mom's first book, *The Frugal Gambler*.

• Set up a separate bankroll for couponing to keep track of your results. Seeing your profits mount will likely make you a fervent believer in coupons.

• Check the fine print on the coupons for blackout dates, restrictions, and expiration dates.

• Make a game plan to maximize your time; organize your coupon sorties by area, so you're not over-lapping or backtracking as you run around town.

• Carry your coupons with you at all times so you'll be able to use them when your plans change.

• Carry legal picture identification, which is often required to redeem a coupon—e.g., a passport or driver's license. Check the details; some offers require out-of-state IDs.

• Build in extra time for delays on coupon runs. Try not to get frustrated or impatient if things don't go exactly as you planned. Casinos withdraw offers and cancel coupons without notice. Be flexible and calm and remember to have fun.

• Bet the maximum amount of money allowed for matchplay coupons as long as your bankroll will al-low it. Betting the limit will maximize your returns. You can even step up in class once in a while—that is, bet $25 on a matchplay even if you're a $5-$10 bettor. The power of coupons provides a lot of bankroll cush-ion. But don't overbet your bankroll severely, even with a coupon.

• Pool coupons with friends and relatives and or-ganize a major coupon run. It's not only more fun to share the excitement, it also smooths out the ups and downs of winning and losing. Remember, the more coupons you use, the more likely you are to come out on the winning side.

• Finally, remember that many small coupons can add up to big profit over the long term.

Advanced Coupon Tips from the Queen

• Don't throw out an expired coupon right away; ask someone if the casino will still honor it. Slot club personnel or a host will sometimes extend the date.

• Although you can get many coupons in free casino funbooks and with flyers available from racks around the city, don't overlook the availability of coupons that involve a purchase. The value may be much more than the cost. Here are the best:

The *Las Vegas Advisor* Pocketbook of Values (POV). The judicious use of two or three of these coupons pays for your $50 subscription—and you get the rest of the coupons, not to mention 12 issues of the newsletter and access to the big Web site.

The Casino Perks Coupon Book has two editions, one for gambling coupons and one for dining and entertainment discounts, for $39.95 each. The Gaming Edition is a good value for those who can bet the max $25 for many of the coupons. You can find the exact details of the coupons in each book by calling 888/737-5778, or visit their Web site at www.casino perks.com.

The *American Casino Guide,* by Steve Bourie, is a book that contains many pages of coupons in the back, for casinos all over the U.S. There's a new edition every year; the book costs $14.95.

Casino Player magazine also puts out a coupon book each year that's sent free to all its subscribers.

• Look for ways to use extra coupons. Trade with friends. Some gambling groups on the Internet have coupon-exchange programs. I always collect coupons, even those I won't use, to give to friends and relatives who come to Vegas to visit.

• Out-of-towners in Vegas should always ask at the slot club desk at the off-Strip casinos if there are coupons sent out to locals that they can get. The worst that can happen is they say no. Once in a while you hit coupon pay dirt, because mailings to locals are often quite strong in the coupon department. Sometimes casinos send out entire coupon books to local residents.

These are often powerful enough to make dignified old men go dumpster-diving in condo complexes. On a side note, they also gave me some added ammunition in my friendly battle with Brad on whether to move to Vegas permanently. (He ended that battle by deciding he liked my side best—and here we are.)

• Always investigate if you don't get a coupon mailer one month that you had regularly received. The U.S. mail is not always problem-free. Brad and I have to track down six to eight missing mailings every year. It's a bother, but worth the trouble to collect literally hundreds of dollars we would have otherwise missed.

• Be aware that video poker coupons often have restrictions that are listed only on the rules posted at the slot club desk, not on the coupon itself. Check particularly the policy of the casino on paying for coupons on multi-line machines. A coupon for a bonus for the "hot-card" quad of the day is usually good for one line only, no matter how many quads you have on the multi-line hand. And a few even specify that it must be on the bottom "base" line. With coupons that require you to play max coins to get bonuses on specified hands, watch out for 10-coin (or higher) max-bet machines. Your coupon is worth only half as much (or less) as it is if you use it on a standard five-coin machine. A bonus on quarters, for example, stays the same no matter how many quarters you play per hand.

• Don't expect every casino to have the same coupon policy, or even that policies will be carried out in a standard fashion within the same casino. This story, e-mailed to me by a friend, illustrates this point: "Yesterday, a casino denied my $50-top-jackpot-bonus coupon from their quarterly funbook on my non-sequential royal. The slot supervisor proclaimed that a sequential royal was the top jackpot on this machine. She didn't care that they gave me the bonus on a non-sequential two months ago on the same machines, stating only that I was very lucky to have been paid for it. Later, I found out they'd paid off a coupon on a non-sequential royal on these machines just the day before. I guess each supervisor does whatever she wants."

• Don't overlook keno coupons. Our favorite is one that allows you to play a $2 pick-six game for $1. It's a fun way to bet a small amount and have a chance at a really big jackpot if you catch 6 out of 6. And you will hit some small wins once in a while while you're waiting for the big one.

• Here's a good advanced coupon play. At casinos where your food comps come out of your comp bank dollar for dollar, 2-for-1 or discounted food coupons are a good comp stretcher. Order your food and use the coupon to reduce the bill. The smaller amount will be subtracted from your comp account.

The Ethics of Couponing

I talked about coupon gray areas in *The Frugal Gambler* and suggested that everyone has to draw his own line in the sand. Since that time, I've discussed ethical questions at length with many friends and readers, and the subject always promotes a lively, even heated, discussion when it comes up on Internet bulletin boards.

Take the question of "one coupon per person." That always brings out many different opinions that all seem to come under the heading of "It depends on ..." I had to laugh at one story that was told online that illustrated that casinos do not always frown on coupon hounds. One gambler tried to use two one-per-lifetime coupons at a blackjack table. The pit boss just smiled as he reminded him of the restriction, then said, "Just go down to the next table." As far as the pit boss was concerned, another table represented another lifetime!

Then, for instance, there's the practice of two people making opposite $5 coupon matchplay bets in a game to ensure a winner every time, with no risk. For example, in baccarat one bets on the bank and one on the player. One loses and the other wins every game (except tie games, which are replayed), for a net profit of $5 if the player bet wins or $4.50 if the bank wins.

Most players don't do this, because it embarrasses them to be told they can't. However, I know many aggressive couponing couples, including the Frugal Princess and her hubby, who put their coupons down matter-of-factly in this manner. If they're told they can't do this, one of the two merely moves the coupon to another bet or picks it up until the next hand. If the casino allows it, they don't feel there's an ethical problem.

Whether or not this maneuver is permitted varies from casino to casino and often depends on who's in charge of the game. (By the way, this technique is sometimes used with roulette matchplays—betting opposites of red/black, big/small, odd/even—but it doesn't ensure a winner because a nasty 0 or 00 green shows up every 19 spins on average. Some players like to cover those numbers with a minimum bet to hedge their coupon bets, but that reduces the overall profit expectation.)

One aspect of couponing in which gamblers are quick to line up on opposite sides is the question of whether using one coupon, then leaving a game without playing any more, is the right thing to do. The hit-and-run crowd says that the casino doesn't require additional play and if they play longer without a coupon they're negating, or at least diluting, the value of the coupon. On the other side are those who say that if everyone did this, coupons would dry up, since the casino issues a coupon that has a positive value with the hope that the customer will stick around for some negative play in order to regain what's given up on the coupon. The advantage player counters with something like: "Someone has to pay the electric bill for all those flashy casino lights, but it doesn't have to be me."

I tend to be on the technical side. What's the use of using coupons if you don't maximize their value? On the other hand, if you know Brad personally, you wouldn't be surprised to hear him say, "It just doesn't seem polite to hit and run." So we go back and forth on the issue. Sometimes we use one coupon and leave a table game, excusing ourselves with, "We need to get back to our machines." Sometimes we stay and play one or two more hands if it's a game that has only a small casino edge.

We still laugh over an argument we had quite a few years ago. We were at Palace Station with a coupon to buy in for $15 in coin to get $5 extra. I was sitting at a video poker machine, but I wasn't playing (there was no play requirement with this coupon). Instead, I was busily opening the rolls of coins we had just bought, looking around for a different change booth to cash them. (This was back when I was younger and still believed that I was at war with the casinos and anything is fair in love and war.)

Brad grabbed one of the rolls of quarters and started feeding the machine next to me. I fussed, "I don't want to come in here to get a free five dollars and lose a hundred dollars playing video poker. Besides, we have a two-for-one coupon for the Feast Buffet." (I wanted to get there in time to get the lower lunch price, then sit through the changeover to get the bigger selection they have for dinner).

Brad kept feeding the machine and muttered, "I'm not going to come into this casino and take their money and eat their free food and not give them some play."

Before I could marshal up a good retort, his machine started playing "our song." He hit the royal! By the time he got paid, we had to leave so we didn't miss the buffet-changeover play.

Sorry, Palace Station, but Brad really did try to do the polite thing!

True Coupon Confessions—
I Didn't Want to Tell Mom
by the Frugal Princess

My husband and I had a coupon Mom had given us for free food at the Hard Rock, but we hadn't read the fine print carefully. We were already sitting in the restaurant (on a Saturday) when we noticed that the blackout times were weekends and holidays. Here's where Mom and I differ. She would have left right then and gone somewhere that she had another coupon for free food.

But my hunk-of-an-Army-Ranger husband was hungry and we were enjoying the lively atmosphere at the Hard Rock. More important, we had only a few hours away from our kids and didn't want to waste time driving back and forth between casinos. So we stayed and paid for our meal. Sometimes time is our most valuable commodity.

I didn't tell Mom about this for a long time. But when I did, to my surprise, she said that she understood the good sense in our decision. Wow, I think Mom must be loosening up in her old age!

True Coupon Confessions—
I Didn't Want to Tell Anyone
by the Queen of KuPon

Once upon a time in the distant past when I had just discovered the joys of couponing in Las Vegas, Brad and I each had a 7-5 coupon to use at a downtown casino crap table. When we put down our coupons on the pass line, it turned out that I was the shooter. I rolled a 6. Neither of us took odds—then as now, we were into playing coupons that gave us an advantage and weren't impressed with just getting a breakeven proposition on the odds bet. I rolled 10 numbers before making the 6. Other players who had been betting on the numbers were busily arranging the rows and rows of chips they'd just won (thanks to my hot hand), while Brad and I were content to collect our $14 profit.

We didn't have any more coupons, but the dice were still mine and I was enough of a crapshooter not to give them up in the middle of a roll despite the math. So I put out $5 on the pass line and rolled a 7—frontline winner. Another $5 on the pass line and I rolled an 8, then about 10 more numbers came before I rolled the winner 8. Wow! I'd been rolling for 10 minutes and we'd made $24.

Suddenly, I didn't want to be a disciplined you-only-bet-when-you-have-the-advantage player. I bet another $5, rolled a 10, put $10 behind my pass line bet, then boldly put $5 on the come. I kept rolling numbers. I maintained three come bets with odds riding and kept shooting ... and shooting ... and shooting. For 25 more minutes I held those dice. Finally, after 35 minutes, I sevened out. I grabbed our $295 profit and ran.

I'm usually a strict follow-the-rules sort of gal—but once in a while ...

My Readers ...

I'm always proud when someone tells me he's read *The Frugal Gambler*, then run all the way to the bank with the information he's gleaned. Although the writer of the letter below may have run a little farther than I recommend, it's a good example of what a persistent, organized, enthusiastic couponer can accomplish. Many people don't think it's fun to hustle all over Las Vegas, especially when it's 120 degrees in the shade; everyone has his own idea of what constitutes entertainment. But this letter refutes the idea that couponing is "small stuff."

Two years ago my wife and I decided to put your queenly couponing ideas to work. We started with only $11. First and foremost, we accumulated coupons any way we could. We subscribed to the Las Vegas Advisor *and* Casino Player *and got their coupon books. We were active Internet coupon traders with people in other parts of the country. When a casino gave out a funbook, we got two, one for each of us. We watched the funbook exit area to collect those that people pitched. Some shows have tickets with matchplays attached that people leave on their tables. We'd grab as many as we could on our way out of a showroom.*

Once we acquired our fistful of coupons, we played as many as is humanly possible. At the beginning we had such a tiny bankroll that we couldn't bear any risk of loss and always played as a couple on opposite sides of even-money bets. This meant baccarat betting on player/banker, crap betting on pass/don't pass with a $1 insurance bet on 12, and black/red roulette with a $1 insurance bet on 0/00. This gave us minimum wins of $1 each play with 7-5 coupons, $4-plus with 10-5s, and $9-plus with those 20-10 beauties.

Playing off both sides of the same event bothers many players. I don't see why. If you're worried about casino heat, just plop down the two coupons, put on your best tourist-from-Idaho face, and say, "This is how we decide who chooses where we eat lunch."

... Rule!

*As we built our bankroll, we could safely play black-
jack, pai gow, and big 6 coupons, which involve more
risk. We never played two coupons on these games at the
same time, minimizing the risk of a dealer blackjack or
big pai gow hand. We stopped hedging the 12 in craps
and the 0/00 in roulette when we were comfortable that
our bankroll was safe from short negative swings. Also,
since our bankroll had grown, we no longer played both
sides of a game. We'd just play two events in a row now.
I confess that we were fast and loose with the one-per-
player limitations; if the coupon didn't say "per day" or
some such limitation, we moved from table to table and
played as many as we thought we could get away with.*

*Our favorites were what we call "money-for-nothing"
coupons. Buy in for $20 and get $30 in chips. We bra-
zenly bought in and went immediately to a different cashier to cash in. Some places even skip the chips and just
hand you the extra $10. We cashed multiples of these at
different tables or cages, or waited for different shifts.*

*As our bankroll grew, we began to exploit higher-value
and longer-term coupons: 2-1 and 3-1 blackjack bonuses
could be safely played; $25 and $50 matchplays were
added to our arsenal.*

*Lastly, we looked for good drawing coupons that gave
us a big advantage. A downtown Vegas casino used to
have a whirlwind booth full of swirling money. Six times
a day they drew an entry and someone got 28 seconds in
the booth. There was one entry in each funbook. I saved/
traded/scrounged these for nine months before I made
my big move. I chose a Monday as the day that would
have the least number of entries. There were only about
600 total that day and I had 350 of them. I was called
three times for the money booth that day for a $288 profit!*

*A little over two years later we took the envelope that
started with 11 $1 bills and counted the contents: 22
$100 bills, 35 $20s, and $100-plus in small bills inside.
Our $11 had turned into $3,000!*

*We feel we've taken your tutelage to the highest level.
Thanks for all the help and guidance you have given us.*

A Look Into the Future

Rather than an employee thrusting coupons into your hand as you walk by a casino, they could soon be dispensed by machine. Fitzgeralds in downtown Las Vegas is already doing it both ways. You can get a coupon flyer from a casino representative at the door and you can swipe your slot club card in a kiosk inside, choosing from a menu of coupon options, including matchplay. (Another reason for a couple to have separate accounts!) Some casinos are already putting coupons on the Internet or sending them by e-mail. *Las Vegas Advisor* members can access dozens of "Daily Deals" coupons that can be downloaded from the *LVA* Web site at www.lasvegasadvisor.com.

I can foresee all this evolving into a system that tailors coupons to the tastes of individual customers, using the information that's already being collected in the slot club databases. Perhaps the computer will create a nice little coupon package for Brad and me, with an emphasis on video poker, but also a few teaser coupons to see if we can be coaxed into playing other games.

Finally, I had to stop and think when someone asked me recently, "Will you ever stop couponing?" After a long pause, I answered, "I may cut down, but I can never see myself giving it up entirely."

Call it feminine capriciousness—or primal thriftiness. But I can play $1 Triple Play video poker at $15 a hand for eight hours and lose $3,000, then win $10 on a couponing break and it makes me feel good. I don't expect anyone to understand it—Brad's had 20 years of practice and he doesn't yet.

IV

COMPS—
The Game Within the Game

8

Welcome to the
Casino Comp World

"Gambling is the most personalized business there is. You are separating a man from his money without giving him a product or a service. You had better at least give him a kiss."
—*so sayeth the late Chester Simms, casino manager of the Flamingo Hotel in the early '60s*

Casinos have evolved in many ways since Chester Simms ran the Flamingo. Nowadays, casinos claim, and rightly so, that they're providing a product and a valuable one at that—namely, entertainment. And people are willing to pay—some a little, some a lot—for enjoying the kind of entertainment that casinos provide. However, that "kiss" is still important: The casinos need to sugarcoat the fact that people are paying an "entertainment fee"—their losses. I look at comps as the sugarcoating.

Everyone likes to get something for nothing and that's the allure of comps. Even people who can fully afford to pay for their own rooms and meals get a bang out of it when the casino gives them something free. Sure, to some it involves saving money. But for many, it's just the feeling of being treated like they're someone special.

As I wrote back in the Introduction of this book, I

felt the need to write *More Frugal Gambling* because so much has changed since the publication of *The Frugal Gambler*. Well, nowhere in Casinoland is this truer than in the comp department. Casino comp policies can now be described as the Revenge of the Nerds.

"It doesn't matter how much you win or lose. The casinos will reward you with comps according to how much money you put at risk." For years I said that, but it's no longer always true. The bean counters have taken over. These business-school graduates, with their beady eyes firmly fixed on the bottom line, now tinker constantly with their comp formulas in order to improve the casino's take for the comps they give.

Let's face it, casinos don't hand out comps because their executives like to give away profits. For them, comps are just another means to bigger numbers on the revenue side of the balance sheet. The smart gambler needs to stay abreast of these changes in order to maximize his use of the comp system and to be sure he doesn't pay too much for the entertainment the casino provides him.

The manner in which a dollar player gets comps is much different than the way most quarter players use the system. We've moved up in our level of play since I wrote *The Frugal Gambler*, thus we've learned many new ways to get comps. In short, I know a lot more now about this subject than I did when I wrote the first book.

The Three Comp Systems in a Casino

There are three basic ways to get comps at a casino: through the slot club system; through direct-mail offers that come from a marketing department; and through the casino player-development department, using hosts.

The first one, the slot club, is great for the beginning gambler who's learning the ropes of the comp system. The slot club booth and its personnel might represent the entire length of the comp road for the occasional or recreational low-rolling gambler. The second (direct-mail) and third (slot and table-game hosts) systems should be mastered by more frequent gamblers and those who play on a higher level, in order to get higher-level comps.

Bottom line: A smart gambler should learn to take advantage of all three systems, benefiting from the perks, while avoiding the drawbacks, of each.

But before we get into the advanced and graduate comp lectures in the next three chapters, we first need to review some comp basics here. And for that, we turn to the Frugal Princess. Though Angela has one of the best teachers (if I do say so myself), she has also learned plenty about comps on her own—by playing, paying close attention to details, and most of all, by using the powerful tool of asking.

"A fool wonders; a wise man asks."
—*Disraeli*

The Frugal Princess Covers the Comp Basics

I used to wonder how Jean the Queen was able to get so much for free in a casino: free meals, free hotel rooms, free limo rides from the airport, even free beauty-shop sessions. I never thought I'd be able to get these things myself, especially with my infrequent visits to a casino and my tiny bankroll.

Good news! Even low rollers can get comps.

When I started telling my friends about the casino life and what my mother and I were writing about, some of them didn't even know what "getting a comp" meant. I had to start with the very basics: The word "comp" is short for "complimentary," and a comp is something free the casino gives you for playing its games so you'll be more likely to come back to visit them in the future. The most common are free food and rooms, but we've enjoyed many other kinds of comps: show tickets; logo wear, such as T-shirts and jackets; admission to entertainment of various kinds, such as a wax museum or a water park; and my favorite since I've had kids, free child-care. Many people don't realize that they can get comps or they think that only people who play dollar slots or high-limit table games are entitled to them. Nothing could be further from the truth. Even the first-time inexperienced low-limit casino visitor can get comps.

If you're a recreational low roller as I am, you don't play quarter machines for 10-14 hours a day, or dollar machines at all. You may wonder: Can we go into a casino where we have no history of play, where we reserved our room directly from a reservations clerk, and get comps the first time we stay there?

The answer is an emphatic *yes you can*.

You don't have to be a big bettor to get comps. We never play at a higher denomination than quarters and we've scored many valuable freebies. We even get offers in the mail for free rooms.

However, comps don't come automatically the minute you start playing a machine or sit down at one of the table games. You almost always have to make some effort to get them. The most important thing you have to do is make sure that the casino *knows* you're playing.

How do you do that? Well, if I weren't the daughter of the Queen of Comps, I'm not sure that I would have found out right away that I needed to get a slot club card before I put any money in a slot machine, so the casino would be able to track my play and put me "in the system," which is the database for comp qualifying. I'm certain I would never have asked a blackjack pit boss to be rated so I could get these rewards based on my level of table play. Now I notice so many people playing $1 slot machines—and even higher—without a card, and I want to go up and shake them and tell them how many comps they're missing. Actually, I sometimes wish I could slip *my* player's card into their machine and collect all those free benefits they're wasting.

We know that the more you play, the higher the level of comps you earn, so it's best to concentrate your play, at first, at one casino, rather than playing a little bit at many casinos and not getting to a minimal comp level at any of them. However, when my husband and I are in a major gambling destination, we like to sightsee and travel all over town and we're sometimes tempted to stop and play a little in some of the casinos we visit. Mom has talked about the pros and cons of this earlier in the slot club chapter, but it can be a good idea, especially in Las Vegas—if we *do* join a slot club, even if we don't play at all. This technique gets our names and address into casino databases and will probably produce a few discount offers in the mail, maybe even for free rooms during slow periods during the year.

However, if your time is limited, it's better to establish a core casino where you play enough to regularly get free food, free rooms, and even some higher-level comps, such as invitations to parties. The best time to work on picking up comps in other casinos is after you have one you can depend on to be your base of (comped) operations.

There's no better technique for getting comps than the word Mom is constantly drumming into my head—*ask*. Sometimes Steve and I still depend on Mom for free rooms and food comps, but we're amazed by how much we can get on our own with a small amount of play if we just ask. Be sure to remember to ask nicely, not in a demanding tone. (It's not hard for me to be humble when I ask for a comp, because I always feel like maybe I don't deserve it. I'm too shy to be demanding.)

A rule we strictly adhere to is to never play longer or at a higher level just to get comps if it means overextending our gambling budget. We play at the denomination that fits into our loss comfort zone (nickels and quarters) and only as long as we're having fun and our session bankroll lasts. Then we go to the slot club desk to see what we can get with our points. We don't say, "Let's get x number of points so we can do y or z," which could lead to us losing more than we can afford. It may be more frugal to just pay for what we want.

One of the best comp hints, for beginning and experienced gamblers who fly to a casino destination, is to check out room-air package deals from a travel agency or an airline tour department. You may find that these cost little more than the airfare alone, which gives you the advantage of not feeling pressure to play to a certain level just to try to get your room comped. Then you can concentrate on getting comps for meals at your comfortable rate of play—food comps are easier to get than room comps. And sometimes it's wiser for a video poker player to pay for a room at a reasonable rate rather than spend the time playing to get it comped; then you're free to move around and play at other casinos that have better games or promotions.

If you do prepay a package, however, be aware that you can't get your room comped later. So if you

---

"I Would've Comped You Anyway"

An e-mail from an acquaintance:

Margie and I had been playing blackjack for several hours one morning at Sunset Station and we were hungry. So I asked a pit boss (whom I hadn't seen before) that if it wouldn't be too much trouble, could he please check my rating and let me know how much longer we needed to play to earn a comp for lunch at the cafe. When he came back with the comp, he said, "Even if you hadn't played enough, I would've given you the comp—because you asked so nicely.'

---

plan to play enough to get a comped room, you should book your room separate from your airfare.

"Try to play where you're a big frog in a little pond." This is one of my Mom's best hints. We don't play much at the fancy megaresorts when we go to a gambling destination. We sightsee at them, but when it comes time to risk our hard-earned money, we look for a smaller and perhaps slightly older casino that will appreciate our business, even if it's small potatoes. There we can earn more comps—and earn them faster for the same amount of play—giving us more bang for our gambling buck.

The Queen Discusses Respecting the Comp System

Comps are considered gifts by the casinos, which means that they are within their legal rights to take away your future comp privileges. Similarly, any comp value you've accumulated in the past can be taken away, and you usually have no recourse. Therefore, it's important to be careful not to abuse the comp system. Note: Regulations are different for cashback, or point systems that are cashback equivalents, which you have earned on a stated schedule. The casino can take away your player's card and you won't be able to earn additional points in the future, but legally they owe you for cashback points you've earned legitimately in the past.

There's no clear line between using and abusing comps. In fact, between the two is a large gray area—as there is when you talk about many casino topics. We've slowly moved to a more conservative position in terms of comp use, but not because of a sudden attack of conscience. I think Brad and I under-use the comp system more and more the longer we play. Maybe we're older and wiser and I'm not as obsessed as I used to be. Maybe I tend to be more careful to guard my reputation—being well-known does create restrictions. And other factors are obvious—for example, being locals means we don't need as many hotel-room nights as when we traveled here from Indiana and higher-level play earns us more food than we can healthily digest.

We earned all the comped rooms, food, and entertainment we needed or wanted for years at quarter play. So many of the extra perks we earn at the dollar and higher level aren't things we need or even want. However, Brad says I'm just as nutty about comps as I am about money in general—I always want to save them for a rainy day. Of course, he has an answer for that, "We're now living in that 'future' you've planned for so many years." However, we still have to make decisions all the time about which of our comp requests are reasonable, which ones might be on the outer edge, and which would be obvious abuse.

Yes, I still advocate using the just-ask technique—

you'll usually be pleasantly surprised by how many comps you can get that you didn't know you qualified for. But some people have run too far with this, asking for so much so often and with so demanding an attitude that the hosts consider them pests or, even worse, comp hustlers. Some players who've read my first book immediately expect to get as many comps as I described in those pages—within the first few days or weeks after they start playing. They miss the point that you build on your play, year after year. You establish yourself and your loyalty over a period of time and only then does it become easier to get comps. Believe it or not, we paid hard cash for some of our hotel rooms the first few years.

Comps in Cyberspace
Check casino Web sites for possible comp-earning opportunities before you leave home. I'm predicting this will be a powerful marketing tool of the future.

It pays to learn the comp "rules," especially those that might be unwritten. At some casinos, when your comp status is RFB (room, food, and beverage), you have a dollar limit and it doesn't matter how many people are in your party. For many others, RFB normally covers expenses for only two people, so if you invite others to eat with you, the casino has the right not to comp the extra expense. In these cases we take care to play enough that the extra meals are picked up as a courtesy if I talk to the host about it beforehand.

Likewise, it's usually assumed that if you get a comped room, you're the one who'll be staying in it.

Again, I often make arrangements with a host for a friend or relative to use the room, but we still play enough to qualify for the comp. It's best to clear any deviations from the ordinary casino policy in advance, so the host doesn't think you're abusing the system.

I try never to stiff a casino. I've rarely accepted an offer for a free room or event where I knew we definitely weren't planning to play—not that it would be illegal or even unethical, especially if the offer came as a result of our past play. Occasionally, we've unexpectedly run into a situation where we've gone to a casino on an upfront comp and found that the good machines we were planning on playing had been removed and there was no good substitute game. Even then we try hard not to burn our bridges by not playing at all. We might want to stay and play at that casino in the future if game conditions improve—and we want always to be welcome to return and earn comps again. (Describing customers who'd come in, used food comps, and left without playing in the casino, one employee referred to it as, "They chewed and screwed.")

Many casinos, especially those that cater to out-of-town visitors, require current play to get current comps, especially for free meals. But now that we live in Las Vegas and play mostly off the Strip, we often go to a casino to eat, or see a show, or redeem a cash coupon, and leave without playing that day. Most of our comps are banked indefinitely in these casinos, so we don't have to worry about earning current comps by playing on the same day that they're used. We'll be in action there enough on other days to keep up our rating as good customers.

More Comps Than We Could Ever Use

A controversial area that's ripe for abuse is the selling of comps. Both sides can produce strong arguments supporting their positions. On one side, many consider it an abuse of the system to ask for or take a comp that you specifically plan to sell—room-service liquor in large quantities, show tickets, or expensive gifts. On the other side, players figure that they've earned these comps legitimately by playing up to specific requirements and after they get them, it's their business what they do with them. A comp is a gift, they say. "Have you ever sold a tasteless housewarming present at a garage sale?"

Most gamblers don't get more comps than they can use, so for them, it's a non-issue. However, a significant number of frequent gamblers, particularly Las Vegas locals, play so often or at such high levels that they accrue more comp credits than they can personally use. I've often joked that our waistlines are suffering because of all the food comps we earn.

What do we do with our extra comps? Well, our small condo can only hold so much, so we give away to friends and family a lot of our casino gifts. We share our comps with all kinds of service people who do nice things for us and to whom we'd like to show our appreciation—the hairdresser, the massage therapist, the always-cheerful change girl at our favorite casino, our helpful hosts. We even look for a charity that will find a good way to dispose of some of them. We use our ever-expanding food-comp banks to entertain friends and, sometimes, even treat strangers we might meet in line. (I hate to see a food coupon expire unused.)

We have a large circle of gambling friends among whom we share comps; it's a way to eat and see shows in casinos where they or we don't play. There are also forums and bulletin boards on the Internet where you can trade comps. Many comp coupons we get are non-transferable, requiring that we pick up, for example, show tickets in person with picture ID. We're careful to follow the rules. But once we have the actual tickets, I don't feel it's unethical to give them to someone else instead of letting them go to waste. In fact, I always feel I'm doing a casino a favor when I give away comps: I'm going to play in that casino anyway; the person I invite might become a new customer.

There usually aren't any legal reasons that you can't sell comped show tickets (unless you're scalping them on the street at a price above face value in a place where this is prohibited by law) or any other comp, for that matter. But it's sometimes against casino policy or local ordinances, even if you're selling below retail or face value. The chief problem is that if too many players start doing this, the casinos will react negatively. Some casinos strictly enforce the rule against selling comps; some do so only when the selling is obvious and extreme. Usually, the casino takes action against the abusers only; I've known more than one gambler or group of gamblers who've had their comp privileges taken away or have even been barred from the casino completely. Worse, occasionally the casinos just change the whole comp program and cut benefits. Then everyone is hurt by the actions of a greedy minority.

I don't expect to influence the few who seem hell-bent on ruining the comp system by greedy and selfish practices, but perhaps some of you are making damaging mistakes because you don't realize the consequences. Be careful not to stretch the limits of the comp system. Yes, *ask*—but don't demand. Ask nicely and take refusals graciously; after all, we're guests of the house. Would you invite someone back to your home if he'd been rude or had stolen from you on the last visit?

I may be the Queen of Comps, but these days I try to ask for less, rather than more, than I think we've earned; we're very careful not to wear out our welcome in any casino. I think we all need to go in this direction—or we'll wake up someday and find that there's no way to frolic frugally in our favorite casino playgrounds.

Comps on Cruises

Casinos on cruise ships used to be located in a dark dinky corner with a few out-of-date machines and a couple of blackjack tables. No more. Especially on the newer ships, cruise ship casinos are now large brightly lit areas with all the newest slot and video poker machines and other table games besides blackjack.

But the biggest news is that many now have players clubs and you can earn comps just like you do in any casino on land. These could include free drinks (which are ordinarily expensive even for players), shore excursions, spa treatments, cabin upgrades, cashback (that you spend onboard), or future cruise discounts. In fact, if you play long enough or at a high enough level, you might get your whole cruise comped.

The Norwegian Cruise Line has integrated its improved casino program into a new overall "freestyle" type of cruise, a more relaxed and informal vacation experience.

Carnival, an umbrella corporation with the ships of Holland America, Windstar, Costa, Cunard, Seabourn, and Carnival, has created a player's club that covers all of its 45-plus ships that sail under these brands. To find out more information on their Ocean Players Club, call 800/253-2773 or visit www.oceanplayers.com.

If you want to work with a travel agent who's knowledgeable in this area, I recommend Players Travel Inc. They work like casino hosts, as well as regular travel agents, and can help gamblers wanting to take a cruise vacation to get the most for their money *and* their casino play. You can call them at 800/599-2021 or visit them at www.playerstravel.com.

9

Comps From the Slot Club and In Your Mailbox

"Getting casino goodies in the mail is like manna from heaven."
—an online wag who calls himself (or herself) Biblescholar

Getting Comps Through the Slot Club

The slot club is the branch of the comp system used by most low-rolling machine players. Of course, there are as many different slot club systems as there are casinos, as I discussed at length in Chapter Five. Hence, the mechanics of getting comps through the slot club vary from one casino to another. If you've mastered the principles in the slot club chapter, you'll find that there's *usually* some expedient way to get comps at the slot club booth.

The best scenario is when the booth has a "comp menu" in a club brochure, which lists what comps are available and how many points it takes to get them. When you earn the specified number of points, you go to the slot club or a kiosk and redeem them for the chosen comp. Some clubs, however, like to keep the details of their system secret. So, after you've finished playing, you must go to the club, queue up in what Jeffrey Compton likes to call the "beg line," and ask what comps you've earned. Fortunately, this type of club is dying out, especially in Las Vegas. Unfortunately, secrecy is still alive and well in Reno and Atlantic City.

Advantages of the Slot Club Comp System

Although rooms and food are the most common comps, some clubs offer a large selection of other comps to choose from: movies, child-care, shows, and gift items. Our favorite use of slot club points is to get gift certificates that we put toward what I call "make-your-own comps": Clothes, groceries, gas, electronics, and household items are some of the practical things we've bought with gift certificates from the slot club.

People like getting comps through the slot club system, because it's usually clear what amount of play gets which benefits. The comps are directly related to points, so people aren't made to feel like they're begging; they've earned the comp. Unlike the host system that I discuss in the next chapter, most slot club systems allow players to get comps without the fear of being turned down.

It's an easy process to redeem points for comps. In most cases, you simply go the slot club, where they check your account and immediately write or print out the comp. Some casinos have made it even easier with a redemption program built into the system that allows you to comp yourself right at a machine or at electronic kiosks.

The most convenient comp-redemption procedure is the POP (point-of-purchase) system. At the restaurant, movie box office, or other casino outlet, give the cashier your player's card and the appropriate number of points are deducted on the spot to pay for what you're buying.

You can often get discounts in a casino (what I call "partial comps") with little or even no play at the games just by having a player's card. In many casinos, flashing this card gives you an automatic discount (often 10%) at restaurants, gift shops, and other retail outlets. The card may even get you a heavily discounted room rate. It never hurts to ask if there's a slot club-member discount.

Disadvantages of the Slot Club Comp System

Some club tracking systems are difficult to use and the card reader might say nothing more than "Accepted" rather than giving a point countdown or balance. With these systems, you can find out how many points you've earned and what comps you're entitled to only by quizzing the booth clerks.

Slot club employees don't usually have the authority to stretch the rules or to issue comps that don't come off your points, so using the slot club doesn't give you extras you might get by talking to a host instead.

Some slot clubs have a limited choice of comps, often just for food. The only way to get a comped room or show tickets, for example, is through mail offers or having a host connection.

Some have awkward rules. For example, comp points not used—mainly for food—do not go back into the bank. So if you overestimate the cost of the meal, you lose the unused points, and if you underestimate, you have to pay out of pocket for the rest. And at some slot clubs, notably in Reno, your points expire at the end of the year or if you haven't played for a certain amount of time. In fact, at some casinos, your slot club points for comps expire at the end of your trip.

On top of these negatives, you often have to face long lines at the slot club booth to get your comps.

Getting Comps Via the Mail
Through the Direct-Marketing System

Every time I go to our condo mailbox, I think, "A day without casino mail is like a day without sunshine."

Although you may get food, show tickets, and other freebies through the slot club, the number-one way that most low rollers all over the country, both table and machine players, get room comps is through the direct-mail system. It's also a first-rate method for adding other comps to those you get through hosts.

Typically, you join a slot club or ask to be rated at the tables the first time you play at a casino—at least this is what you should do. You usually pay for your room this first time—maybe you came to town on a bargain airline-package deal that included a room. Or perhaps you searched the Internet for the best rates and prepaid your room reservation. You're prepared to buy all your own food on this trip, though you might play long enough to ask for a food comp from the pit boss or to earn enough points to redeem for a few meals.

Then, a month or two after you get home, you receive a room offer in the mail. It could be for a reduced rate or it could be free, depending on how much you gambled during that first trip. You make a reservation using this offer. Then, after playing some more at the same casino, you get another free-room offer in the mail. Soon you're staying free at this same casino on every trip, always gambling enough to keep the mail offers coming.

Next, you decide to start the cycle at another casino, playing enough to get the free-room offers from them. Now you can stay twice as long, two or perhaps three free nights at each casino, always making sure you play enough at both to keep the offers coming.

278

If you want to start staying longer periods, you repeat this cycle at other casinos. At some, you'll find that because your history of play covers a longer period of time, even though you don't increase play, you begin getting better offers, perhaps for more nights or upgrades to a suite. You learn that the offers vary, depending on the time of year; slow times not only bring free-room offers, but extra goodies as well: free meals that don't come off your points, free show tickets, logo wear and other free gifts, even a reduced-rate or free room for a friend.

If you build on this plan for many years, you might find that you can stay in a casino free as long as you want to keep playing casino games. Maybe you can do it 191 days in one year—as Brad and I did the last year before we decided to unpack our suitcases for good in the condo we bought in Las Vegas.

Advantages of the Direct-Marketing Comp System

Similar to the slot club system, you don't have to deal with a host, so for the shy person the direct-marketing comp system is a convenient and non-threatening alternative.

Taking advantage of mail offers often keeps you from having to redeem slot club points, so you can save them for other comps—or for cashback if it's offered. Point requirements for rooms are often proportionately higher than for food and other comps, so it's gravy when a free-room offer shows up in your mailbox.

Some casinos, especially smaller ones, use a less complex formula in making comp offers by mail, often just basing them on actual coin-in (machines) or money put at risk (tables), rather than on win/loss figures and other factors that the host system more frequently uses these days. But this is changing fast. I've heard many reports concerning two people who've given the same amount of play, where the loser gets a nice mail offer and the winner gets zilch.

It's not uncommon to get more generous offers through the mail than you could with the same play under the host system. Although marketing tends to employ a multi-tiered schedule of play requirements to determine the value of the various offers they send out, the range within one level can be quite broad and you can get a good offer even if you just barely make it into a level. These offers can also be more generous because they factor in a specific time period. You'll get better offers for weekdays than for weekends. It's amazing what goodies marketing will use to entice players during the slow days of mid-December. And when the country is in a recession, some casinos send free-room offers to all slot club members who are still breathing.

Direct-mail offers often consider your long-term history at the casino. I've seen some send out free-room offers to former regular players who haven't been in their casino for several years. In fact, some marketing departments are patient and optimistic; they continue to send invites for a year or two to people who use their free-room offers, but don't give any play at all—although you can't count on this.

Mail offers might even provide you with free benefits in casinos where you've never played. With the consolidation of casino companies, there's a lot of cross-property marketing going on. We've received generous offers, with free room and food, even cash coupons, from a casino up at Tahoe owned by the same company as one that we play at in Las Vegas. Also, hosts move around frequently and take their little black books with them; sometimes these names are added to a new casino database. *Voilà*—an offer from a casino whose front door you've never even walked through.

You may get to double-dip in a casino promotional-mail goodie dish. Different departments in the same casino sometimes send out their own offers, apparently not consulting with any other department. We've been the happy recipients of two promotions from the same casino for the same month (one from the slot club and one from marketing), so we never complain about this lack of coordination between the various casino departments. As far as we're concerned, let each supervisor continue to jealously guard his own mailing list and plans.

Working From a Distance

Here's how to get into a casino's database and possibly score mail offers before stepping through their front door:

1. Join the slot club by phone or online.

2. Visit the casino Web site and sign in as a guest.

3. Write for information before your visit. (As an added benefit, you'll sometimes be sent coupons, funbooks, or small souvenirs.)

4. Apply for casino credit. At some casinos, applying for a line of credit will bring a mail offer, often for a free room for two or three nights, even before you join the slot club. (A caveat: Be sure you can handle casino credit lines with discipline. It's all right to stay on these offers without tapping your approved credit line, but do not take markers at a casino without showing any play. Casinos don't look favorably on customers taking an interest-free cash advance to play at another casino or to make purchases.) Although applying for a line of credit may help get you some comps at a new casino initially, future comps will be based much more on the amount of your play.

Disadvantages of the Casino-Marketing Comp System

Sometimes the free room offered by marketing is not as free as they want you to think. Though you won't have a room bill at the end of your stay, your comp account may be charged, even if it puts your comp credits into the red. In this event, you can't get any meal comps from a host during your visit until you play enough to get back into the black. Sometimes the mail offer states this, usually in the fine print; other times it comes as a surprise when you're turned down after asking for your first meal comp.

This happened to a player I know. He was sent an offer for free airfare and three free room nights. After playing several hours and losing bundles of money, he asked three different employees for one buffet comp and was denied all three times. "I was good enough for a free room and airfare, but giving me a lousy buffet was out of the question!" How did he react? After one night, he checked out of that casino and stayed somewhere else. That casino lost two days of his action over one buffet comp.

This is mainly a problem for people who play at a higher level and use the host system in conjunction with direct marketing. We never ran into this sort of thing when we were playing at the quarter level and we never had mail offers decrease any of the benefits we earned through the slot club system.

Not all casinos send marketing offers to all of their customers, preferring to stick to their specific target markets. For example, some Las Vegas neighborhood casinos don't send mailings to out-of-town addresses, no matter how much a customer has played. I have a friend who lives in Reno, works in Las Vegas, and plays almost exclusively at Las Vegas locals casinos. It's the rare marketing department that sends him even a slot club newsletter, let alone free-room offers. On the other hand, some Strip casinos don't mail to locals, since they're targeting tourists. In other parts of the country, casinos favor targeting particular zip codes.

Direct-mail offers are undependable. Although some properties have a regular schedule and you can plan on receiving offers every month or two, at least for free rooms, most casinos send their offers out on an irregular basis. Therefore, you can't rely on them as your only source for comped lodging, especially if you're not flexible in your schedule for casino visits.

It's difficult to determine how much play gets what kind of marketing offer. This is one area where, no matter how experienced you are, you'll never know all the answers. First, every casino has its own guidelines. Second, these guidelines are usually guarded as secretly as the details of the casino surveillance system—occasions on which I've gotten a casino host or high-level executive to share this information with me have been rare indeed. Third, even if you found out the guidelines, it wouldn't do you much good, since they change as fast as the weather at the top of Mount Everest. Casino executives are known for their job mobility—and every time you get a new Director of Marketing, you get a new marketing plan.

People have been known to go crazy trying to figure out how a casino sends out its promotional offers. I've found that it reduces stress to just consider this as one of the gambling-life's mysteries.

Since we always have separate accounts, Brad and I have tried experimenting with different amounts of play on each card, then studying the different mail offers we receive. We've actually had some success in formulating a rough idea of how much play is required to get the offers we want. Generally speaking, the more you play at one casino, the more offers you get. However, this is not always true. Maybe we've played heavily on Brad's card for a period of time and not played on mine at all. Guess who gets a free-room offer. Not Brad—no reward for him. But I get a we-want-you-to-come-back offer.

Probably the most surprising offer came to Brad after he'd been on a lucky streak at a very small casino, including hitting three royals in 24 hours. He was winning so much that we joked that he ought to take a rest from playing in this casino before they threw him out. But what came in the mail in just a couple of days? A letter congratulating him on his jackpots. And attached at the bottom was a coupon for a free room and $10 in cash the next time he visited. I guess this was a we-want-a-chance-to-get-our-money-back offer!

Mail offers often aren't sent far enough in advance to give customers time to make adequate work-schedule and travel plans. This was my biggest pet peeve when we were staying in casino rooms for long periods of time. Why can't casino marketing departments plan ahead? It's more difficult to get time off work on short notice and the best bargain airfares are usually gone if you don't book a couple of months ahead. Back when we lived in Indiana, we used to get good offers that came in the mail *after* we'd already left to go to Las Vegas. Nothing is more frustrating than finding a terrific offer from a casino you would have really like to stay at after you've arrived back home.

There's no easy remedy to this problem. It's no use to call ahead and try to find out what mailings are being planned—it's usually "in committee." Back in the days when I depended on free-room offers, I often went ahead and made airline reservations early so I could get the best price, hoping that I was guessing correctly about the offers from past experience.

Sometimes you're pretty sure you'll be getting a

promotional room offer from a casino that sends you regular mailings, but you don't want them to run out of rooms before you get that letter—like on busy holiday weekends. Here's what you can do. Go ahead and reserve a room at that casino at the regular rate and if later you get a promo offer for a lower rate or free room, you can call up and change the high-rate reservation to the free or reduced-rate. You can almost always do this *if* the specifications of the offer fit. I called this my book-cancel-rebook routine.

Hints for Mail Offers

• You're usually not required to play during the time of your stay unless it's stated on the invitation. This means they won't look at your playing record upon checkout and charge for the room if no play is shown. And if you have a long history of play on other visits to this casino, not playing on this one might not hurt your record. However, not playing when you're staying on a free-room offer is usually the way to stop the glittering offers from this casino lighting up your mailbox.

• Your speed of response in calling and accepting room offers is crucial. Often, all the rooms set aside for a particular offer are booked quickly. However, if you call as soon as you get the offer and still find all the rooms gone, you can sometimes convince a supervisor to find a promotional room for you.

• In establishing yourself at a number of casinos in order to get mailings, try to play enough when you first get your slot card to get to the minimum redemption level for cashback. Some veterans feel that this may be the key to getting entry-level mailings. Many casinos base their mailings on frequency of play *and* long-term playing history, another good reason to concentrate your play at one or two core casinos.

• If you want to get a high-level offer from a top resort-casino where you've never played, concentrate your heaviest possible play during one day. I've known some high rollers who got extremely lucrative mailings for a long time after just one big-play day.

• Read carefully any mail offer for a free room. Some casinos require a credit card to hold the room, but don't charge it. Others charge one night's cost to your credit card, even with a free-night promo; when you check in, the front-desk clerk is supposed to remove this charge from your card. Be sure to ask for a credit receipt at this time. If it's forgotten, there's often a hassle to straighten it out later by phone.

I've seen a few free-room offers that have a no-cancellation feature. They charge your credit card for one night and, even if you cancel the reservation far in advance, they won't issue a credit. (That's one way casinos occasionally report occupancy rates of higher than 100%.) On the other hand, we've found that in some casinos, if you're a very good customer, you won't be asked for a credit card to hold a room reservation, but they request that you cancel a day or two in advance as a courtesy if at all possible.

• If you receive a combination cash/free-room offer (where you can't get one without the other) and don't need the room, you can always book the offer, check in, get the cash, and check out later the same day.

The Growing Complexity of Casino Marketing

One of the problems of working on a book over a long period of time, especially on a subject where I learn a new wrinkle every day, is that I have to keep adding qualifiers like "usually," "often," "as a rule," and "in most cases." When I first started this section on comps, though direct marketing has more complexities than the slot system, it seemed to be simple for the ordinary player to use.

However, some of the things I wrote a year or two ago are not as sure now as they were then. Take that first bullet under "Hints for Mail Offers." I wrote, "You're not required to play during the time of your stay, which means they won't look at your playing record on checkout and charge for the room if no play is shown."

So what happens? I read a post on an Internet gambling bulletin board in which a player tells of receiving an offer from a fancy Strip casino for three free room nights, but then notices in the fine print that he has to earn a specified number of points or his room will be charged to his credit card

In all the years we've received free offers through direct marketing, I never came across such a practice. So in goes a qualifier: You're *usually* not required to play during the time of your stay.

Part of the reason for the change in direct-mail offers is a trend in casinos to consolidate all marketing efforts into one department, so "casino marketing" is becoming an umbrella term that includes all departments connected with marketing: the slot club, direct mail, and the host system. With the help of new computer programs that can crunch enormous amounts of information, the whole system is becoming more integrated and complex.

Take the concept of factoring in whether you win or lose to determine comp levels, a common practice in the host system. This element now might show up in the amount of bounce-back offers you get through the slot club system or how often you get a free-room offer in the mail. With the integration of the three systems, many times these days you'll get a room offer in the mail and it's unclear just what department it came from.

Therefore, although the next two chapters are concerned mainly with the host system and the advanced information needed to use it skillfully, even if you want to keep the comp game as simple as possible, you'll find ideas that will help you better understand all three systems.

10

Do You Need a Host?

"Our job is to make our customers as happy as possible while they lose their money."
— *casino host*

"A good host is one who makes you feel like you're more than just a wallet."
— *casino gambler*

Player Development?

The third department involved in granting comps to players is what the casino usually calls "player development." Here, I exercise my author's privilege to go off on a brief rant. I *hate* the term player development. It gives me visions of wild-eyed scientists in the casino basement, madly working with multicolored fluids and rows and rows of test tubes, cooking up a potion to add to the casino's free drinks that will turn a sensible deliberate conservative nickel-playing Iowa hog farmer into a reckless loud-mouthed money-flinging red-eyed high-limit slot fiend.

Even more sinister, I see psychologists, advertising mavens, market researchers, and efficiency experts sitting around a large boardroom table discussing how they can get gray-haired retirees to dig into that deep dark part of their wallet, take out the $20 stashed for emergencies, and try to hit that progressive jackpot they figure is due.

I can develop myself—my physical being, my character, my mind—all by myself, thank you. I don't want to walk into a casino and feel I'm part of an experiment.

What happened to the warm word "host"? Having a host in a casino gives you the feeling that you're coming into a place that's personal, inviting, friendly, a place that's—well—like home. So, since my name is on the cover of this book, I'm going to take the liberty of throwing out the expression player development for the rest of these pages and refer to this as the chapter on the host-based comp system.

Mistakes We Make

A correspondent sent me the following e-mail: "My wife and I are quarter players and we get all of our rooms and food comped through the slot club and mailed offers. Why do we need a host?"

Until fairly recently, Brad and I could have asked this question ourselves. Does that surprise you? After all, we've been frequenting casinos for nearly 20 years. We're experienced in obtaining an edge. Shoot, this is my second book on how to play smart when you gamble. So, it stands to reason that we always know the right thing to do when we're in a casino. Right?

Wrong.

Obviously, we made mistakes in the first years of our casino visits. Back then, we did all the wrong things that novice gamblers do when they first come to Las Vegas. We played too many hours a day and lost too much sleep. We chose the marathon-session technique and didn't take bathroom and meal breaks until our stomachs and bladders were crying out in pain. We took everything we read about gambling at face value and actually bought a few sure-fire get-rich-quick systems.

But perhaps our biggest mistake was that we never

used a slot host when we were quarter video poker players. Although we eventually reached the point where we could get all of our rooms and food comped indefinitely, with a lot of extras like show tickets and gifts, it required a tremendous amount of time and effort. I kept elaborate files of casino mail offers and complicated schedules of potential comps and I endlessly juggled dates and venues, moving frequently from one casino to another to take advantage of them all.

It's not that we didn't know about hosts; we did. However, I thought we weren't big enough players to merit their special attention. Of course, I know now that a quarter player who puts in long hours, as we used to do, may be feeding just as much money into the machines as casual dollar players. And hosts now even have (gasp!) nickel players in their valuable-customer black books. You may think you're small potatoes if you play nickels, but if you're a heavy player at max coins on the new multi-line machines, you may be surprised how much money you're putting through them. You may even be a bigger bettor than an infrequent dollar player.

I also didn't realize something else until after we graduated to dollar machines and started enjoying the services of hosts: Although we became experts on how to stay and eat free in a casino on our own, we could have done even better, *and* with a whole lot less effort, had we tapped into the host system back then.

For example, some of you might remember the first account of our comp adventures when the *Las Vegas Advisor*, back in 1993, chronicled our winter stay of "50 Nights, 49 Free." I bet if I'd asked a host, I could have gotten that one orphan night comped, as well.

Keep in mind that although comps are awarded according to how much you play, every casino has its own comp schedule, which takes time to decipher.

Most hosts respond willingly and cheerfully when I ask them to explain the comp requirements for various things I want. The approach, as always, is crucial. I never say, "Can I have ...?" Instead, I simply ask, "How much play does it take to get ...?"

In this chapter, I describe how to establish relationships with hosts and the ways in which a host can help you get more benefits than you would by just using the slot club system or depending on mail offers. These extra perks and benefits aren't arranged according to levels of play; not all casinos even offer them all. I'm merely giving you some examples, gleaned from either first- or second-hand experience. I hope they open your eyes to possibilities that you may have been missing.

(By the way, hosts can be men or women. However, most of our hosts have been women, so I refer to them throughout the book as "she." Also, a female host is never called a hostess; that term is used in casinos for a woman who seats you at a restaurant, and sometimes for a young woman who works in VIP Services.)

Advantages of the Host System

Using the host system enables you to reap more comps than just using the first two systems described in Chapter Nine, especially if you're a dollar-and-above or very heavy quarter player.

In many casinos, some types of benefits are available only through a host and using the host system does not decrease your slot club benefits or your direct-mail offers. So learning your way around the host system can make the whole comp system more flexible for you and be a great supplement to the other outlets for securing comps. A note on the Internet put it this way: "Getting comps at the slot club booth is like paying full price. Getting comps through your host is like buying on sale."

The benefits go beyond the purely financial. Having your own host has great psychological impact. Good host programs are committed to a VIP approach—and everyone likes to feel important.

Disadvantages of the Host System

Some smaller casinos don't have hosts. In that event, you can sometimes ask for a room or food comp from a slot supervisor, slot club supervisor, pit boss, or casino manager; someone is almost always around who has comp-writing authority. Other times you're limited to using your slot club points or waiting for a mail offer.

Unless you play at an extremely high level, in most casinos you have to take the initiative and look for a host. In my opinion, this is one of the main weaknesses in the system—the casinos should have their hosts looking for you. Many players are just too intimidated or have the perception that you have to be a high roller to qualify for host treatment. (I believed that myself early on.) The majority of gamblers are not comfortable making that first contact themselves.

A few casinos have slot club representatives out on the floor looking for players who aren't using a club card. But in many of the larger casinos, even those with advanced player-tracking computers (which a host can use to see where gamblers are playing the machines at a high enough level to be getting comps), often no contact by a host is made. I've had more people complain to me that they've gone to a new casino and played the dollar machines for a couple of hours with their player's card inserted, even in a high-limit room, and never had a host come over to welcome them, much less ask if there was anything the casino could do for them.

The host system is often difficult to use, since details about how it works are not readily available to the public. It's a system that punishes the shy players and rewards the aggressive ones. Why do casinos continue with this secretive system that frustrates players so much? Apparently, some casinos believe that people will play more if they don't know the exact comp requirements, and are simply hoping they'll reach some lofty level of benefits. Personally, I think they just get disgusted and move to a casino where they know exactly how much play it takes to get what they want.

Sometimes it seems like you're just haggling with the host, which can leave you feeling belittled rather than rewarded. The comp system was set up by the casino, but too often the hosts act like it's the greedy players themselves who thought the whole thing up. Many players feel like they're begging just to find out the basic details of an overly secretive comp policy.

My take on the disadvantages of the casino host system doesn't just come off the top of my head. It's based squarely on my own experiences and on my e-mail. I probably get more questions on this subject than on any other. "Why haven't I seen these hosts you talk about?" And, "Isn't a host only for really big gamblers?" And, "I wouldn't have the nerve to go up and ask a host for anything; what if she turned me down?" However, you can get so many more benefits if you use the host system that it pays for most frequent casino visitors to spend some time and effort to learn how to get around the disadvantages. That means first learning the basics.

The Host Basics

How Much Should I Play Before I See a Host?

This question has no single answer. Each casino has its own parameters for its host system. For organizational purposes, I like to divide casinos into three general categories, enumerated below (though keep in mind that this is a subjective evaluation and you have to take into consideration factors such as location and nearby competition).

1. Top-level casinos—These are usually the largest and classiest operations, with luxury hotels attached and many extra amenities. They're often the newest—although some are classic veterans. They offer the broadest range and highest level of comps; therefore their host systems are usually geared to the heavy dollar-and-up machine player and the table player who makes at least $50-$100 bets. A rough rule-of-thumb might be that a $1 machine player should probably wait until he's played three to four hours and a $5-machine player perhaps an hour before approaching a host.

2. Low-level casinos—These are usually the older and smaller casinos in a jurisdiction; they often look tired, if not actually rundown and shabby. They sometimes don't offer accommodations and if they do, they're basic no-frills rooms. Many don't even have a host system, but if they do, you can approach a host after an hour or two of quarter play or a few minutes at the dollar machines. You can often get a comp after an hour or so of $5 table play. Some of these casinos have a hard time competing in the age of big and glitzy casinos and are glad to see (and comp generously) anyone who looks like more than a minimum-bet gambler. Still, others in this category run on low profit margins and can be pretty stingy about comping anything.

3. Mid-level casinos—If you can't place a casino in either the top or bottom categories, you've got what I call a mid-level casino, by far the majority. Because there are so many of them, the range of comp benefits, and thus the range of betting requirements, is broad.

In strong local markets in Las Vegas and on riverboats, comp requirements are usually based on a longer-term history of play, while casinos with a fly-in market give out comps on a trip basis.

However, regular dollar players, even those playing only a couple of hours a day, will find that they're warmly welcomed by the hosts in most mid-level casinos, and heavy quarter players might also be surprised at the number of benefits they can receive. The minimum bet to get rated for table-game comps usually ranges from $10 to $25 per hand.

Where Do I Find a Host?

I can't count how many people have told me that they've played in casinos for years, have never seen a host, and wouldn't know if they fell over one in the aisle.

If you've seen hosts in action and even used one on occasion, you still might not be sure where you fit into a particular casino's system. If you're planning on staying or playing in a casino, you should talk to a host to find out. You can phone or ask to meet one *any time*, just to inquire about the requirements. Simply call the casino's toll-free number and ask to be connected to a slot host. Max Rubin's book, *Comp City*, has excellent information on "Scouting Casinos" by talking to a host before you go.

What if you're in a casino, have played awhile, and wonder if you've logged enough time or action for a comp? How do you find out?

One thing you can do is to go to the slot club desk and ask to speak to a host; one can usually be paged and will meet you right there at the booth. Most larger casinos have a host office somewhere on the premises; just walk in and talk to a host on duty or a clerk will find one for you (sometimes it's called the VIP office, although any level of player can get information there).

Avoiding Telephone Tag With a Host

Many hosts now have casino e-mail addresses. I save a lot of time by using this for routine communications, such as responding to a tournament invitation. E-mail can be used to ask brief questions or for requesting that a host call you if you need more time to discuss comp matters. I prefer to ask a host to call me, either putting this message in a short e-mail post or leaving a message on her voice mail, so she can respond at her convenience, rather than having her paged in a noisy casino and waiting until she's found.

Of course, like everyone else who's wired these days, many hosts now have cell phones that allow you to call directly. But I still hate to bother her when she's busy—so I'm brief and ask her to call back at her convenience.

However, the best way, in my opinion, is to stay at your machine and tell a change person or floorperson you'd like to speak to a host as soon as possible. Floorpeople can get a host your message by relaying it to a supervisor or by using their own pager.

Having a host meet you at your machine has several advantages. First, they're often very busy and can't always respond to pages immediately—so you can continue playing during a possibly long wait.

Second, if a host sees you actually playing, she may write you an immediate comp based on the coin denomination you're playing, without bothering to go to a computer to check your past play record. This is why I suggest meeting a new host when you're playing at the highest denomination you ever choose in that casino.

Don't try to pull a fast one here and play for several hours on quarters, then move to a $5 machine and

---

Taking Notes on Business Cards

Always ask *any* host you meet for a business card. The cards usually include direct phone numbers and e-mail addresses. I often add personal notes on the back. I have a large file of host business cards I've collected over the years. It helps me remember names and makes for a rich source of possible future contacts when hosts change casinos or we need one in a casino where we've never played before.

---

slow-play until the host arrives; you'll get nothing but a hustler reputation when she checks the computer.

However, if you've been switching back and forth between quarter and dollar play, ask for a comp while you're playing a dollar machine. This may score you a higher-level comp—e.g., a meal for two in a better restaurant instead of the buffet or perhaps expensive show tickets. For room-comp requests, a host almost always checks your past-play record on the computer.

One high-roller friend of mine makes scouting for a host a careful science—because once you're assigned to a host, he says, it's often difficult to change later. Although I've found most hosts quite easy to work with, a few shouldn't be in a customer-relations job. Also, some hosts are so scared of losing their jobs that they tend to stay at the low end of the range of comps they're allowed to give; this is why some savvy players look for a host who's been on the job for a while and is comfortable in giving comps at the highest level possible. In large casinos that have a host hierarchy, "executive" or "senior" hosts usually have more experience and more authority to grant better comps.

It's good to find a host who fits your personality. Some players feel they can do better with a host of the opposite sex. But regardless of gender, it's always advantageous, as it is in all relationships, if that indefinable element we call chemistry is good between the player and the host.

How do you find a generous host rather than a timid bean counter? My high-roller friend is good at going into a casino and observing hosts in action and assessing them, but most players have neither the time nor the experience for this. However, if you know someone who has used a host in a certain casino, you could ask for his recommendation. Networking, both with gambling friends and casino employees, is an important tool for experienced gamblers.

If you're on gambling bulletin boards on the Internet, you're in luck. I'm on a couple of big boards where all I have to do is ask for a host recommendation at a particular casino anywhere in the U.S. and within the day, I'll have anywhere from two to a dozen posts giving me names and experiences with the good, the bad, and the ugly. This can be an important search, because for a heavy or frequent player, a generous host can mean thousands more dollars worth of comps every year.

How Do I Get Comps Without Feeling Like I'm Begging?

When the host arrives at your machine, stop playing, smile, and introduce yourself like you would to anyone new you're meeting. Don't feel like you're in an inferior position or that the host is some kind of god. Remember, comps aren't charity; you earn them as a reward from the casino for putting your hard-earned money at risk. Casinos include the expense of giving out comps in their marketing budgets, so they expect to give them out. Hosts are hired for that very purpose.

One Internet friend described it well: "Think of your gambling action as a bank deposit and comps as earned interest. Your host is simply a friendly bank teller who checks your account and pays you some of that interest when you ask for it. The more you play, the more interest you earn. And after you've shown yourself to be a good loyal customer, you can expect to be rewarded even more. Instead of the toasters, book bags, pen sets, or traditional bank incentives, hosts can now offer (or again, give you when you ask) such goodies as room upgrades, party and tournament invitations, show tickets, and more."

On the other hand, a good host is not just another impersonal casino clerk. Once you've met, she often becomes more like a good friend. When you visit, seek her out and behave like an invited guest in the home (the casino) of a friend. That's what you are. Just like good friends, good hosts like to be generous and helpful, especially to players who are willing to play and behave properly.

"But I'm afraid I'll ask for more comps than I've earned and I'll feel so embarrassed when she says no."

There's a very simple way to avoid the bugaboo, which almost everyone fears, of being turned down. First, remember a host hates to say no. I stressed this in *The Frugal Gambler* and I'll stress it again: Use language in your interaction with a host, whether at the first meeting or one that occurs many years after you meet, that doesn't require a yes-or-no answer:

• "How much longer would I need to play to get two comps for the buffet?"

• "I was wondering how many hours I need to play at the quarter level to get my room comped."

• "Can you evaluate my play and let me know what comps I'm entitled to?"

These non-questions are neutral enough that you shouldn't experience any sort of discomfort. They make the host's job much easier as well. An added bonus is that you get valuable information that will help you in the future to know better what the requirements are in that casino.

A good attitude goes a long way in smoothing your encounters with hosts. Hosts follow guidelines, not strict rules, so they have some leeway. But remember, hosts are human, not casino robots. Be demanding and picky and you'll find yourself with only the minimum for your level of play. Be friendly and appreciative and you'll be amazed at the comps you'll be readily offered.

Benefits From Knowing and Using Hosts

Room Comps

Let's say you've been getting all your rooms free through mailed offers from the casino or by using your slot club points. What can a host give you that you're not already getting?

First, you can have your host personally make all your room reservations, even for mailed offers from other casino departments. Maybe the invitation you receive in the mail is for a specific date, but you want to go a few days earlier, later, or even a different month. Or you get a room offer for three nights, but you want to stay four or five. Depending on your past play, the host may be able to accommodate you.

Also, hosts get credit for the number of nights they book for their customers. By letting them make all your reservations and customize your stay, you're actually doing something for them. Imagine—thanking your host by letting her make your vacation arrangements for you!

At many casinos, regular customers can get a room

through the host and no points are taken from their slot club or comp accounts. A host can often secure a room for you even if the regular reservations clerk claims the hotel is full; almost all casinos hold back a block of rooms for comped players that can only be booked through a host. Sometimes a host is able to upgrade you to a better room or even to a suite, after looking at your play history. Or she can okay an earlier check-in or later check-out time, at no extra charge—handy on those days you have an early or late flight.

Sometimes a host can get a room for your friends. Now that we have our own place in Las Vegas, we don't use room comps as often as we used to, but we have a lot of visiting friends and relatives who do need them. I call up a host and tell her I have friends coming in and at what level they play, if I know it. At the least, the host can, as a courtesy to us, offer our friends the casino rate until she can determine if their play warrants a free room. And recommending new customers to your host is another way to show your appreciation for her effort on your behalf.

What if your friends don't play? On occasion, I've explained to a host that we needed a room for nonplaying friends, but that we would play enough to cover their comps. Hosts always seem to appreciate honesty in these matters.

Occasionally, if Brad or I have been ill or we've had lots of family in town, we don't have time to put in as much playing time as we usually do when we stay in a comped room. We explain the situation to a host, and we've never been docked for our room and food and it has never gone against our history of loyal play.

One of my friends who plays heavily told me that a host at her favorite Las Vegas casino comped her son, who wasn't a gambler, a two-night stay during a time he was in town without her. Again, this was a courtesy because of her past play.

Hosts often have the authority to give out comped rooms "on the come," which means on speculation. Not all friends or relatives of frequent gamblers necessarily become regular customers, but some do. The casino takes a shot at converting referrals to regulars with comps, which it writes off as an advertising expense. Actually, when a casino isn't fully booked, giving out a free room costs them very little.

Sometimes, if a host knows that you often recommend her casino to other gamblers, she'll be able to stretch your comps a little further than your actual play warrants. Some of our hosts have promoted us to a higher level after we sent many referrals to stay and play at their casinos.

Having a host comes in handy during an emergency, as this story related by a friend illustrates:

"My wife and I spent Super Bowl weekend in Atlantic City—a hectic weekend for the A.C. casinos. Unfortunately, we had to fly home on Sunday, and we would miss the big game during our flight. After checking in, we were told that the plane had a mechanical problem and we would be delayed a half-hour. The delay was extended three times. We had no way of knowing if or when the plane would leave and we were getting nervous about flying on this troubled aircraft. That's when the host became so important.

"I whipped out my cell phone and called the toll-free number on the back of my player's card. At my request, the operator quickly connected me directly to my host. I explained that we were stuck at the airport and asked if she could help us out. It was a great feeling when she said that she would be happy to find us a room (even though the hotel was theoretically fully booked for the Super Bowl.)

"Looking back, we were really glad that we'd cultivated that host relationship. We watched the game, played some blackjack, and caught the first flight out the next morning."

Food Comps

In most casinos, anyone can go to the slot club desk and use points for meal comps. But at some, if you ask a host for the comp, she can write it out for you and no points are deducted from your account. (These are known as "courtesy" or "off-record" comps.) You need to check the casino policy and it's all right to ask the host about it. Simply say, "Can you write food comps that do not come off my account or do I have to go through the booth?"

Even if you don't save points, there can be an advantage in going through the host to get your restaurant comps. At too many casinos, you must know the exact dollar amount you'll need for your meal if you get a comp at the slot club, because unused points don't go back into your account. Any amount not used is lost. The best way to play it is inconvenient at best: You order, eat your meal, and when the bill comes, you trudge down to the booth, wait in line, and get a comp for the exact amount of the bill.

A host, however, may be able to give you a comp for an open amount and the restaurant fills in the exact amount that you spend. It may still come off your points when the copy of the comp goes back to the slot club, but it saves you the awkwardness of leaving your guests or partner as hostages after the bill arrives while you make that trip to the slot club booth.

The host can also make reservations for you at a restaurant that you've been told is fully booked. Just as they do with rooms, casinos often hold back a few tables in the better restaurants for comped customers.

In fact, in Atlantic City, some Asian restaurants don't accept paying customers at all. The only way to eat there is to get a comp. They do this to give Asian players some sense of exclusivity, but non-Asian players can get the necessary comp from a host if their play deserves it.

Sometimes a host can approve a comp even if you don't have quite enough points to get one from your slot club account. Winding up on the positive side of a host's leeway is one of the benefits of having a good relationship with her. You can always ask a host for a line pass even if you haven't played enough for the meal itself to be comped. It takes very little play to get a line pass, you feel like a VIP when you can go to the front of the regular line or join the shorter comp line. And who knows? If you ask for a line pass, the host might just upgrade you to a full meal comp—this has happened to us many times.

Show Tickets

One service of a slot host is to give customers comped show tickets. This can rarely be handled at the slot club, especially with major shows. As with rooms and restaurant reservations, if you're a good customer, your host can usually get you show tickets even when a show is sold out. Again, casinos reserve sections for comped customers and these are usually prime seat locations—an added bonus.

It's much easier to get a comp for a show at the property where you're staying, but it's also possible for your host to arrange comped tickets at another casino, especially if the two are owned by the same corporation (or stray billionaire). With so much recent consolidation in the casino industry, this opens up the opportunity to get comped show tickets even in different areas of the country.

And yes, it's still possible for your host to get tickets to a show at a completely unrelated property, but it's not as easy as it used to be. At one time, when Las Vegas casinos were smaller and fewer, the hosts all knew each other and they informally swapped show tickets. Now you have to be a fairly heavy player for a host to go to the trouble (and for the casino to pay the hard cost, known as a "bill-back") of arranging a show at a competing property.

If you know how to play the game, show tickets can be one of the easiest comps to snag, even if you're a light player. The following doesn't work for a popular show that sells out in advance, but many shows in casinos everywhere have empty seats every night. Performers don't like to play to empty seats. Casinos want their performers to be happy. So wait until 30-45 minutes before showtime, then see a host. She'll probably have unsold tickets, possibly in hand, that have just been released to her to get rid of. If she doesn't have tickets with her, she can easily call the box office, and if she sees at least some play on your club card, she'll be happy to let you fill up one or two of those empty seats.

If I need additional tickets, I ask. It's not uncommon for us to get two additional tickets for another couple, or even four or six extras if we have a family group in town and we have a good history of play in that casino. The host can't always grant these requests, of course. But sometimes she may be able to arrange for you to buy the seats you need in better locations than you could get through the box office.

Transportation

The ability to get comped transportation varies greatly, depending on whether it's a low-level or a high-level property. A little grind joint in downtown

Vegas won't offer the same transportation options and refunds as the latest megaresort on the Strip, although it pays to ask, since it's not always easy to guess which casinos offer this benefit.

Ask the host if the casino provides complimentary transportation to and from the airport, and if it does, can she arrange it. Sometimes it's a limo; other times it's a van. Some casinos are generous with limo comps, though as always, it depends on which casino and what level of play they consider high enough to provide it.

I have some low-roller friends who stay at what I would consider a mid-level casino out on Boulder Highway, far from the Vegas Strip. Their host arranges a limo to take them to the mall or downtown or even to the Strip. Getting a limo to competing properties is unusual. A better play, if you're switching from one casino to another and your action qualifies, is to call the host at the receiving casino and ask her to send a limo to pick you up. Nine times out of ten, she'll be glad to snatch you from the competition.

Once, while staying in Reno, I was preparing to walk to a doctor's office a couple of miles away. Because I love to walk, I didn't think of asking for a ride. When the host heard about my plans, she was appalled and insisted that I take the limo.

At the higher levels of play, you can ask a host about getting a refund on your airfare, but be forewarned that this is one of the toughest comps to snag. Slot hosts are usually not authorized to give this, but they'll talk to a supervisor about your play rating and deliver the message from on high. If you aren't sure whether you've reached airfare-reimbursement levels, or you don't even know whether your casino offers them (you might be surprised that this is a perk not just at megaresorts), talk to your host in the way that was described earlier, seeking information but avoiding questions that require yes-or-no answers. Perhaps part of your airfare will be rebated. Sometimes the casino will rebate airfare to big losers even if they haven't quite played to the required level. On the flip side, some will never comp airfare for trip winners no matter how big they play.

Note: If you can't score high-roller airfare comps through your host, all is not lost. Some casinos offer travel programs that allow the use of slot club points to pay for airline tickets. It's a good way to give low rollers or medium-level players a chance to get their airfare for casino visits comped. And some casinos occasionally send good customers direct-mail offers that include coupons for airline tickets.

Credit

In many casinos, the host takes care of you if you want to set up a credit line (although you can almost always go straight to the cage and pick up an application). In the larger properties, a host will offer to sit down with you so the paperwork is done quickly. We recently had a host establish a credit line for us and we never left our machine! Casinos love customers with credit lines.

Problem Solving

If you have a problem at a casino, this is the time when a host can really shine. Say you check into your room, something major is wrong, and the front desk insists no other rooms are available. A host can make a new room materialize out of thin air—and it might even have transformed into a suite. Maybe there's been a computer malfunction and your slot club points haven't registered accurately; a host can see that your point balance is corrected. There's an overcharge on your hotel bill at check-out and you're having a problem getting it taken care of; turn it over to your host.

We have frequent problems with coupons—expired coupons, lost coupons, even coupons that were never sent, but should have been. A good host can often reinstate or secure them. Over the years, using a slot host has put hundreds of dollars in our pocket from coupon recovery alone.

The same has proven true for promotions. One year on Valentine's Day, a casino was giving a $200 bonus for a royal flush in hearts. Brad was playing alone that day and wasn't aware of the promotion. When he got home and told me he'd hit a royal in hearts, I asked about the bonus, which he hadn't been paid. The next day we both went back to the casino. Chatting with the host, I mentioned that Brad had gotten a royal in hearts the day before, but hadn't received a bonus. The host called the supervisor who'd been on duty the day before. She felt sure that the royal had been in spades, and Brad wasn't 100% sure it was in hearts, so we just let it go. Then, a half-hour later, the host returned with the picture they'd taken of Brad and his royal. Sure enough, it was in hearts. We were $200 richer because a host had cared enough to dig through the previous day's files.

Individualized Service

We've had free babysitting arranged for our grandchildren. We've been given extra invitations to VIP parties so we could bring our out-of-town visitors. We've had free gifts we were entitled to stashed and saved when we had to miss a special promotion. And most of our hosts, knowing how I like to plan ahead, take the time to inform us of future promotions we qualify for long before we receive the mailed notices.

One host came around to ask if there was anything she could do for us, noting that we weren't using many of the comps we were earning. I told her we weren't into gourmet dining.

"Well," she responded, "what about something nice from the casino retail shop?"

I'd heard of using comps for casino gift-shop purchases, but it's so rare that I hadn't thought to ask. Thanks to my host, I now have several expensive new outfits.

Sometimes hosts provide concierge services, particularly in smaller hotel-casinos with no such specialized service. One host arranged a picnic basket for a group taking a helicopter tour. I've known people whose host helped them plan their wedding—from reserving the chapel to ordering the cake. Other hosts have facilitated family reunions and group trips. Even when the concierge does these things, a host is often included in the plans to give them a more personal touch. One host told me that she sprinkled rose petals on the bed of a honeymoon couple.

And although no casino employee would ever publicly admit to it, I've been told stories about hosts giving extra-special service—arranging companionship for high rollers. Although no casino would risk its license by comping this, I've heard that introductions are sometimes arranged, a practice that's perfectly legal.

Your Relationship With a Host

Some players don't like the host system at all; they think a host is pretending to be their friend for purely mercenary reasons, a kind of "hired friend." Since the host works for the casino, which in the final analysis wants to take your money, the whole relationship seems artificial and insincere to them. One poster on the Internet put it this way: "I'm not an experienced host schmoozer—I feel like I need a shower to rinse off all that syrup after I talk to one."

There's some validity to this position. Some hosts do come off as overly friendly. I remember one high roller telling me about his first encounter with a host in the high-limit slot area of a large megaresort. She came up to him at the $25 machine he was playing, panting as though she'd run from the computer in her office clear across the casino when she saw such a big fish in play. "My name is Tiffany ... and I want to be your new best friend." And another player's reaction: "*Puh-leeze* stop hovering over me while I draw to a $30 flush (Come on! Come on! Aww, darn!). It's not going to bring us any closer, trust me."

Although the host *is* employed by the casino to make guests want to play there (and eventually lose their money), most hosts I've met genuinely like people and they're as outgoing in their life off the job as they are on. The friendly attitude isn't merely a professional mask. Of course, they've learned that they must sometimes put on a happy face even if they're feeling stressed or lousy—but we all wisely do that on occasion in our public activities. I've found that if you're a respectful, understanding, and non-demanding customer, they often do become bona fide friends, rather than just friendly professionals—not because they have to, but because they want to.

Although I strongly advise you not to be demanding in your dealing with hosts, you have to take the initiative in making yourself known to them. Unless you're playing at a very high level, in many casinos the hosts will never seek you out. Hosts are there for you, but you need to be sure they know what you want. Common sense and good manners will help you walk the sometimes fine line between using the comp system fully and appearing greedy. However, as you tread carefully and slowly on this path, you'll soon learn how to ask appropriately—which pays off with big dividends.

A good relationship with hosts has that important side benefit that I've mentioned before: Hosts tend to move from property to property. When one of our hosts changes jobs, we sometimes find that we have instant VIP treatment in a new casino where we may have never played.

Rewarding Your Host

Many players develop such good relationships with their hosts, they want to give them gifts or tips for services rendered. Before you offer a tip or gift, you need to ask the host or a casino supervisor whether this is allowable. In some states, the agency that oversees gambling and casinos has specific regulations that cover this and if there's a no-gift rule, it's strictly enforced by the casino or they could be heavily fined. However, in Nevada and many other states, it's left to the individual casinos to determine the tip and gift policies.

At some casinos, hosts aren't allowed to take any gifts at all; it's a strict rule and they can be fired if they violate it. Other casinos forbid their hosts to accept *cash* gifts, a policy that avoids the problem, at least partially, of hosts being bribed for comps. Some only allow gifts that can be shared at work, like candy and other food items. Others impose a limit on the monetary value of the gift. On the other hand, some casinos have no policies that restrict what a host can accept.

Even if a casino has a no-tip policy, exceptions are usually allowed. One host told me that some gamblers from other cultures are insulted if he doesn't accept a gift. So, although his casino has a general no-cash policy, he's instructed to use his judgment and accept even cash gifts under those circumstances. Some casinos with a no-gift policy allow the hosts to accept them, but they must turn them over to a supervisor who donates them to charity.

I've read many articles about suitable gifts for hosts. Often the same items are mentioned: candy, perfume, and scarves for women; ties, tie tacks, and cufflinks for men. I wondered if those were the things they really wanted, so I did the logical thing—I talked to some of my hosts. And did I get an education! It turns out that many gifts hosts receive are definitely unsuitable and unusable. Of course, hosts have good manners—they're going to act appreciative of anything you give—and they do really appreciate the spirit behind the gift. But here are some ideas they gave me that will allow them to *sincerely* love a gift you give them.

• Unless you're sure of their tastes and preferences, perfume, costume jewelry, and clothing items such as scarves and ties can be a very iffy choice.

• Candy is *not* highly welcomed—they get far too much of it and almost all of them are watching their weight, men and women.

• They're overwhelmed with knickknacks that either don't fit their home decor or they have no room for.

• Liquor can be a good choice *only* if you know for sure it will be appreciated. Just because a host works in a casino where the liquor flow is constant doesn't mean she isn't a teetotaler. She could even be a recovering alcoholic.

• If casino policy allows it, *cash* is the number-one gift of choice. I suggest you be classy about this; don't slap a bill in her hand. At least put it in an envelope; you can always get one at the front desk. Better would be to include it in a thank-you note.

• Gift certificates are usually allowable even if cash gifts are not—this is the number-two gift choice. A gift certificate to a fine local department store is most welcome; hosts have to buy a lot of clothes to keep up a good appearance. They also have everyday needs and wants just like the rest of us, so we often hand off certificates we've earned from slot club points for Easter hams, Thanksgiving pumpkin pies, holiday turkeys, grocery stores, discount stores like Wal-Mart, and hardware stores like Home Depot. Phone cards come in handy for anyone and video or bookstore certificates are always appreciated. An out-of-town friend earned some gas cards for a local station and gave them to his host. We've been surprised by how many hosts like logo jackets from other casinos or even the inexpensive T-shirts we always have in abundance—the large sizes are popular for the gals (or their kids) to sleep in.

• Even if gifts aren't allowed, sometimes hosts can accept something that can be shared with the whole department: flowers, homemade baked goods or regional food specialties, handmade craft items to decorate their office (but make sure they're professional-quality, not something your kid made in Brownies or Cub Scouts). Instead of candy, think "healthy"—fruit, nuts, low-cal snacks.

• Sometimes we make an inexpensive bet at the sports book—especially when we know the host's favorite team—and give him the ticket.

• Sometimes you get to know your host, and even her family, quite well. If you know your host has kids or grandkids and you know their ages, you could choose a gift for them. Likewise, you can present a gift for the wife of a male host or the husband of a female host.

• We often share our surplus comps with our hosts: show tickets from other casinos; an extra free hotel room for them to have an overnight getaway from home; food comps from other casinos. Many hosts don't gamble themselves and, since they usually work full time, they appreciate a free meal out. Remember, hosts live a regular life outside the casino. Many have families. Most have budgets. So they appreciate comps just like you do. Some of our hosts get lucky when Brad and I receive duplicate gifts from a casino; we get one to keep and one to give away, as we did recently with two DVD players.

• One of the best gifts you can give a host is to just show your appreciation for what she does for you. Put a message of thanks on her voice mail or in e-mail. Or why not write a letter to her boss, effusing about what a good job she's doing? Many hosts tell me that this is the tip they appreciate the most.

• Another gift you can give is to show your loyalty. I often recommend my hosts to other players— and that's a big gesture, because a host lives and dies by her black book and always wants new names. This is a great way to contribute to the host's job security and possible advancement. One regular gambler I know has on several occasions alerted a host from a smaller property that there was a job opening at a larger one. Now *that's* giving your host a career boost.

You don't have to deal with hosts for long to realize that they're in a position to give you thousands of dollars in comps over the years, so it's only natural to want to cultivate a good relationship with them and show your appreciation with gifts. And human nature being what it is, doing so will probably get you more in the long run. When gift-giving is permitted, always take care never to give even the impression that the gift is a bribe or pressure to get more comps than you've earned. Many of the hosts I talked to emphasized that they didn't appreciate *any* gift under those circumstances. It not only makes for an awkward situation, it can threaten their job security.

What Not To Ask For

Don't hesitate to use the services of hosts; that's what they're there for. But don't abuse the privilege. I always emphasize that, even though I'm noted for the number of comps we've gotten over the years, I want all my hosts to be able to say that I underused their services, rather than stretched them to the limit. I know that if I'm careful not to bug the host all the time, especially with little requests, I'll more likely get those special comps I want once in a while.

Never ask a host to do anything that's illegal or against casino policy. You don't want to be the cause of her losing her job. And always remember, hosts cannot get involved in a dispute about game rules, jackpots, or anything that falls within the province of the pit bosses or casino managers.

Divorcing Your Host

As I was writing this chapter, I got an e-mail from a friend on the East Coast:

"A few years ago, we developed a relationship with a slot host at an Atlantic City casino and she's turned out to be a dud. She rarely returns our calls and forgets to give us the dates for invitational tournaments. She's usually off on the days we visit. We haven't heard from her in over a year. Is it acceptable to request a change of slot hosts and if so, how do we go about this without causing hard feelings?"

Good question. As this example demonstrates, not all hosts are magical or even attentive. It takes a lot of good judgment and people skills to be a host. I'd love to tell you that hosts are infallible, but obviously, that can't be true. Hosts sometimes show a lack of common sense, understanding, and tact when dealing with customers.

It's easier to understand this when you realize that hosts are continually bombarded with requests for comps, many of them way out of line in proportion to the asking party's play. Not all customers subscribe to the concept I promote of being nice to a host; a few are extremely demanding and rude, even threatening, sometimes taking out their frustrations on the host when they're losing. You should realize that if you're a new customer, you'll have to win a host's trust. This is usually easy to do if you have the proper attitude.

Another problem for many hosts is that they simply have too much to do; casino management gives them too big a customer load or drowns them in so much paperwork that they can't provide the kind of personal customer service they'd like to. Also remember that hosts don't make casino policy. They merely carry it out. So don't be too hard on hosts who can't or won't give you what you're after. Their hands might be tied.

However, you're not married to your host and it *is* possible to change if it's obvious you're not getting the service you reasonably expect. How you do this depends on the organization of the host department.

In a large system with many hosts, you're often coded to one of them specifically, usually the one you had contact with the first time. After this, you "belong," and your play will be credited, to this host, even if you book a room through another department or get a comp from another host—when, for example, your host is off duty. This is particularly the case when there's a host incentive program in place that gives bonuses for individual performance (see box on the following pages).

In this sort of highly organized department, sometimes you'll find it difficult to change hosts; it might take a request to a department supervisor to get recoded, or even a written letter to a vice-president. In many cases it will take a great deal of persistence and follow-up. The real problem is that your old host will fight to keep you. It's like trying to change your car salesman in the middle of a deal: The first one feels entitled to the commission. Asking for a change in hosts can lead to an awkward situation, because the supervisor will want to know your reasons for the request

---

How Does a Casino Know ...

There's no industry standard for evaluating and paying casino hosts. I've talked to a host who worked in a small casino for $9 an hour. He called it "very poor pay for the amount of work and situations that we were asked to resolve and evaluate." On the other hand, celebrity hosts, those who bring in high rollers to the Strip megaresorts, might pull in $150,000 a year, or more. And a few of the highest-level hosts who bring in the whales command mega-compensation for the mega-business they attract. That leaves a large salary range in between these extremes, probably with a majority clustering around the middle.

Some casinos offer bonuses or incentive programs, but this is closely guarded information that's rarely shared with a customer. It's taken me many years and many conversations with insiders to get the general information that you're reading here.

Bonuses, if offered, are usually given quarterly or yearly. They can be based on subjective merit evaluations, but they're more often based on "production" figures. That is, player losses. These numbers may be figured two different ways, using either the customer's actual loss or by using theoretical loss, which is the average loss associated with the games they've played.

If the bonus is based on losses, the host may get a

---

and you may not wish to go into them. Even if the request for a change is routinely handled, you may not feel comfortable if you'll still be seeing your ex-host frequently (which is more likely in a smaller casino). This is one reason that some savvy players scout carefully before making a choice in a casino where they know it will be difficult to change at a later time.

Fortunately, the host structure is not as rigid as this in many casinos. In some, the whole department may

---

... that the Host is Doing a Good Job?

percentage of the actual losses sustained by his or her customers. When you lose $20,000, the host may add $200 to his end-of-the-year bonus check. However, a host's player losses are offset by the wins. If you come back next time and win $30,000, it erases the previous loss. The host won't owe the casino a percentage of the extra $10,000, but the win brings the balance down to zero.

If a host's performance bonus is based on theoretical loss, whether the customer actually wins or loses is not taken into consideration. This is a good program, in my opinion, because it rewards the host for doing what she should be hired to do: bringing in as many new players as possible and keeping the present ones happy so they'll continue to play at the current casino instead of moving down the street or across town. Also, hosts whose bonuses are based on actual losses have to root for you to lose, while pretending to hope that you win. Hosts can genuinely root for you to win if their bonuses are based entirely on your action.

But whether or not there's a bonus system in place, you can be sure that almost all hosts are being evaluated and promoted according to the amount their customers play. This is why they value customer loyalty as much as they do gifts and tips.

---

work more as a team, even though each host still wants to have as high an individual job-performance record as possible. In these casinos we usually have a primary host who takes care of most of our comps, such as rooms and invitational-tournament reservations, but we know other hosts well and use them when our primary is off or busy. In smaller casinos with only a few hosts who work together closely, we consider all of them our hosts.

So what should that dissatisfied letter writer at the beginning of this section do? I would suggest that he start looking for another host by talking to a few that he sees often when at the casino. It's always good to have a host who works the same shift as you do. When he finds one that seems to be serious about taking good care of her customers, use the magic word, *ask*. The player might say that he and his wife would like to establish themselves with a new host that they can talk to more often, then ask how they should go about doing this. He doesn't have to badmouth the other host to get the point across.

The Door to More Comps

Whales—those highest of high rollers—can ask for and receive pretty much anything their hearts desire. Low rollers may not be given everything, but they can get much more than they realize. I've had hundreds of e-mails over the last six years since *The Frugal Gambler* came out, telling how my magic word, *ask*, has opened the door to the hitherto-unknown amazing benefits and privileges in a casino. Who's standing at that door? Someone you just might need—a host who has the power of the pen and can make even a low roller feel like a VIP.

320

11

Finding Your Way Through the Comp Maze

"Are you a fish that can take the bait without getting hooked?"
—*Royal Cat, a big player and expert on comps*

It's difficult to generalize about comps. You're probably tired of hearing this, but it's necessary for players to always remember: Every casino is unique, and comp-system details vary more than those in any other area of casino operations.

Although, in previous chapters, I've tried to thoroughly explain the three basic ways to earn comps, it's impossible to cover every possible contingency. So to help you navigate the sometimes rough paths of these systems, this chapter concentrates on player pitfalls. Many of these are most often faced by gamblers who use the host system. Still, even players who get comps through the simpler systems—the slot club and direct marketing—are not immune to some of these dangers.

Playing Requirements

One of the basic problems facing someone who wants to get into the comp system is learning the playing requirements for getting to a specific comp level. Over the years, I've seen few casinos publish their comp specs outside of what can be obtained through the slot club. One exception was the Four Queens in downtown Las Vegas, which years ago had a neat menu describing the various comp levels, what it took to reach them, and the benefits you were entitled to when you did.

Of course, you can ask a host, who will usually give you some details, but there's rarely an exact schedule. The key word here is "guidelines." The host usually gives you a *range of play* for the various comps you want.

In some casinos you have to pull teeth to get even a general answer in this area. That's usually related to changing criteria. The younger bean counters hate to give away anything. Maybe they'll have an old-school mentor, someone who got his training during many years in the operations trenches dealing with real live casino customers. The mentor can teach the beanie the things that he didn't learn in grad school—how comps build customer loyalty over a long period of time and how you can't expect to balance the books on every customer every month, or even every quarter.

Unfortunately, in today's casino, this combination—the practical knowledge of the casino veteran and the business acumen of the new keepers of the books—contributes to ever-changing comp policies. The two philosophies are always pulling away from each other.

It's a fact that the seat-of-the-pants comping of the old days gave away too much of the casino's profits.

In *Comp City*, Max Rubin tells the whole story of a time when players were granted comps based on how much front money they brought on a trip to a casino or what their credit lines were. Of course, people brought a lot more front money or applied for a lot higher casino credit than they intended to bet and spent more of their visit enjoying their luxurious comps than actually gambling. Little data was collected or analyzed to determine just how much the casino was getting back from the comps that flowed so freely to players. Well, the bean counters and computers rule the comp kingdom now.

The table-game comps were the first to be examined and the simple old formulas—you risk X number of dollars anywhere in the casino and we'll give you X number of dollars worth of comps—were fine-tuned with more complex calculations. Then, when the analysis of machine games was given over to the marketing computer, a much higher level of intricacy was possible. Although casino information systems vary in their capabilities, from the simple to the complex, the technology exists to take into consideration all of the following:

• specific machine played;
• how much the casino projects it can win from the average player on a specific game;
• your skill level in playing that game;
• what coin denomination you're playing;
• how long you play;
• the frequency of your play;
• whether you've won or lost during a period of time;
• your long-term history of play at that casino;
• the color of your hair.

Again, just kidding about that last one. But it makes my point that sometimes the whole formula is so complicated that even the hosts have to stammer and stutter when asked for simple playing requirements.

My answer to this problem is formed from a combination of lots of questions and lots of learning from experience. Trial-and-error isn't the most efficient way to learn something, but it seems to be the only way that works in figuring out how to get comps in the host system. I can see some of you running back to the good ol' slot club system already! But hold on; I'm not abandoning you. Here are some hints that will help. (Max Rubin has done a good job of discussing the table-game comp system and how to use it efficiently, so I'll address mainly the machine player.)

Denomination and Duration Factors

Dollar players are often rated slightly higher than quarter players, even if the quarter player puts in more than four times the hours. The way to get around this is to avoid the top-level casinos, which worship the dollar player, and go where the quarter player is appreciated and rewarded for his actual coin-in instead of being labeled by denomination.

Occasionally, you'll come across a casino that penalizes you for mixed play, especially if you're rated as a dollar player and drop down to quarters. This shouldn't matter—total coin-in should be the deciding factor—and it's yet another example of a casino policy that actually drives players away. But if you find out—a host will usually tell you if you ask why you aren't getting as many comps as you used to— that your quarter play is dropping your rating, you may want to save quarter play for another casino.

Another factor that seems like it shouldn't matter, but often does, is the length of time played. And to confuse us more, if you play at the dollar-and-up level, it goes the opposite way than in the mixed-play example. Although point accumulation is usually based on coin-in—you'd earn about the same number of points playing a $5 machine for one hour or a $1 machine for five hours—you'll sometimes get more comp credit for the $1 play, because that large five-hour time factor is added into the comp equation.

So if you have a choice of playing at a higher level for a shorter period of time or a lower level for a longer period of time, sometimes it's better to choose the latter. Because I'm busy with a heavy writing schedule, I have to resist the temptation to hurry up and qualify for a particular comp, such as an invitational slot tournament, even though our bankroll would allow us to play a higher-denomination game; I don't want to be hit with the time penalty.

Caution: If you're in a casino that rates you for comps strictly by time on a machine, you can play *very* slowly. But be aware that some machines time you out after just a couple minutes with no play.

The Daily-Average Trap

Be especially careful when casino benefits are based on your "daily average." This can be a *huge* danger area, not only for players who use the host system to get comps, but also for someone who depends on bounce-back cash from the slot club or room offers through direct-mail.

The obvious meaning of daily average is as follows: the amount of action (coin-in or slot club points earned) divided by the number of days you play. If you're staying in the hotel where you're playing, this might be figured as a whole-trip average. But whether it's called a daily average (for a day visitor) or a trip average (for the multi-day tourist), it's quicksand territory.

325

The main problem comes in determining what a casino considers a "day" or a "trip." A high-roller friend of ours is an expert in avoiding this problem. Writing under the *nom de plume* of Royal Cat in *Strictly Slots*, he supplied a long list of ways you can run afoul of being "tripped," meaning doing something that the casino might count as a day or a trip, even if you don't actually put money into a machine.

• Sticking your slot club card into any casino machine or kiosk, even just to view your point balance.

• Presenting your card in a table-game pit.

• Any slot club transaction, including checking point balances, redeeming cashback, having free play put on a machine, or getting a comp for your points.

• Use of *any* coupon that has your account number on it, including gift shop or buffet discounts.

• Playing on your card later in the day after checking out from the hotel, triggering a second trip rather than a continuation of the first one.

• Inquiring about or paying off a marker.

• Making a reservation for a hotel stay or event, even if you later cancel it.

• Signing in to a VIP lounge.

Even if you're careful to avoid all the above, you're not safe—and you won't always know that you've triggered a day or a trip. Royal Cat talks about the possibility of getting stealth-tripped by going into a VIP lounge with a friend who gives his name to the guard at the door; she recognizes you, jots down your name, and later enters it into the computer. Or you sit down and play blackjack for a couple of minutes, not bothering to show your card; the pit boss recognizes you, looks up your number in the computer, and suddenly a trip is generated without your knowledge.

Welcome to the new casino world ruled by computer technology. Although cooperation between various casino departments is sometimes good for players—for example, you get credit for both machine and table play to get to higher comp levels—you can see that a complex computer system that links all departments can be used to punish players if one department uses this information in an illogical way.

To further complicate the problem, you have to know what actual hours are considered a day in a particular casino. One person I know played at a casino from 11 p.m. until 1 a.m., earned 100 points, and wondered why he had only a 50-point daily average. He didn't realize that that casino ended its day—and accounting—at midnight.

Conversely, many players have been penalized on their daily average by assuming that midnight is the end of the day. Often this is the case, but some casinos start and end their day at 2 a.m. or 4 a.m. or 8 a.m., sometimes basing this on the time their slot club opens or closes. Most riverboats that aren't open 24/7 consider a day as the time from when the boat first opens in the morning until it closes early the next morning, even though that covers two dates.

Tourists staying for a period of time at a casino where their status is based on a trip, rather than a daily average, need to be sure of the definition used for a "trip." Usually a trip ends after there's been no action for three days, but some casinos start you on a new trip after just one day with no play.

Following are a few tips that a savvy machine player can use to avoid being punished by an unreasonable use of technology (hopefully, casino executives will read this and see how irrational rules keep gamblers from playing as much as they'd like in their casinos).

Never engage in walk-through play in a casino that worships the God of Daily Average. If you can't give a substantial amount of play in one of these casinos, don't give any. For example, when you get in from the airport late your first night for a three-day stay, or you have only an hour on the day you check out before you go to the airport, don't ruin your average by playing for a short time. Sometimes a host is authorized to take these short periods into consideration, but you can't call and explain to a computer when you're sent the next room offer based on a ruined daily or trip average.

Instead, play next door where your action will be welcomed, whether for long or short periods of time. Alternatively, some couples with individual slot club accounts, as I always recommend, solve this problem by using one card for major comp play and the other for these short sessions in the same casino.

This situation presents itself frequently and can be a problem even if you never ask a host for a comp. Maybe you suddenly stop getting mail offers from a casino marketing department, even though you've been earning the same number of points on each trip. This could happen for many reasons, such as a change in head honchos or casino policy, but you might think back and try to remember if you've spread your play over a longer period of time on recent trips. There may be a minimum daily average necessary to get these mailings—and you just got caught in the daily-average trap.

With all my experience in this area, I still can't avoid this problem completely. Here's a recent example.

Say a new casino opens near our condo in Las Vegas. It would be handy for us to establish ourselves there and perhaps drop playing in one or two more distant casinos. But we first have to see whether this new casino offers the same benefits we've been getting elsewhere.

We discover that there's no cashback, so we have to depend on bounce-back cash. And there aren't any brochures to help us determine what it takes to get certain amounts, so we have to experiment.

After our early play, the casino starts sending frequent free-play coupons, sometimes three, four, or five times a week. Okay. We're not pikers; we don't just play out the free play, then run. Every time we use a free-play coupon, we play for an hour or two—so we're generating some serious weekly coin-in.

Then our free-play-coupon amounts start decreasing. Meanwhile, we have friends who are generating the same coin-in as we are each week, but all in one day. They get much bigger free-play coupons. Oops, we were caught in the dilemma of getting tripped for using a coupon, but not playing or having a low daily average.

RFB

"RFB" stands for Room, Food, and Beverage. With "full RFB" you receive free rooms; room service; free food in all the restaurants, including gourmet; and free drinks at the bars. With "limited RFB" you usually get free rooms, free food in the buffet or coffee shop, and free drinks at the bars.

Comps Turning Into Pumpkins

Watch for the expiration point for comps. Policies vary a lot. While some casinos allow you to bank comps indefinitely, the trend seems to be toward time limits and some are exasperatingly short. A few casinos expire your comps at the end of every day or each trip. At some casinos, it's difficult getting even a limited coffee-shop comp on a current trip until you've played some. It doesn't matter that your plane was delayed and you got in after midnight half-starved.

329

This is a trend that definitely needs to be turned around. If I've given a casino some decent play on my last trip and can't get a host to make an exception, I'm likely to start hunting for another casino.

Remember that benefits in customer comp banks are debts of the casino and shareholders do not look favorably on debt. Jeffrey Compton gave this warning in a *Casino Player* article called "Comp Optimization": "Sometimes, usually about the time financial statements are being prepared, the casino MIS (Management Information System) gurus do a mass comp-account adjustment, wiping out dormant dollars in the belief that most players will not notice—and those who do, get a sincere apology and benefits restored."

Fortunately for Las Vegas residents, some Strip casinos (but not all) modify this expiration policy for locals. And the off-Strip casinos usually offer a comp system for locals that allows us to bank our comps indefinitely.

Room-Rate Games

Watch for casinos charging your comp bank for a room at rack rate, which can be twice as much as the casino rate, therefore requiring twice as much play. And speaking of the casino rate, a few of the larger Las Vegas resorts have abolished this long-established custom. You either qualify for a comped room or you pay rack rate. Fortunately, in this climate of heavy casino competition, I don't think this is a trend that will take hold.

Trusting Casino Words

Be careful when a host says she'll "take care of everything." To her, that phrase could mean a casino rate, not the free room that you might expect. Many hosts bend over backwards to please their customers, but they're only human. Sometimes they promise more than they have the authority to give and have to back down later. Sometimes they have second thoughts and worry that they won't be able to justify to their boss what they promised.

You can try to be specific with a host, but some casinos just won't be pinned down in advance about what it takes for various levels of comps. Many people who don't like surprises ask for food comps as they need them rather than charging them to their room, particularly if they aren't sure how much their play will get them in total comps at the end of their stay.

However, here's a warning from an Internet bulletin board: "Some casinos won't write a direct food comp for someone staying in-house. They want you to charge the food to your room, so they can evaluate the total at check-out time. Of course, if they then refuse to comp part or all of your meals, it's too late for you to eat elsewhere. So I only comply with this policy at casinos where I'm sure there won't be a problem."

Other people don't want to have to bother the host for every meal they eat or event they attend. They prefer to play at their comfort level and charge to their room the amount they can afford to pay if it isn't comped. Then they talk to the host about the total bill once, just before they leave, and are grateful for whatever's comped. And judging by my mail, the average player who's done most of his gambling where he's staying is surprised, even overwhelmed, by how much *is* comped.

There's another problem with casino words, one that's serious and showing up more frequently, although, I'm happy to say, is certainly not widespread. This is the problem of a casino pulling comps after they've been offered up front, because a player is winning or the casino suspects he's a skilled advantage player.

Typical is a story I heard of a blackjack high roller who was promised full RFB up front, then won a large sum of money during his stay, and his credit card was charged for all his expenses (more than $8,000) *after* he checked out.

Some have suggested that it pays to have an agreement in writing up front—for example, your check-in slip should indicate that your status is RFB. Then you could dispute this credit-card charge, after which it becomes an issue between the casino and the credit-card company. Others have suggested either using a credit card with a very low credit line or leaving the minimum cash deposit the casino will accept in lieu of a credit card. This limits your risk.

Most of us ordinary gamblers will never face such a crisis, but even in simpler circumstances, it always pays to have as much in writing as you can. As one wag said, "Oral agreements aren't worth the paper they're written on."

Are Your Comps Hard or Soft?

You need to know the difference between hard and soft comps.

Soft comps refer to amenities for which the casino does not have to put out hard cash. Instead, the expense is absorbed by departmental budgets. These comps are given routinely for goods and services from on-property outlets owned by the casino: rooms, meals, shows and events, golf, and shopping.

Hard comps refer to amenities for which the casino has to put out hard cash. They used to mean off-property expenses, such as airline reimbursement, sightseeing tours, fishing cruises, golf outings, or sporting events in other venues. In the old days, it used to be easier to get most comps, because the casino owned everything on the property. Hosts didn't have gamblers asking them for comps for a gondola ride on the canal in a mall or admission to a shark aquarium, a roller coaster, or a wax museum! Today, there's no clearly defined division between soft and hard comps now that so many independently owned concessions, retail stores, and restaurants are located in the new megaresorts. In fact, some casinos own few or even none of the restaurants in their own buildings. Even the limo service may be outsourced.

For example, a show comp may be a hard comp if the show is "four-walled," meaning the casino has leased out the showroom and has to buy tickets from an independent company for its comped customers. Usually, leases are written in such a way that the casino gets a special pre-arranged discount when it writes a comp for the show, but the line between hard and soft is still blurred.

Also, there's still some old-fashioned cooperation between casinos. Some hosts have working arrangements with hosts at other casinos, so there's a lot of trading back and forth, especially for show tickets. And due to the consolidation of casino ownership, there's the opportunity to receive a variety of comps because several casinos are in the same system.

How can you know whether the comp you want is soft or hard? First, you have to remember the difference. A good mnemonic is: A *hard* comp is probably *hard* to get.

Can you tell by the dollar amount of the comp? It's not a good test. I know of one casino where the hosts can't give you a comp for an afternoon show that requires only a purchase of a $6.95 drink, although they can give you one for $200 to spend in the gourmet restaurant.

One good rule of thumb is: If you can't charge it to your room, it's probably a hard comp. This is often true of beauty salons and spas. It doesn't mean it's impossible to get a comp for a spa treatment, but you can be sure it takes more play. The only way to find out how much more is to talk to a host.

Of course, if you play at a high enough level or lose enough, you can get just about anything comped. But for most gamblers, even some who play on a fairly high level, there's one comp that's definitely hard— sometimes "impossible" describes it better: telephone charges. I'm not talking about the long-distance charges I put through the hotel operator; I don't expect the casino to pick up those personal expenses. I can even live with the usual policy of not comping in-room movies and tips. But even after being comped for hundreds of dollars worth of luxury room nights, meals, and other perks in a visit to a casino, at check-out there's still an unremovable $5.50 charge for a few local calls and one to a toll-free number. It's become a game for me over the years to see if I can ever get these pesky telephone charges taken off by a host. Considering my 99.9% lack of success in this endeavor, maybe it's time to find another game. A few casinos don't charge fully comped customers for local or toll-free phone calls (although they may charge it to their comp account), and the lofty whales are never charged for phone calls. But even among the many big players I know, I've heard precious few success stories in the telephone game. Many avoid this frustration by using calling cards at a payphone or their cell phones with plans that have no roaming charges.

Laptops and Long-Distance

Be prepared for phone-fee shock if you travel with a laptop computer. There's usually a $1 (or more) fee each time you dial your Internet provider, even if it has a local access number. This fee is charged every time you dial the number, even if you get a busy signal. And increasingly common now after a basic period (commonly 20-30 minutes), you're put on the clock, with 10¢-25¢ *per-minute* charges relentlessly ticking away. This is true, again, even on local calls.

And if you have to use a long-distance access number dialed directly through the hotel switchboard, well … let me tell you what happened to a friend of mine. He was at a convention in a hotel-casino in Puerto Rico, where the company president logged onto his e-mail account frequently, just as he did whenever he travels anywhere in the U.S. "Imagine the look on his face at checkout when they presented him with a $3,000-plus phone bill."

Making "Theo" Your Friend— Comps by the Numbers

Although many people wrongly think they can't get comps because they aren't high rollers, others go to the other extreme and think, also wrongly, that if they lose $100, the casino will give them $100 in comps. Casino comps are a rebate of *part* of player losses, the percentage varying from 10% to 40%, depending primarily on the amount of competition a casino faces.

Most casinos now use a mathematical formula to calculate how much in comps a player should receive. They take the amount of money risked multiplied by the casino's edge multiplied by the comp percentage.

Let's illustrate this with a $25-a-hand blackjack

player who plays 50 hands per hour for four hours. This player puts $5,000 into action ($25 x 50 x 4). The casino figures it has a 2% edge overall in blackjack, so $5,000 x .02 = $100, which is the expected casino win. Since this casino is on the Strip and faces stiff competition, it has a 40% comp rebate. So .4 x $100 = $40, the amount the player is entitled to in comps.

This formula works the same way for slot and video poker players, but all machines are not created equal and savvy machine players need to understand the meaning of the word "theoretical," usually called the "theo"—the god worshipped by casino executives.

When your host tells you your comps are based on the theo of the slot or video poker machine you're playing, she means that her comp guidelines are based on a percentage of the amount the casino will *theoretically* win from all the gamblers who play that game. Many players win in their sessions, many more lose in their sessions, but adding up all the results, the casino will win a certain percentage of the coin-in. That percentage is the casino's theo. (From the opposite point of view, it's the theoretical loss of the player.) Of course, this differs from any one player's actual loss for any session or trip.

How does a casino get the theo for each of the thousands of machines on the casino floor? Is there a different percentage for each machine based on the actual hold?

It's not really broken down into that many pieces. There may be one average figure for all machines. Or a casino may have one figure for reel slots and another (always lower) for video poker. Even casinos with complex computer systems commonly use just 10-15 different theo percentages within which each machine is classified. Most casinos use the figures from the manufacturers to set the theo on VP machines, which is usually around 2% lower than if everyone played computer-perfect strategy.

In a perfect world, a player would know the theo of the machine he's feeding. He would also know the percentage of the theo that the casino is giving back in comps. Then he could figure how many dollars in comps he's earned. For example, $20,000 coin-in x a theo of 2% = $400 x a 25% kickback rate = $100 in comps earned. Simple, isn't it?

But the casino world isn't simple and the comp system rarely employs a simple formula. Maybe the bean counters have decided to base comps on an either-or system—the larger of 25% of your theoretical loss *or* 10% of your actual loss. Or they may factor in denomination or time played, or use any of the other factors we've talked about in the last few chapters. Sometimes you can get the formula from your host, but it's mostly a deep dark secret.

Whether you can figure out the system or not, it always pays to choose a game where skill is a factor, then study to gain that skill. To quote Jeffrey Compton, "Just because the casino computer says that, on average, you should be losing 3% of every dollar you play doesn't mean that you have to make the prediction come true." If you're playing the correct strategy on a good video poker machine, you will, over the long term, most likely lose less than the average player does. And if comps are based on the theo, you have a chance to get as much as those who lose much more. In short, theo can be your friend.

Comp Secrets From the Queen

• If you want to eat at a nice restaurant, but are afraid you haven't played long enough for a full comp, you can try asking for a "limited comp." These are usually for food only, no booze, or are limited to a certain dollar amount. (Do your expensive drinking at the tables or machines where the cost is only a tip.)

• Try to use coupons to reduce the expenses that you hope to be comped at the end of a trip. Take your 2-for-1 meal coupon into the restaurant and you'll only have a charge for one meal.

• If you've had bad service or something inconvenient happens to you in a casino, write to the hotel general manager or a casino boss and explain what went wrong. They'll often send you comps to try to make you forget about the bad experiences and come back to have good ones. Obviously, you shouldn't make things up, but rather than doing a slow and silent burn about something displeasing that happened to you, it's better to write a letter.

A story from an Internet board: "By chance I met a high-level executive at the casino where we were staying. I introduced myself and politely told him that I thought the new buffet needed improvement. I went on about how much we liked his hotel and how we chose it for our tenth wedding anniversary. By this time he had his comp pad out. We scored an unlimited coffee shop comp with two rounds."

Not all of us would feel comfortable with this technique, but complaining politely and constructively to the right people is one way to vent frustration *and* snag some extra comps.

• Despite all the talk these days about being politically correct, sexism is still alive and well in casinos. A woman will generally get more comps with a male host—and vice versa.

• If you ask a host for something that you know from past experience is reasonable and are turned down, wait for the shift change and ask a different host.

Although casinos have set policies, hosts often differ in their interpretation and administering of them. They do have wiggle room. Maybe the second host is wiggling in a direction that will allow her to issue the requested comp.

• To avoid unexpected expenses when the bill comes, ask your server what your comp includes before you order. If limited, your comp often doesn't include dessert or an appetizer. On an open or unlimited comp you can order whatever you want within reason—one appetizer, main course, dessert, and drinks. But be sure to make sure it includes *alcoholic* drinks.

• Most casinos' slot club and table-game systems are still separate. Sometimes it pays to ask for show tickets and food comps while playing at the tables so you can save your slot club points—especially if they can be used for cashback.

• It's true that most casino customers should never play *just* to get a comp. One reason for this is that it's too psychologically painful to lose more than the comp is worth. However, this is not necessarily a hard-and-fast rule. An advantage player often plays at a particular casino specifically to get a particular comp. As long as he can find a good game and doesn't overplay his bankroll, he won't be shattered if he loses more than the comp is worth. He was going to play anyway, and he knows that all his play goes into one pot and he'll likely come out on top in the long run.

• What if the slot club meal comp you get from redeeming your points doesn't double as a line pass and there's a long line at the restaurant? Go straight to a host and get a comp for just one person. A group can almost always use the comp line if at least one person has been comped through the host system.

• Try not to overplay at one casino. If you've already put in the number of required hours at the tables or the machines for the comps you're getting, in most cases your play will be worth more the rest of that day at another casino where you can build up comps for future trips.

• Mix and match all three comp systems to your advantage. Some gamblers avail themselves of a marketing room offer at a mid-level casino that requires a small amount of play. Then they play at other casinos to get gourmet meal comps through the host system. Or they get a deluxe room at an upscale casino through the host system and use their slot club points for meal comps at other casinos.

• If you ask your host primarily for soft comps, which cost the casino little to nothing, you can often get special comps that will make your casino visit more convenient or pleasurable even when your playing level is low. Examples include an early check-in or late check-out; tickets to a show that isn't going to sell out anyway; line passes for restaurants where you aren't using comps; a Saturday-night check-in when that's usually not permitted; an upgrade to a suite when the hotel isn't full; on-property movies; or meals in casino fast-food outlets.

• To get the most comps, limit your stay in any one casino to five nights. A casino figures that most people bring enough money to last three to five days. They want that bankroll to last you the whole time, but they want to get it in the end. Then they want to replace yours with a fresh bankroll. Most casinos don't look favorably on comping a player longer than five days, especially quarter players. There are exceptions, of course, and sometimes it might be fine to stretch it to seven nights if you play heavily. But if you ask to stay longer periods, unless you have a very large credit line, a casino might start thinking you may be a blackjack or video poker player skilled enough to survive in a casino for a long period.

• Take advantage of the fact that casinos tend to be very generous with room and food comps when they first open and are trying to make a good first impression and build their database. On the other hand, don't be surprised when you want to go back a few months later and the comp requirements are much higher, probably more in line with competing casinos. (There can be exceptions here—some new megaresorts have high comp requirements when they first open since they know they'll have instant heavy occupancy from customers who chase the newest and biggest thrill.)

• Be aware that at some casinos there's something called a "cash comp." You may have a lot of incidentals on your hotel bill, like phone calls, tips, or in-room movies, but the casino policy is not to comp these. Perhaps you haven't played quite high enough to get airfare reimbursement, but you were close (or you flew in on a frequent-flyer ticket that has no price to reimburse). You can ask your host if you qualify for a cash comp. Max Rubin calls this "walking money." Try asking for this when you've had a big losing trip—you're more likely to get extra consideration then.

• Some casinos like to see you play to your comp level early. If you're on a three-day comped trip and plan to do all your playing on the third day, don't be surprised if you get a call from your host on day two, telling you that your comp status is in danger.

A player on an Internet board related an incident in which his room was comped up front by a host at a small casino. He was surprised when he had a phone message from the front desk in the middle of his stay saying he was going to be charged casino rate for his room. When he checked with the host, he found out that because of a computer error, his play was not being recorded, so she thought he was stiffing the casino. Fortunately, the host immediately straightened out the problem.

• If you're getting some or all of your final hotel bill comped, be sure to verify that your host is taking care of it the day *before* you leave. Don't wait until the last minute to find that there's been a communication problem or that the host isn't available to handle this with the front desk.

• Even if the host says she's picked up all of your room and meal charges, make sure you get a copy of the actual bill before you check out. Sometimes the host's instructions to cover these won't make it through to the front-desk billing department and you may see those charges still active on your bill. You'll have to ask the front desk to contact the host before check-out to clear this up. If you fail to do so, it's possible for the host to get a credit issued after you get home, but it usually involves a telephone hassle.

• To get a visit comped up front at a casino where you've never played, talk to a host and refer to other casinos where you've played, particularly those that are on the same level or higher. It's especially helpful if you've played at a sister property; in fact, having your home host call the host at the new casino is often the fastest way to get up front comps. However, many casinos won't promise you up front what they'll comp. You may have to go in at the casino rate and be on probation, with the level of your comps decided at the end of your visit, based strictly on your play.

• If you live in or near a large city, one of the easiest ways to get no-hassle comps is to go on a junket. These package tours, using chartered flights, are sponsored by independent operators or individual casinos and go to many casino destinations, including Atlantic City, Tunica, Biloxi, Foxwoods, Elko, Laughlin, and

Las Vegas. They can be as short as one (long) day, leaving early in the morning and coming back late at night, or as long as four days. If you're a low-level unrated gambler (or don't gamble at all), you can pay a flat fee that usually includes the flight, ground transportation, baggage handling, and your room. This fee is usually much lower than what you'd have to pay to put together a similar trip on your own, so you'll already enjoy some discounted benefits. As your level of play goes up, your benefits will increase, including free meals, shows, and other goodies. At some point it won't cost you a thing to travel on this junket trip. Looking in the Sunday travel section of most large-city newspapers will provide leads on casino junkets that run in your area.

Don't Worry, Be Happy

Finally, I need to stress one last idea about comps. Everything I've written in these last four chapters is general information. It's *not* gospel, or carved in stone. Take these generalizations and gingerly apply them to your own experiences.

As we've seen, casinos change comp policies more often than Elizabeth Taylor changes husbands. Comps are rarely issued on an exact mathematical basis, even when there's a strong casino policy. Hosts are human. If the casino has 10 hosts and one policy, you'll have 10 interpretations of it. In fact, a host can interpret the same policy differently herself from one day to another, depending on how well she slept the night before, whether she just got chewed out by a boss or was commended or got a raise. And the subtle chemistry between a host and a player often influences comp decisions.

So don't be surprised when what you've read in

this book, or stumbled across on the Internet, or heard about from your brother-in-law's mother-in-law's experience, isn't what you experience when you try it.

My recommendation is to always get as much information in advance as you can. Then, even after asking every question you can think of, don't be surprised if the unexpected happens.

Getting comps is not an exact science. In fact, it's quite political. Just ask ask ask—always nicely nicely nicely—and hope for the best. Many times you'll get more than you expect. But once in a while, even the Queen of Comps gets less than was promised. When this happens, after exhausting all avenues of questioning, I simply shrug and say, "You can't win 'em all."

Remember that comps are a gift that the casino has no obligation to give. You can't force anyone to give you a gift. If a casino disappoints you, your best option is probably to leave and go to another one. But don't let one or two unfavorable incidents or uncooperative employees sour you on a casino, especially if it just opened. If we never went back to a casino where we once had a bad experience, we wouldn't have any place to play! If, after two or three visits, you're still not enjoying yourself, you can put that casino on your personal blacklist. (Of course, if a casino on our blacklist suddenly puts in $5 full-pay Deuces Wild with a .5% cashback slot club, we would return so fast and furiously that rude employees, uncomfortable chairs, lousy food, and no ambience would disappear from our memories like magic!)

Brad and I never take for granted that the casino will give us something. This helps our attitude in less-than-favorable comp circumstances. In fact, after all these years, when we get an especially nice comp, Brad often shakes his head and says, "How can they afford to do this?"

We feel we get more comps than anyone deserves and we always consider them offerings of friendship that we appreciate. So on occasions when we don't get something we think we've earned or were promised, we just say to ourselves, "Well, this time it didn't work out like we expected. But hey, we've gotten so much good stuff in the past and there's so much more good stuff to come, we still feel very lucky."

V

CASINO FINANCIAL SMARTS

12

Money Matters

"Not counting our losses, we're ahead"
—overheard in a casino

If the old expression, "Money makes the world go round," is true, it's doubly true in the casino world. No matter how many comps and coupons or how much credit you have, you need real money to gamble with on the casino floor.

I'm often asked, "How much money should we take with us to the casino?" Of course, there are as many answers to this question as there are people who ask it. And how much money you should take to the casino depends on many factors: your disposable income, temperament, goals, and choice and knowledge of games, to name a few.

For people who already have a large gambling bankroll, this isn't a burning issue. However, for most casino visitors, just asking this question implies that they don't have as much money to risk in a casino as they'd like.

How to Get It

Every wise gambler has a specified fund for gambling. You can call it your "gambling bankroll" and use it for nothing else. Or you can call it your "entertainment budget" and use it for all your leisure activities, including gambling. No matter what you call this fund, however, it's wise to follow two basic bankroll guidelines, predicated on the principle that a wise gambler hopes to win, but faces the reality that he often loses.

• Don't use money that's needed for the necessities of life; pay your bills first.

• Don't gamble with money that will lower the quality of life for you or your family if you lose it.

Okay, you're a responsible gambler, but you never seem to be able to scrounge up enough money for even a small bankroll. Do I have any advice for you? One of my best suggestions can be summed up with one word: budget. Some people list bankroll in their financial planning, along with food, insurance, and retirement saving. Similar to an old-time Christmas Club, the gambling bankroll entry is funded when you take a certain amount of each paycheck and put it into a separate savings account. A two-income family might decide to set aside all or a large portion of the smaller income. Many people set up automatic transfers, reasoning, "If I never see the money, I'm not tempted to spend it on something else." This can be especially effective when you get a raise, then automatically transfer the extra income, so you don't get used to it in your regular budget.

I know one couple that's totally committed to growing a gambling bankroll. She volunteers for overtime on her job and contributes all that money to their bankroll. He moonlights as a handyman and painter and puts all this extra income in. She says that they tend to be a little more careful with their gambling money when they recall the extra sweat they've put into earning it. That's a great way not to go on tilt in a casino.

If you're living up to (or beyond) your means and you're bound and determined to save up a gambling fund, you might try scrimping on other expenses. You can't, obviously, cut out the necessary expenses: groceries, the rent or mortgage payment, or the proverbial shoes for the baby, but you can cut down on or forego non-essentials, such as dining out, movies and videos, new clothes, cell phones or pagers, and the like. Meanwhile, you can spend some time finding coupons or taking advantage of rebates for the items you must buy, then earmark the money you've saved for your casino vacations.

One gambler told me he went without using air conditioning in his car one whole summer—in hot California—so his gas expense was lower and he could save the difference to add to his bankroll. A desire for a gambling bankroll might even provide strong motivation for heavy smokers and drinkers to quit.

And almost everyone gets a big windfall once in a while—an inheritance, a bonus check, an income-tax refund, even a slot machine jackpot. That can be instant-bankroll time. It finally all comes down to deciding on your life priorities and being disciplined about your resolutions.

How to Bring It With You

Taking a Chance with Cash

Some people prefer to have all their fun money— and that's what most gambling money should be—in cash. They like the feel of the bottoms of their pockets or purses when they bulge with big wads of bills. And it's the easiest way to carry your bankroll into the casino. With all due respect to Elvis, cash is king. Of course, you're also most vulnerable when carrying cash: You could lose it; you could be robbed of it; it could even be confiscated by police or airport security (under the omnibus crimes of money laundering or cash-transaction infractions).

On the other hand, there are ways to protect your cash. The first rule is: Don't flash it. I'm constantly amazed by how many gamblers pull out wads of C-notes and peel off bills to buy in at the tables, get coin for the machines, or simply purchase a newspaper at the sundries shop. Yes, there are times, especially at the tables with the pit boss watching, when it's tactical to expose a big bankroll, but in most cases it's unwise. If the wrong person gets a glimpse of it, it could cost you that money or, worst-case scenario, your life.

It's best to keep only enough money in your wallet or pocket to pay for what you know you'll need in the near future. You can carry the rest of your cash (along with travel papers, airline tickets, and the like) in a thin money belt, sold at any luggage store.

Once you've carried your cash into the casino, you can get a free safety-deposit box at the casino cage and use it as your private bank to deposit and withdraw money as your gambling fortunes go up and down. You can also deposit the money with the casino at the cage, signing markers at the tables (the papers you sign when the casino issues you money off the credit line) or simply going to the cage to withdraw all or part of it as needed.

You can also stash extra cash in an in-room safe, though these days there's often a hefty daily charge for their use. Some guests opt to hide their cash in out-of-the-way places in their hotel room, but I figure a professional thief knows all the good places, too. If you do decide to hide it, don't forget where you put it! A friend told me that he once had to tear his hotel room apart to find his cash—he forgot that he'd taped it to the inside of the toilet-tank cover. This friend also told me that another time, he was idly flipping through a Gideon's Bible in his hotel room and found 20 twenty-dollar bills that someone apparently had put there for safekeeping—then forgot to retrieve. When I was younger, I thought people made up stories like that; now I've experienced just enough senior moments of my own to believe anything when it comes to the memory department.

Cashless Safety

If you're squirrely about carrying large amounts of cash around, there are other ways to get money from your bank to the casino and back that provide a little more security.

For many years our vehicle of choice was traveler's checks. They're universally accepted, so they're as good as cash most everywhere, which is convenient. You can cash them in any casino, though a few may have a daily limit for new customers. They're replaced if they're lost or stolen, so they're much safer than cash. We've always used a bank or belonged to a credit union that didn't charge a fee for the checks, so it was also a frugal method for us. If you're a member of the American Automobile Association (AAA), you can get a limited amount of American Express Travelers Cheques for free. If not, all banks sell them, albeit often with a hefty fee. A final advantage is that traveler's checks can give you an easy way to budget your casino-vacation money; you can buy them in denominations that will help you keep daily or session stop-loss limits.

If you don't have a problem controlling your

spending, a good idea is to use a debit card from an account at your home bank. That will save you from pulling money out before you need it and losing the interest. If you want some help in self-discipline, you might want to get a debit card for an account that contains nothing but your gambling bankroll for a current trip. That way you can set a total loss limit before you leave home.

Another good option is a money-management account with an online broker, such as TD Waterhouse. You get a free ATM card good for up to a $1,000-per-day withdrawal with no cash-advance charge (though you might have to pay a fee at the ATM you use). The big plus here is that you get money-market interest rates while your money is waiting for you. You can also sometimes make special arrangements with your bricks-and-mortar bank to increase the daily amount you can draw from an ATM machine.

It's possible to wire money to a casino, although the bank fee is usually high, so you wouldn't want to do this for a small amount. You have to warn the casino in advance that it's coming and find out what information they need for the transaction, but the casino will hold the money for you and hand it over when you arrive. You can either take all of it at once or deposit it at the cage and tap into it as you need it, as described earlier.

A Line of Casino Credit

Getting a credit line at a casino is a great way to manage your gambling money. For the self-disciplined, it's one of the most frugal methods, as you get to use the casino's money interest-free. It lets you avoid the problem of carrying a large amount of cash. Also, in our case as Las Vegas locals, it saves us from having to make frequent trips to the bank. However, keep in mind that any money you get from the casino is a loan, which you're expected to pay back within a specified time, anywhere from the end of that particular visit to 60 or so days after you sign for the money. For the more cautious, a better use of a credit line is as a pre-approved check-cashing station. If you take a marker, you write a check and pay it off before you leave to go back home, whether you live around the corner or halfway around the world.

The bad thing about casino credit is that you may be tempted to use it when you shouldn't. Casinos often grant credit limits up to the balance in your bank accounts, even higher if you have a clean record covering past credit transactions. The bean counters are interested only in whether you have the resources to pay back your markers and don't care a whit if that money is already earmarked for your necessary expenses. Stories abound about gamblers with credit lines at several casinos who start to chase their losses and suddenly find that they've gone way beyond their normal limits. So it's wise to get a credit line only for the amount you have budgeted for your gambling bankroll—that is, what you can afford to lose.

Another disadvantage is that if you lose a lot, you can often, with a small wait, get the casino to extend your credit line 10% to 50%, again opening up the temptation to lose more than you intended to. Therefore, if you have a weakness for overdoing the gambling, I suggest you avoid credit play completely.

A marker usually looks just like one of your own checks—"Paid to the order of XXX Casino" with your signature on the bottom line. If you don't pay back the marker in the required length of time, the casino sends it to your bank for payment, just like any regular check. In fact, in many casinos where we have credit lines, we've arranged for this to be done automatically at the end of the specified time, saving us the bother of going to the casino before the due date and writing our own check. Of course, we always have enough money in the bank to cover the marker.

If you get into financial trouble and your debt becomes overdue, it turns into a serious matter. Although casinos may be patient for a reasonable length of time if a gambler is making a serious effort to take care of the debt, they pursue unpaid markers vigorously. And they have various means at their disposal, from dunning phone calls to collection agencies to the District Attorney pressing charges. Since a casino doesn't want to lose a good customer if the financial problems are only temporary, they'll sometimes negotiate a reduced settlement of the debt, especially for good customers. But you have to show them some speed first.

What if you simply can't pay the marker, or refuse to? It depends on the size of the unpaid debt, the size of the casino, and most importantly, what state the casino is in. Traditionally, state courts have not helped casinos enforce the collection of gambling debts; this practice is a holdover from the time when casinos were illegal. However, Nevada has declared, and it has been held up in the courts, that markers are checks and as such, nonpayment can subject those who default to civil and criminal prosecution, the same as if a bad check were written to another business.

How to Manage It

An Internet gambler asked, "Do you have any advice on money management in Las Vegas? My usual plan of losing every cent I can get my hands on is not very effective."

I wasn't going to talk about money management in this book. I did so in the last one, in quite a bit of detail, and the subject has been beaten to a pulp in gambling literature for many years. However, I still get frequent pleas for help in this area and I continue to read bad information put out by charlatan gambling writers. So I'll discuss the subject again briefly.

First of all, remember this basic undeniable mathematical fact: A money-management system cannot make you a long-term winner in a game where the casino has the edge. That is, money-management as it's most commonly cited in books and magazine articles is not a valid technique for *winning* money. But most people who ask me about money management are really asking, "How can I make the money I bring on a gambling vacation last the whole time?" The really ambitious ask, "How can I come home from a gambling vacation and still have some money left so I don't feel like an absolute loser?" I'll let the Frugal Princess address these questions.

The Frugal Princess on Lasting Longer

Steve and I take only cash and traveler's checks to Las Vegas and other gambling destinations. It's always money we can spare after all our financial obligations have been taken care of. We never take a checkbook, credit card, or ATM card—even a frugal princess can be tempted in a casino.

I've heard of many creative plans that are successful for people. One of the most popular is dividing a total bankroll into equal daily or fixed-time portions and stopping when the allotment is gone, switching to non-gambling activities until the next scheduled session.

A more appealing idea for some is to allot at least half of a bankroll for the first day and play till the cows come home—or until you lose the whole half. Most people who don't get to gamble frequently want to play a lot the first day they get to the casino. If they lose the first half, they get a good night's sleep and go sightseeing or shopping or pursue another non-gambling activity, but don't gamble at all the second day. Then they go back to playing on a bankroll that's divided into the number of days left on the trip.

Some plans involve locking up certain wins, like high-paying quads in video poker or slot jackpots over a specified amount. Some like to put their windfalls in sealed envelopes to take home, or even buy traveler's checks and mail them home so there's no temptation to put those funds at risk again. Those on the equal-portion plan discussed above lock up any balance left at the end of a session as take-home winnings.

The advantage of all the above plans, and any plan really, is that you've thought about the subject ahead of time. You arrive at the casino prepared, which is a prime requisite for a wise casino visitor. Now, all you have to do is summon up that second requisite: self-discipline. *Sticking to* a plan is much harder than *making* one. This is one of the values of having a gambling buddy—you can encourage each other to follow through on your resolutions.

The Queen Adds ...

I have one last comment—actually a strong opinion—on money management in a casino. Most gamblers lose their money too fast because they're playing at too high a denomination relative to the size of their bankroll. Regardless of the level you're playing at or the game you choose, step down in denomination and notice how your bankroll—and thus your fun—lasts longer.

What to Do if You Win It

Now here's a "problem" we'd all like to face more often than we do—hitting a big jackpot. What do you do after all the hoopla is over and you're standing there holding thousands of dollars in cash just paid by the floorpeople?

Remember, you can usually request that the casino write you a check for the jackpot instead of giving you the cash. Or you can take part of the jackpot in cash and part by check. Be aware that you must make this request when the casino employee *first* shows up at your machine. Once the cash is brought out to put in your hand, it's too late to decide that you want a check. Government regulations I discuss later in this chapter (put in place originally to try to thwart drug-money laundering) prohibit a casino from writing you a check in exchange for cash.

If you hit only a medium-sized jackpot and the payoff is a quiet event, you can probably disappear into the crowd without being noticed. However, I suggest you look around every once in a while to make sure that no one's following you and go straight to your room or car. If you're alone or in the least bit uneasy, ask the floorperson to summon a security guard to escort you to wherever you need to go. You can also go to the cage to get a safety deposit box to put the money in until you decide what you want to do with it next.

What To Do if It's All Gone

At some point on one of your trips to a gambling destination, you might find yourself out of money and wondering what to do. Maybe you've been careless,

What Do You Have to Give the Casino ...

Casinos will not pay out a machine jackpot of $1,200 or more—the W-2G trigger amount—until they see the player's ID. The preferred form of identification is a government-issued document that contains a photo, like a driver's license, passport, or military ID card. Some casinos might be a little more flexible, particularly if you have a player's card so your name and address are already in the computer system, but you can avoid a hassle and a wait if you carry acceptable identification in a casino.

A side note. We've found it useful to keep copies of our driver's licenses. We've lost the originals several times in the 20 years we've been visiting casinos. Some days it seems like they're in and out of our pockets a dozen times, having to constantly show ID in a casino for some purpose or another—redeeming coupons, joining slot clubs, and collecting jackpots. Having duplicates saves a lot of time in the interim if we lose, and have to replace, the original. Customers who don't have ID and are not known in a casino will have their jackpots held until they can produce identification.

The casinos may also ask to see proof of your Social Security number—on your driver's license or a Social Security card itself. Again, there's sometimes some flex-

inebriated, losing big, under-capitalized for your bet size, or a victim of any number of other disasters or combinations thereof. Whether you've forgotten your money, been pick-pocketed, trick-rolled, or just thrown your last buck at a fearsome losing streak, after you reach for your wallet and find nothing in it, you'll probably repeat the forlorn words of the first question ever asked: "Well, what now?"

This is no time for a lecture. You need some ideas—and quick! There's always the possibility of panhand-

... When You Hit a Big Jackpot?

ibility here; some casinos merely ask what your number is. Or the casino might be able to check your player's card information or past W-2G records. However, if you have ID but refuse to give your number, the casino must, by law, withhold 28%-31% for federal taxes. Be prepared—you never know when Lady Luck will tap you on the shoulder.

If you're lucky enough to end up with so much cash that you don't want to travel back home with it, here are a few options. If you have a bank account at a large national or international bank, you can head for the nearest local branch and make a deposit. Las Vegas, for example, has Citibank, Bank of America, Wells Fargo, and the like. If you don't have a bank account, but you do have a credit card from a bank, you can also make a large payment on your credit-card balance. That gets the cash out of your hands, and if it puts the account into positive territory, you can either leave the balance there while you use it up with purchases or request the card issuer to send you a check for the balance.

You can also buy traveler's checks to carry or send home. Here again, membership in AAA comes in handy, allowing you to go to one of their offices and purchase them for free.

ling. The only cost here is to your self-esteem, unless you run afoul of the law.

Here are some less humiliating no-cost options. If you're carrying personal checks, you can usually cash one at the cage of a major casino. All you need is a valid photo ID and a major credit card. Many casinos impose a check-cashing limit of $100 or $200, but you usually aren't required to be a guest at the hotel. If you're a guest or a known player, some casinos may okay cashing a check up to as much as $1,000. However, for checks larger than that, you'll need to have an established credit line.

A friend of mine told me about a smart move she made after forgetting to go to the bank for cash before leaving home on a trip to Las Vegas. She carries a AAA Visa card, which allows her to charge American Express traveler's checks with no purchase fee at any AAA office. The checks are charged to the credit-card account as a purchase, not a cash advance. There might even be a free float for whatever the grace period is on the card, usually up to 20-25 days. Now that's frugal— a method you can use routinely, not just in a pinch.

But free options are limited. Here are the high-cost fixes. If you have a credit card, you can get a cash advance at any bank. You'll be paying a very high interest rate from the nanosecond you complete the transaction, plus a fee of up to four points on the amount of cash you take. Even so, it's better to get the cash advance from a bank than from the instant cash-advance machines lurking near every casino cage. If you must use this dreaded option, what I call the worst machines in a casino to play, all you do is insert any credit card in the slot, then enter how much money you want. If the amount is approved, you go to the cage, show ID, and retrieve the green.

My friend Bill Burton, the guide at www.casinogambling.about.com, compiled this revealing report about these true no-armed bandits:

"I recently visited an East Coast casino and inquired about the finer points of taking a cash advance on a credit card. The casino charges a certain amount just for issuing you a check from your credit card for the cash advance, depending on how much you want. To get a $500 cash advance, this casino charges $21.99. That's 4.4% up front. Most credit-card companies hit you up for a fee equal to 3% of the cash advance, which will come to $15.66. Think about it: You're already down $37.65, or 7.5%, before you even sit down to play. That's a big edge. It's like sitting down at a $5 black-jack table and losing eight hands in a row or getting nothing back after putting nearly four rolls of quarters through a slot machine. If this happened on a game, most of us would head for the hills real fast!

"But we're not through yet. The following month your credit card bill arrives. Your balance is $537.65, and you find out that on top of the 3% you had to pay, the interest rate for a cash advance is 5% higher than the 14.9% you normally pay for purchases. Your new rate is 19.9%. If you pay the minimum $15 a month, it will take you five years ($854) to retire the debt from that one cash advance of $500 in the casino."

My friend Max Rubin, author of *Comp City*, adds, "Cash machines keep a running log, complete with addresses and amount taken, of every chump who uses them. The machine company adds that information to its database. That's some pretty private information. You probably don't want your name on a mailing list labeled 'Degenerate Gamblers Who Can't Control Themselves and Make Really Stupid Decisions about Money.'"

I cringe every time I go by one of these instant-cash monsters. And then I hear that a company has developed the technology that allows you to insert your credit card in a slot machine in exchange for cred-its. I shudder to think about the cost of this dangerous "convenience."

You may decide to bite the bullet, eschewing a gouging by a cold impersonal machine to face human judgment—telephoning a parent, sibling, son or daughter, or friend and asking them to wire you money through Western Union. As Max Rubin observes, "This is where you find out if there's anyone left in the world who cares about you." Western Union offices are conveniently located in casino towns, sometimes even in casinos themselves. Check the Yellow Pages. The fees can be fairly high—and so can the embarrassment. But at least, if you connect with a sympathetic soul, you can be quickly pumped up with cash again.

As a last resort, pawnshops are always a place to get emergency cash. If you have anything worth hocking, you can get, perhaps, 30%-40% of what it's worth. You'll also pay a small service charge (usually around $5) and a big interest rate (usually around 6% a month—yes, that's 72% a year). You'll be given a receipt you can use to reclaim whatever you pawned within a set period of time (usually around four months). If you don't buy it back in the allotted time period, the pawnshop is free to sell it to anyone who comes along.

I said you didn't need a lecture on money. But I have to say that the sensible thing is to bring enough to see you through your casino vacation, and be careful with it. The alternatives are dicey at best. Being broke anywhere is not fun; being broke in a casino is a real bummer.

How to Handle It When The Government Wants to be Involved

That the government is interested in much of what happens concerning money in a casino is a fact that can't be ignored. If you spend time in a casino, especially if you play at more than minimum-bet levels, you'll find this out fast enough. Just winning a slot jackpot of $1,200 or more—not an uncommon event, even for a quarter-machine player—requires that you provide your Social Security number, which is used to generate a tax form, a copy of which is sent to the Internal Revenue Service. And it goes much further than this.

Most people know, at least vaguely, about the "$10,000 cash law." They think it affects only drug dealers and criminals who try to launder or hide ill-gotten gains. However, $10,000 today isn't as much as it used to be and many average citizens find themselves filling out, at a bank or other financial institution, government-required Currency Transactions Reports (CTRs). And guess what? That's right, casinos are considered financial institutions.

I. Nelson Rose, one of the top authorities on gaming law, recently wrote an eye-opening article called, "Casinos as Spies for the Federal Government." Here's how it begins:

"Warning to All Casino Patrons:

"If you win big, are a high roller, or do anything that a casino or the government regards as suspicious, you will be reported to the U.S. Treasury Department's Financial Crimes Enforcement Network, commonly known as FinCen. The information will be made available to the IRS and your local law enforcement agency. … The casino will not always tell you when it files these reports; in fact, under some circumstances, it is not allowed to let you know that you have been reported to FinCen."

So even if you never have a transaction in a casino that comes near $10,000, you can't assume you're home free. Federal regulations require casinos to make out "Suspicious Activity Reports–Casinos" (or SARCs—the government loves alphabet soup) on *any* activity, no matter the amount, that a casino employee "has reason to suspect."

And then there's Regulation 6A, the rules that govern the way casinos handle money. For example, you cannot decide you have too much cash to carry safely and ask them to write you a safer-to-carry check, because Regulation 6A forbids it.

If you deposit fifty $100 bills in the cage, but don't use them, when you take the money out, you cannot have the casino give you back 49 hundreds and the rest in $20 bills. Regulation 6A requires that they give you back your money in the exact same denominations as it went in. You would have to take the fifty $100s and, in a new transaction, ask for small bills.

Some casinos are so afraid of running afoul of both federal and state regulations (and the huge fines that result—as I write, MGM Mirage has just been fined $5 million for violating cash-transaction reporting) that they enforce much higher standards just to be safe. Many times I've been stuck with many old or damaged $100 bills that the video poker machine bill acceptors reject, but can only get four or five of them exchanged at the cage at one time.

And many casinos require their employees to routinely file reports on any "unusual" transaction of more than $3,000. Professional video poker player and author Bob Dancer wrote about having to show ID and give his Social Security number at an out-of-the-way Nevada casino when he went to the cage to cash in $3,200 in $5 tokens from a machine that was not in sight of the cashier. If a cashier had seen him play for several hours, he says, he would have been exempt from this money-laundering precaution, which regulates cashing out with "minimal or no gaming activity."

I had a similar experience once. During one long session I had experienced an amazing streak of good luck on a $2 coinless machine, but all my payoffs racked up as credits because they were each under the $1,200 W-2G trigger for a single-jackpot hand. After many hours, I cashed out and Brad took my $7,000-plus ticket to cash in while I stayed at the machine to update our gambling log. Suddenly, a slot tech appeared and said he needed to check my machine. (This didn't surprise me—it's often policy for a casino to check for a malfunction when there's a series of wins on one machine.) Brad told me later that he was told this was the largest ticket that had ever come into the cashier. They finally did cash it. They could have easily checked my slot club card record on the computer and seen that I'd been playing for many hours, but I wouldn't be surprised if I'm now on a government "suspicious-gambler" list somewhere.

Speaking of the government, the money matter of gambling and taxes is so complex, ambiguous, and fraught with pitfalls that I've written a separate report titled *Tax Help for the Frugal Gambler*. It contains complete information on accounting for gambling wins and losses on the federal and state levels, plus sample tax forms, sample gambling logs, input from Marissa Chien, a financial planner and tax preparer with a particular expertise in complex gambling-tax issues (contact her at 702/207-1040), and much more. As always, call Huntington Press to order; the 77-page report costs $25.

13

Let Me Give You A Tip

"Bribery will get you everywhere."
—an age-old expression

Money makes the world go round. It lubricates all the cogs and gears of day-to-day commerce, negotiation, transaction—in short, the vast majority of interpersonal interaction. And if money is the oil, then cash is the STP additive, making sure that the oil turns those cogs and gears as smoothly as possible. And there's no place on Earth where more people expect the passing of a little cash to smooth the way than in casinos.

The custom of tipping permeates every area of the gambling business. I always feel a little jarred, so to speak, when I see the tip jar next to cash registers in casino gift shops. People actually put money in cashiers' tip jars—just to reward someone who takes their money and gives them change.

Tipping is a subject that's always been problematic for me (I'm sure to no one's surprise). All my life I've saved money by paying the lowest possible price for anything and everything. So you can readily see my dilemma: You don't *have to* tip. So to never tip might seem like the appropriately frugal road for me to travel. However, *being frugal isn't the same thing as being cheap or stingy.* Therefore, I've always tipped when I felt it was the customary, the useful, or the right thing to do.

On the other hand, there are so many tipping situations in casinos that I find the whole thing to be a challenge. And I've witnessed tipping extremes. Some players tip so much that they give away all their profits and can never come out of a casino a winner. Perhaps this level of tipping makes them feel important or loved. I don't know. Other people never tip at all, neither inside nor outside a casino. They're often judged by others to be tightfisted or miserly, but they obviously don't care what other people think.

Ultimately, whether they're inside a casino or out, all people have their own opinions about tipping. There's no clear right or wrong. We're all influenced by how we were raised, what we were taught about money in our formative years, and how we feel about money today. Each of us has to make our own decision and this is influenced by many factors.

Tipping—A Personal Decision

One factor is basic personality. My husband, for example, is naturally a generous person. My own generosity, by comparison, is sometimes tempered by a frugal nature. I probably don't tip enough at times, while Brad sometimes tips too much. In that way, as in so many others, I figure we balance each other out.

I've noticed that gratuity-giving patterns depend on many external factors. People who've worked in tip-earning positions, no matter how long ago, are apt not only to be generous, but also empathetic with service people.

Translating Casino Tip Talk Into English

Duke off—Share the tip money. "Dealers sometimes have to duke off a percentage of their tokes to the floormen."

George—A good tipper. "Mr. B is a real George."

Grease—Tip money. "Grease the bellman a buck a bag."

Stiff—To not tip, or someone who doesn't tip. "Don't stiff the cocktail waitress or she'll think you're a stiff."

Toke—A tip. "The dealers complained that the tokes were down last month."

From which part of the country or world you hail also determines tipping patterns. I have a friend who is more frugal than I am in many ways, but he always tips on the high side. When I asked him why he does this, he answered, "I guess it's because I'm so used to doing it in New York."

Germans, Australians, and Canadians are notorious among American waitpeople, taxi drivers, and bellmen for not tipping, because it's not the custom in their countries. (Of course, driving 120 mph on the Autobahn is allowed in Germany, but I don't see too many Germans importing that custom here.)

Certain occupational groups have predictable tipping tendencies. Doctors and dentists, fairly or unfairly, have a reputation as stiffs, and I've heard Las Vegas waitresses talk about how they hate to have a teachers' convention in town. Ouch!

Specific Tipping Locales and Situations

Following is a list of places in a hotel-casino where you'll be expected to tip. In addition to general hints,

I've added some examples of creative tipping that can get you more of what you want.

Buffet—Although most people are comfortable about knowing how much to tip in a regular casino restaurant—the same as they do in a non-casino eatery—many wonder what to do in a buffet. We feel the servers in a $6.95 buffet work just as hard (or harder) than those in the high-class $25.95 spreads. Again, this is a personal decision, but we don't tip in a buffet according to the price of the meal. We tip a minimum of $1 per person dining for average service, more if we're given extra service. We also tip more if we stay a long time and deprive the server of another set of customers who might tip. We also tip extra when we're with our grandchildren and leave a messy table to clean up.

Front Desk—Here's one of the best examples where tipping up front can work miracles. The front desk clerk can often mysteriously make a room materialize, or make arrangements for you to keep your room, when the hotel is otherwise "sold out." These employees can also upgrade you to a better class of room, often at no extra charge.

An e-mail correspondent who regularly works the front-desk clerks for better rooms suggests the following: Be friendly from the beginning, but don't tip up front; it might offend someone not accustomed to it or it might seem a little too blatant. Still, you can covertly communicate that you have money in your hand, perhaps with a little twinkle in your eye. Say something like, "We'll be staying here for a week and would really like to be comfortable. Any chance of getting into a mini-suite?" Or, "Any chance of getting into the Centurion Tower?" Don't use the term "upgrade" or mention the cost of your original reservation or of the room or suite that you're asking about. If your request is granted, after registering, thank the clerk and discreetly hand him or her a folded bill. Some don't want to leave it to chance that the clerk will get the message that a tip is forthcoming, so they use a similar approach, but have some bills folded in their hand in such a way that the clerk sees them from the outset.

Another e-mail correspondent has what I think is an even more sure-fire system. Before he goes to check in, he buys $300 worth of chips—11 green $25 chips and five red $5 chips. Then he walks up to the front desk and sets the chips on the counter as he checks in. This way he looks like he was just playing green-chip black-jack before getting around to taking his hotel room. Usually the clerk keeps glancing at that stack of chips. So when he asks for an upgrade, more often than not he gets it. As he thanks the clerk, he slides her a couple of red chips and says, "Try your luck when you get off work." The real beauty of this strategy is that he has total control over how much he tips, depending on the level of the upgrade and the eagerness of the clerk. Plus the whole thing looks utterly spontaneous.

Bell Desk—Bellmen expect a dollar a bag minimum—you might sneak in one shopping bag "free," but don't think six shopping bags don't count. If you hand over your bags to a bellman when you're not going straight up to the room and want to be sure they'll be delivered right away, tip him then and there or you might find that you have to call for them when you finally get to the room.

Free Transportation—We always tip the driver of a free casino shuttle at least $1 per couple, and $2 if he keeps us entertained or provides informative commentary. If you get a comped limo ride, you'll usually feel cheap if you don't tip $10-$20, or higher for long rides, even if a taxi would have been less expensive.

Housekeeping—We don't stay in hotel rooms for long periods of time like we used to, so we have a regular practice for short-term stays of leaving $1 a day for the maid.

I also still like to give our maids a day off sometimes, as I described in *The Frugal Gambler*, with their appreciated tip being the words, "No service today." Some have questioned me about that practice since then. "Does that actually give the maid a break? Maybe the supervisor just gives her another room to clean." One friend commented that she would hate to think she was trying to give the maid less to do, only to find out that the housekeeping supervisor's opinion was, "If there's time to lean, there's time to clean." I head off this potential problem by finding out if a hotel requires maids to phone in from each room in order to prove she was there. If she is, I tell her to come on into the room and make that phone call.

Hosts—Tipping here is a very complex issue and there are so many considerations that I've devoted a whole chapter to it (see Chapter Thirteen).

Tipping While Gambling

Let's assume you're an average and knowledgeable tipper outside the casino. You tip a standard 15%-20% in restaurants, or more if you receive extra good service. You know to give the skycaps at the airport at least a dollar for each bag they handle for you. Still, you might be a little confused about the tipping protocols in a casino, which are a bit more complicated and unfamiliar than in the restaurants, valet parking lots, and taxicabs you may be more used to.

Brad and I rarely play table games any longer, video poker having replaced blackjack for us. If you want to be a savvy table player, you should read *Comp City* by Max Rubin. In addition to giving you sound guidance on how to play the games smarter by using the comp system, Max's book covers the art of tipping, including ways that tips can increase your bottom line while at the tables. Simply stated, you can tip a table-game dealer in two ways: by giving him a chip or two directly or by betting a chip for him as you're betting your own. Pretty straightforward.

Since I write a lot about machine play, people often ask me to provide guidelines for tipping at the machines. "We know the tipping customs in the usual places, but we have no idea what to do in a casino when we hit a thousand-dollar jackpot on a slot machine and suddenly people appear out of nowhere, expecting to share in our good fortune."

Here are some tipping ideas if you play slot machines or video poker. Some I've used personally, while others have been suggested by others. Perhaps you'll find a combination of techniques that will help you form your own tipping guidelines.

Resisting Tip Pressure

First, always remember tipping is voluntary. You, the player, are in charge of this monetary transaction; it's your decision what to tip. Employee hints, blatant or subtle, should be stringently ignored. These include profuse congratulations on small hand-pays, the sudden appearance of several employees when a big jackpot is being paid, and the particularly irritating practice of being handed the last hundred of any payoff in twenty-dollar bills.

The problem of tipping pressure is often the result of a lack of actual gambling experience by casino employees. Most employees on the lower levels don't make enough money to be able to afford to gamble, even if they want to. If they do play, it's usually on a limited basis at low denominations. Therefore, they're overly impressed when they see someone win even $1,000. They figure they'd have to work two or three weeks to bring home that much money—and here you've won it in just a few seconds. Many have no idea how much you may have put into that machine today, or machines like it for the last couple of years. It doesn't dawn on them that maybe you've lost much more than the $1,000 jackpot they're paying off. When you're playing dollars and hit for $4,000, or even more at higher denominations, most casino employees think that this is all the money in the world and you certainly can *afford* to tip large amounts.

The new multi-line games have radically changed what a player considers a jackpot, but casino personnel have no clue about what winning or the long term means. When we play $1 Deuces Wild on a Ten Play machine and hit four deuces on one line for $1,000, we don't look at this hand-pay as a jackpot; we often lose more than that on the adjacent machine while waiting to be paid. But even on the traditional one-line quarter Deuces that we played for many years, when you hit four deuces and are hand-paid the $250, every experienced player knows this is, at best, just a brief winning interlude, not a jackpot.

So understand and accept the fact that employees always hope for big tips; after all, they're human. Don't judge them too harshly, but don't feel pressured by them, either. You're a gambler, not a contestant in a popularity contest.

Another element of tipping strategy to remember is that the money you spend on tips, whether gambling-related or not, can add up when you're on a casino vacation. This is especially true if you're comped for meals; 15%-25% of restaurant bills, particularly in gourmet rooms, can really eat up the cash. In fact, tips are our largest expense in a casino. That's why you need to have a little discipline and not go wild with the granting of gratuities. You need to think, soberly, about how much it's going to cost you to tip for all the service you receive on your trip, then include that expense in your vacation budget.

Planning Ahead

The best way to determine how to deal with casino tipping is to plan your toke attack in advance. If you gamble with a spouse or pal with whom you share a bankroll, you should agree on the procedures. Brad and I vacillated on our tip policy for many years. Then one day we sat down and settled on a basic strategy. It wasn't a rigid list of absolutes—it contains a range of dollar amounts—but it gave us a guide, which saves us from the stress of having to constantly make tipping decisions on the spot.

This advance planning also helps insulate us from being intimidated by tip hustling. Hand-paid quarter-and-above royal flushes, for example, are paid off in $100 bills and most floorpeople peel off the last hundred in $20 bills. You certainly don't want to start handing out hundreds, but you might not even want to pass around twenties. That's why we always have lots of small bills (ones and fives) handy when we play. We never tip out of our jackpot winnings. In the rare case we run out of small bills after we're paid, we politely ask for change for one of the twenties. (And it's perfectly acceptable, when an attendant comes to your machine after you hit a jackpot, to request that you be paid completely in big bills.)

Many people use a percentage system for their tipping on top jackpots, generally ranging from .5% to 2%, but most commonly 1%. They might tip $10 for a $1,000 jackpot; $40 for $4,000, etc. Brad and I tend to tip on a graduated percentage system, starting at $10 (1%) for

$1,000, but decreasing the percentage as the jackpot climbs, with $20 (.5%) for a $4,000 payout and a maximum of $50-$60 for higher jackpots of $8,000-$13,000.

As for tipping on mini-jackpots or small hand-pay amounts and machine fills, there seems to be no average or consensus. Some players stick to their percentage schedule. Many don't tip at all for these and this is a reasonable policy, since the amounts are usually relatively small and depend on how many credits a machine can accumulate, rather than whether they're real jackpots. Some of the old machines in some casinos lock up and require hand-pays, or spit coins and require frequent fills at extremely low amounts. This is one reason we like the new coinless machines, which usually rack up credits for all wins up to the W-2G amount ($1,200). That means even a $1,000 royal on a quarter machine doesn't require a hand-pay. This kind of machine cuts down tipping expenses drastically.

Brad and I sometimes use a spread-it-around tip system, especially when we plan to play a long time in one day and expect frequent hand-pays or machine fills or when we're at a casino where we play often and many of the employees give us special service. We get a couple of rolls of dollar coins (the new brass-plated dollars are good here) and give out *one* coin to anyone who does anything for us (except for a major jackpot). This includes filling the machine, making a small hand-pay, watching a small hand-pay (security), cleaning up around our machine (the porter), or bringing us drinks.

At first, some employees look at the dollar coin scornfully and think we're being cheap, but soon they get the idea and can't wait to come around and do something for us. Talk about instant machine fills, fast hand-pays, and extra promotional goodies, like drawing tickets.

We like this spread-it-around idea even for major-jackpot tipping. In some casinos where we play often, we know what system the employees have concerning tips they receive. Some keep all their own tips, but many places have sharing arrangements. However, we usually ignore this factor when we hit a big jackpot and just try to share our happiness with as many employees as we can.

I don't really care if a casino rotates the change people to do hand-pays. But since I don't like to give one big tip to a change person I've never seen prior to her arriving to count out my stack of hundred-dollar bills, I might lower the tip for the new hand-payer, then see how far I can spread the joy by offering $5 to everyone who shows up—floorpeople, supervisors,

---

"Get Those Girl Scout Cookies Away From Me!"

Believe it or not, sometimes tipping creates tension among the employees and can backfire on the tipper. I know a blackjack player whose wife is an executive with the Girl Scouts. He tells a story about the time he came to town with a bunch of Girl Scout cookies and gave away several boxes (one at a time) to various floorpeople and pit bosses at a downtown Las Vegas casino. He got such a good reaction that on his next trip, he brought more cookies—but this time no one wanted any part of them.

It seems word had gotten back to a boss that the floorpeople had taken gifts (a $3 box of cookies, for cryin' out loud) from a player and he chewed them out roundly. On the second trip, when my friend tried to pass around his cookies, the employees reacted as if he were trying to give away radioactive nuclear waste. He wound up using them to toke valet parking attendants and maids.

---

security, whoever. Some may not be allowed by casino policy to accept tips, but they're happy I offered.
Whatever tip money is left over I distribute to other
employees who've made my day pleasant—the hard-
working porter who keeps our machine area clean, the
bathroom attendant who always has a cheerful greet-
ing for me, the cocktail waitress who brings me hot
tea *and* a bottle of water at the same time, the friendly
change girl who's been rooting for a jackpot on my
machine all day.

This system, especially in a casino where you play
frequently, can give you a reputation as a George at
the same time you're staying well within your tipping
budget.

Other Important Tipping Factors

Even with planned tipping guidelines, most players stray from them under special circumstances. For
example, they might tip less (or not at all) if service is
extremely slow. I've often been tempted to do that
myself. But then I remember that the employees in
charge of hand-pays and fills aren't always at fault;
they're scrambling. It's management's problem for
understaffing and I don't want to punish the wrong
person. However, I definitely won't tip someone (with
no guilt feelings whatsoever) who treats me rudely or
has a bad attitude.

Conversely, we often tip extra for special service
or particularly friendly attention. This usually happens
in a casino where we play frequently. We see the same
change people and other employees so much that we
get to know them. Many have been nice to us over a
period of years. They've never hustled us for tips and
have always been visibly grateful when we did tip,

whether big or small. Once in a while we find one who's going through a very difficult financial time. Then a bigger tip goes under the category of charity.

How much time a gambler spends in casinos is also a factor in deciding on tipping levels. A person who gambles infrequently may feel that he can tip more generously. Maybe he goes to a gambling destination only once a year and being a generous tipper adds a feel-good element to his vacation. The frequent casino visitor, or maybe a Las Vegas local, has to look at the total annual bill for tipping and might decide that he can't afford to be as generous as he was when he was just a sometime visitor. A video poker player whose main purpose in a casino is to turn a profit always figures tokes into the total expected return of any play and might decide he has to tip on a more restricted schedule.

Most people have a range of tip amounts and go to the higher end when they're winning and the lower when losing. I don't feel particularly benevolent when I'm losing heavily—you'd have to be a saint to feel generous when you're in the hole for a couple thousand! Similarly, if I'm down four or five grand playing dollars when I hit a $4,000 royal, I don't feel like tipping as much as I usually do—or as much as an attendant might think I should. So I might say something like, "I can only give you ten dollars now, because I had five thousand in this machine before I hit the royal. If I hit another jackpot and get even or ahead, I'll tip you more." And I keep my word.

Of course, you're not obliged to explain any tip, but I find that the floorpeople are more understanding when you share your feelings honestly, and it mitigates some of the awkwardness you might feel. (On the other hand, I don't whine to the employees constantly about losing. That makes them callused fast: "If you can't stand the heat, get out of the kitchen …")

Following Casino Rules

Each casino has its own tipping policies, which cover who can and who can't take tips. There's no standard here that you can depend on. Sometimes a security guard is allowed to take a tip; sometimes this is forbidden. Sometimes hosts can take tips; sometimes it could get them fired. I've found that the smaller the casino, the more employees who can take tips—probably because of the lower salaries overall. Privately owned casinos, as a rule, seem to allow more tipping than larger corporate-run operations.

People in casino management are usually prohibited from accepting tips—there's a demarcation line on the slot floor among the change people, floormen, and supervisors. It's the same in the table-game pits with dealers, floormen, and pit bosses. However, this line is not drawn in the same place at every casino.

To cope with the diversity of policies, I've found a few good tipping tactics that have worked for me in the past:

• You can ask any employee about the tipping policy at the casino: "Are you allowed to take tips? If so, are there any specific limits? Do you have to share tips with anyone, either as a casino policy or through private arrangements you make among yourselves?" If you don't want to ask the person you want to tip directly, you can ask another employee, such as a supervisor or a co-worker.

• You can offer a tip to *any* casino employee and they won't be insulted (they know tipping is a way of life in casinos). Even if they have to refuse it, they appreciate the gesture and the good will generated may benefit you in some way in the future.

• Many employees take and appreciate tips even if it's against casino policy, but only if you do it discreetly. How do you do that? Ask for a home or mailing address so you can send tips or gifts there. Slip a tip in a thank-you card, give it to someone in the casino, and tell him to open it at home. Invite the employee to meet you at a casino restaurant where there are no surveillance cameras, and give a small gift that can be slipped into a pocket or purse. Don't refer to the gift in e-mails to the employee's company address; the computers might be monitored.

• Even if there's a no-tipping policy for some classes of employees, many of them can still accept non-cash items that don't seem like tips, like sports or race book tickets, comps or coupons for meals or shows at another casino, and inexpensive casino logo items like T-shirts.

The Brad Scott Tipping Guide

Many people tip attractive service workers more than unattractive ones, especially of the opposite sex. Brad likes to tip unattractive people more; he thinks they won't get their fair share.

Brad has been in Las Vegas for so long he hardly knows how to act when we travel to a non-casino destination. He feels as if he should tip anyone and everyone who does anything for us. A porter is mopping up in a mall restroom? Hand him a dollar. A security guard at a jewelry store holds the door for us? Give him a buck. Someone gives us directions at the gas station? Toss him two. The teenager is emptying the trash bins at McDonalds? Why, he needs a reward!

Brad is such a good tipper that it could be aggravating to a frugal soul, but I've learned to appreciate his generous nature most of the time. He knows when it starts to bother me, though. It's when I start calling him George.

The Bottom Line

Finally, remember there's something you can give *all* casino employees who serve you—something that's valuable to them and doesn't cost you any money at all. You can treat them with respect and honor their dignity, no matter what job level they're on. A from-the-heart "thank you" with a friendly smile may be the most appreciated tip of all.

Theory & Practice—
The Queen on TV

Editor's Note: Jean Scott doesn't just practice what she preaches, she practices it for the whole world to see. The following article, which originally appeared in Strictly Slots *magazine, was written by Anthony Curtis.*

Think of it as a perk of the business. When you achieve a certain level of notoriety as an authority in the gambling world, you're bound to get the call. It's the chance you've been waiting for. Your 15 minutes of fame realized. An opportunity to immortalize yourself—assuming you know how to program your VCR—with an appearance on television.

It's exciting. It's glamorous. But most of all, it's nerve wracking. The fear, of course, is that you won't perform up to par. You'll mangle your words. Or worse, if you're demonstrating your gambling technique, you'll lose while the cameras are rolling.

I've been there. In one of my first TV appearances,

I played high-stakes blackjack at Harrah's. It wasn't pretty. I lost 19 out of 24 hands in a half-hour nightmare, dumping about $2,700 along the way. Luckily, a Harrah's exec got cold feet just before the taping and made me agree to "play for fun." He wasn't pleased to see that all of my losses had to be returned after the session. But while I dodged that particular bullet, losing like that on camera surely wouldn't sell too many books or newsletters.

On the flip side, doing well in front of the cameras can lead to a major bonanza. Olaf Vancura, author of *Knock-Out Blackjack*, scored big when he got his chance on a Discovery Channel documentary called "High Stakes." Olaf was filmed employing his count and winning a contest among several other skilled blackjack players. The day after the show aired, I logged onto Amazon.com and was stunned to see that *Knock-Out* was the #4 best-selling book in the world!

Olaf certainly made the most of his chance. But even that timely performance was nothing compared to the on-camera exploits of Jean Scott. There's just something about Jean Scott and TV. When the cameras are rolling, she's nothing less than a casino killer.

It began in 1995 when Jean was the subject of a "48 Hours" piece. She'd had a horrible run of luck during the taping, losing at the video poker machines to the tune of about $2,000, a tidy sum for a short span playing quarters. Time was running out and even a thousand-dollar royal wouldn't get her off the hook. What happened next, though, was amazing. Knowing that she had hundreds of tickets in a drawing for a car at the Stardust, Jean dragged the "48 Hours" people down to the drawing area. In the face of huge odds (thousands of tickets were in the drum), her name was drawn. Pow! The "48 Hours" crew was ecstatic as their subject drove off with a new Mercury Mystique.

A couple years later, Jean was on a shoot for "Hard Copy," playing single-line Deuces Wild. The cameraman revved it up and within minutes, Jean popped again. This time it was the second-best hand possible: 4 deuces, paying $250. To top it off, the deuces were dealt. More good fortune on national television.

Next up was "Dateline." Jean was coaching correspondent Bob McKeown on a 9/6 Jacks or Better $5 Triple Play machine while he played with $1,000 of NBC's money (and her slot club card, of course!). They were dealt 9♥9♣8♣6♣5♣. McKeown saw the pair of nines and wanted to hold them. Jean pointed out the 4-card straight flush and explained that it had a higher expected value, even though it was a long shot. Conceding that they were likely to lose $75 on the play ($25 on each of three lines on the Triple Play), McKeown held the inside SF and hit the button. He pulled a flush on the bottom line, zilch on the top line, and the 7♣ on the middle line. The hand paid $1,400. The fortuitous draw was seen nationwide on the "Dateline" broadcast and it sent *The Frugal Gambler* to a dizzying #2 on Amazon—only one of the Harry Potter releases kept it out of the top spot.

Jean does lots of interviews for lower-profile shows and true to form, she's come off luckier than normal on those, too. But it's the big ones that seem to start her engine. Not long after the "Dateline" shoot, word reached me about another one of her big small-screen conquests. This time the Travel Channel was following Her Frugalness and she was hot again, hitting four 4s and four aces on a 4-line Double Bonus game. Then came a dealt flush with four cards to the royal. Jean instructed the camera crew to position itself for the potential windfall. She discarded the odd flush card and, sure enough, up popped a royal on one of the lines. Uncanny!

Fact is, Jean doesn't even have to be *in* a show to steal it. I found this out last summer while working with the Travel Channel at the Palms. Jean wasn't involved in the shoot, but she was there playing, because the Palms was running a juicy multiple-point special. All of a sudden the cameramen filming me stopped and ran off toward Jean's machine. Turns out she'd just been *dealt* four deuces on a $1 Five Play machine—a $5,000 jackpot! The director recognized her and wanted that footage in the show. In an instant, my interview turned into her interview. Like I said, there's just something about Jean Scott and TV.

Postscript

I've now come to the end of writing two books about frugal gambling. I must say my main feeling is relief.

You, on the other hand, might be feeling overwhelmed. Many people told me that they felt that way after reading the first book. They wanted to become smarter casino visitors, but I'd given so many suggestions, they didn't know where to start.

Slow and Sure Wins the Race

Relax. First, I don't expect every gambler to use every suggestion I make. As Brad says so often, "No one wants to be as frugally nutty as you are."

Remember, we developed the information in these two books over a period of nearly 20 years. We've had varying goals during that time, thus we've employed a number of frugal concepts. We don't use every weapon in our arsenal every time. Some were more effective when we played quarter video poker, while others became more applicable when we went up in denomination. Some techniques are useful only when we play blackjack or coupons.

Furthermore, when I originally came to Las Vegas in 1984, I didn't know *anything* that I'm writing about today. And I certainly didn't learn it all on that first three-day visit. It came to me gradually, over nearly two decades. My knowledge and experience grew with every visit. It's true that my purpose in writing both of these books was to shorten the learning curve for other casino visitors, but it's still a plodding process, not instant magic. You'll have to learn from your mistakes, as we did and still do. You'll have to adapt to changing casino conditions, as we continue to do. Your education will never be complete, as it never will be for us or anyone.

So, how do you cope if you feel overwhelmed by so much information?

I suggest that after you've read the books the first time, pick out a few of the basic ideas I emphasize. If you're a machine player, you might decide never to play a machine again unless you've joined the slot club and can use a tracking card. If you play table games, you might decide never to put any money down until you ask the pit boss about having your play rated. Or you might decide to study a book mentioned in the "Resources" so you can learn how to play a game with better odds.

Then try adding one or two new techniques on every visit. Many readers tell me that they re-read *The Frugal Gambler* frequently—often on the plane to a gambling destination—and they always find some useful idea that they'd overlooked on earlier reads. Don't try to swallow my books whole; you'll definitely choke. Take it slowly, one bite at a time.

My hope is that the more knowledgeable you become, the more fun your casino visits will be. Whatever other goals you have, never forget that your main purpose in visiting a casino is entertainment.

Ethics

I didn't include a chapter on ethics in this book, as I did in the first one. Instead, I tried to sprinkle some ethical considerations throughout as they pertained to the area being discussed. But I want to emphasize once again how important it is to be true to yourself.

I trust I haven't given you the impression that anything goes in a casino. My casino activities are merely one part of my total life experience and I try to hold myself to the same high ethical standards and moral principles in a casino that I do everywhere else.

I do advocate using the casino system in such a way that will maximize your benefits. Notice the word is "use," not "abuse." I would never approve of your twisting my suggestions to do anything unethical or illegal. I encourage you to learn all the details of the casino system so you can be sure to receive all the benefits that are available, but I expect you not to break the rules in order to get something you didn't earn or deserve.

Farewell

Now, I bid you all a frugal goodbye, with the hope that I can see every one of you sometime. Then I can autograph your book personally with this wish:

Skillful luck to you,

Jean Scott

Resources

The cornerstone of the success Brad and I have enjoyed in the gambling arena is information. We're not looking for one big win; we don't play progressive slot machines hoping to get supernaturally lucky and hit a life-changing jackpot. We know that the best way to be long-term winners is to grind out the small wins—and that means using literally hundreds of small money-making and money-saving ideas.

Luckily, plenty of resources—books, periodicals, Web sites, and e-mail—are available for just this purpose. The following is a list of the sources I rely on to make me a more knowledgeable gambler. It's organized by time—the sources I check daily, weekly, and monthly, or refer to continually, for help in making Brad and me consistent long-term winners.

Daily
1. The *Las Vegas Review-Journal*. I read this morn-

ing newspaper thoroughly to keep up with the ever-changing Vegas scene—the dirty-hands copy when I'm in Las Vegas and the online version, found at www.lv rj.com, when I'm not. I check the casino ads in local newspapers—in Las Vegas or wherever I visit a casino—since this is often the first place I find out about good promotions and important slot club benefits or changes.

2. E-mails from Skip Hughes' Video Poker List and the Lodestone group. This is a fantastic and active source of VP and casino information, not only for Las Vegas, but also for most other U.S. gambling destinations and beyond. I religiously read and process anywhere from 30 to 75 e-mail messages a day from here. Go to www.vphomepage.com to sign up, not only for the forum but for access to a site packed with information that will help you gamble smarter and enjoy your casino visits more.

3. *Fantini Daily Gaming Report*. This online gaming-investment newsletter is full of the latest news concerning the casino industry. It's mostly for investors, but the coverage often includes casino tidbits that I glean to my gambling advantage. Sign up at www.gaming investments.com.

Weekly—More or Less

4. *Gaming Today*. This weekly tabloid contains detailed coverage of sports and race betting, general gambling, and Las Vegas entertainment and happenings. I disagree (sometimes strongly) with the theories of some of the gaming writers, but I love to read the features where I might find some breaking news or insider information. This tabloid is a freebie available in numerous Las Vegas locations, such as casino sports books (it comes out on Tuesdays and you have to be quick about picking one up; it disappears quickly). You can also

subscribe to the online version at www.gaming today.com.

5. Freebie magazines and newspapers in Vegas and in other gambling venues I visit. I never pass a counter or rack of these ad-driven free periodicals without checking to see if I have the current copy. I pore through them looking for coupons and other money-saving stuff. Some of these also have online editions.

6. Casino promotions information online. We usually make more money taking advantage of promotions while we play video poker than we do on the games themselves. I used to check many sources to find out where the best promotions in Las Vegas were taking place. One was Scot Krause's column detailing Las Vegas promotions and I still check it every Monday to see what new ones are in store for that week: www.americancasinoguide.com/Promotions/VE-GAS-VALUES.shtml. Another source for promotions, "Player's Edge" by Jeff Compton and Bob Dancer, is the first thing I read on Fridays in the "Neon" entertainment section of the *Las Vegas Review-Journal* or online at www.lvrj.com/lvrj-home/opinion/packages/columnists.

But these days, my primary source is the *Las Vegas Advisor* Web site at www.lasvegasadvisor.com. Scot Krause updates the coupon and funbook listings and the "What's News" page almost daily and I help him update the "Bonus Points" page as soon as the casinos announce the new schedules. Sign up for the free weekly e-letter *Las Vegas Advisor Lite*, which is a truncated, but valuable and timely, version of the *Las Vegas Advisor*. This is your one-stop site for the most practical, useful, and current information on Las Vegas anywhere. And it keeps getting bigger and better.

7. *Viva Las Vegas*. I'm a big fan of Billhere's free weekly e-mail newsletter that distills Vegas news you

site often to see the unbelievable list of free, or almost free, things you can order: www.billhere.com.

8. *Everything Las Vegas.* Another free weekly e-mail newsletter, this one is chock full of information about all things Vegas. Its biggest asset is its numerous links to other Web sites where you can get the full stories of current happenings around town. Sign up by sending an e-mail message to mrvegas98@aol.com.

9. Other good Web sites and forums I check whenever I have the time: the *Las Vegas Advisor* Web site's Forum Board. I wish I could get to this active Internet forum more often, but I do log on when I can. It's only open to *LVA* members (another value-added bonus to the cost of a membership) and is packed with updates, trip reports, Q+A's, and spirited discussions of current issues in gambling and in Las Vegas.

http://groups.yahoo.com/group/vpfree. This free Web site concentrates mainly on video poker in Las Vegas and has valuable information especially for locals. I like the links it gives to many weekly and monthly online gaming columns.

John Grochowski's gambling columns. John has an accurate mathematical take on gambling and he has the knack of translating the often difficult concepts into layman's terms. You can find John's columns on the Web at www.suntimes.com/index/grochowski.html and http://data.detnews.com/casino/columns/grochow ski/previous.hbs.

www.casinogaming.com/columnists/dancer/ index.html—weekly articles about VP by Bob Dancer.

www.rgtonline.com. An abundance of gambling news and articles about playing all kinds of casino games. I don't agree with some of the writers' views at times, but mostly you get helpful gambling information.

www.smartgaming.com. A good site hosted by

Henry Tamburin, one of gamblings most prolific writers. I especially like his *Blackjack Insider*, a free blackjack newsletter. There're also hotel bargains (updated regularly), gambling tips, and a list of Las Vegas events.

www.wizardofodds.com/index.html. The first site I turn to when I have math questions about any casino game. This site is loaded with gambling information, all of it based on sound math principles. Also valuable is the long list (more than 100) of other gambling sites he recommends.

I don't exactly read the following Web page; I write it. But every Friday you can get a piece of my mind in "Frugal Fridays" on the *LVA* Web site, www.lasvegas advisor.com. This is my most enjoyable writing job, since I literally get to say whatever's on my mind— and with *my* mind, you never know what's gonna be on it next! But it always has something to do with frugal gambling and casinos.

Monthly

10. *Strictly Slots*. I suck up like a Shop-Vac every iota of gambling info in this excellent monthly magazine. A must-read for anyone who ever puts even a nickel into a casino machine. Subscribe at www.casino center.com.

11. *Casino Player*. I've had a long affair with the *Player*, the original gambling consumer magazine, first as just a reader, then as a contributor. I feel as if *Casino Player* and I have grown up together. I always learn something new from every issue, especially with such quality contributors as Anthony Curtis, Arnold Snyder, Jeffrey Compton, Bob Dancer, Frank Scoblete, Frank Legato, Adam Fine, Melissa Fine, and Henry Tamburin. Subscribe at www.casinocenter.com.

12. *Las Vegas Advisor*. If I've been having a long-term affair with *Casino Player*, I've been married to the

Las Vegas Advisor. I've been contributing to, and my gambling adventures have been immortalized by, the *LVA* for 12 years now. It's been ranked among the best travel-destination newsletters in the country by the *L.A. Times.* Enough said. Subscribe to the online and/or snail-mail version at www.lasvegasadvisor.com, or call 800/244-2224.

13. *Casino Journal* and *Global Gaming Business.* I also read the foremost gaming-industry trade magazines to get other-side-of-the-fence info: the casino's point of view. I want to know all about my opponents' plans! www.casinojournal.com and www.globalgaming business.com.

14. *Video Poker Player.* This online magazine by Skip Hughes and John Kelly (Lodestone) is packed with practical and specific VP information, presented in a hilarious style that makes it the ultimate laugh-and-learn gambling read. Subscribe at www.vphome page.com.

15. *Video Poker Times.* Published every other month by Dan Paymar, this hard-copy newsletter has well-grounded-in-math information about the VP scene, particularly in Las Vegas. www.OptimumPlay.com.

16. *Midwest Gaming and Travel.* Covering travel, casino, and gambling information in—where else?—the Midwest area, the content includes Indiana, where we spend some of the summer escaping the searing Vegas heat and need localized casino help. www.mid westgamingandtravel.com.

17. *The Dealer's News.* This is a little monthly newsletter for Las Vegas casino employees that's full of juicy insider tidbits about the jobs and lives of dealers, pit bosses, casino managers, and other casino employees. www.thedealersnews.com.

18. Blackjack Forum Online. Arnold Snyder's Web site offers all kinds of information on blackjack, as well

as one of the most lively gambling forums discussing blackjack and other casino games. www.bjfonline.com.

Books

19. *Comp City—A Guide to Free Gambling Vacations.* Max Rubin is the funniest gambling writer I've ever read, and his book, *Comp City* ($19.95), is a jewel in any gambling library. Max shows you how to get $1 worth of comps for every 10¢-30¢ in casino losses. High and low rollers alike, and especially table players, can get lots of ammunition to use against the casino's assault on your wallet.

20. *American Casino Guide.* I highly recommend this nationwide casino guide ($14.95) by Steve Bourie, updated every year and indispensable for anyone who goes to casinos around the country. It also contains a substantial casino coupon section in the back of the book.

21. John Grochowski books. As I mentioned above, John is the gambling columnist for the *Chicago Sun-Times.* He's mathematically accurate and precise, has an excellent handle on the nuances of all the games, and focuses on those that are beatable. He's also emerged as an expert on new casino games. His books include *Gaming—Cruising the Casinos with John Grochowski* ($11.95), *Casino Answer Book* ($12.95), *Slot Machine Answer Book* ($12.95), and *Video Poker Answer Book* ($13.95).

22. *Knock-Out Blackjack.* For those of you who like playing blackjack, *Knock-Out Blackjack—The Easiest Card-Counting System Ever Devised* by Olaf Vancura and Ken Fuchs ($17.95), can improve your game to the point where you're getting more in comps than you're giving up at the tables.

23. *Slot Expert's Guide.* If you're a slot machine player, you'll want to pick up John Robison's *Slot*

Expert's Guide to Playing Slots ($6.95). Even though slots are almost never beatable, this book provides valuable information on how to play the reels at the lowest cost.

24. *Million Dollar Video Poker*. This is Bob Dancer's tell-all narrative about how he and his wife Shirley won $1 million in a six-month period playing high-stakes video poker (they won half the million in one night, hitting $100,000 and $400,000 royals). If you've ever wondered about the life of a professional video poker player, this book will answer all your questions, and then some. It's available for $16.95.

25. *Burning the Tables*. Though this book focuses on high-stakes blackjack, the author, Ian Andersen, is to table games what Bob Dancer is to video poker. There's lots of relevant—and irreverent—information, useful to anyone who gambles, whether in a casino or playing the game of life. It's available for $27.95.

All the above books can be purchased from Huntington Press by calling 800/244-2224 or by logging on to www.greatstuff4gamblers.com.

Resources for Video Poker Players

Special resources specifically for VP players are discussed in Chapter Four. They include these "frugal-approved" products that can be ordered at the Web site www.frugalgambler.biz (the only place you can order my books personally autographed).

26. *The Frugal Gambler*, my first book. Although I talk about all casino games and many gambling subjects in this book, it still contains the best introduction to video poker, since I also introduce the basic tools of a successful VP player: slot clubs, comps, and promotions.

27. The *Frugal Video Poker* 2-in-1 software program, developed by Jim Wolf. This is both a tutor and a strategy generator for almost any VP schedule you will find

in a casino. It's easy for use by a beginning VP player, particularly the feature that figures slot club benefits, and it has many advanced functions that will be appreciated by serious VP students who want to analyze special situations and use advanced math functions.

The *Frugal Strategy Cards,* developed by Skip Hughes. These colored-coded laminated cards give a simplified strategy for many of the common VP games. Each strategy is easy enough for the beginning player to learn and suitable for the majority of gamblers to continue to use as they become more experienced. Most players will find that they can play much faster and more accurately and therefore achieve a higher return using these cards than trying to decipher the much longer and more complicated strategies.

These and other good VP resources can also be ordered by calling Huntington Press or browsing the www.greatstuff4gamblers.com Web site.

Finally

As I was compiling this list, someone told me that I need all these resources more than the average casino visitor, because I'm also a gambling writer. So I looked over the entries to see what I would drop if I quit writing about gambling and just gambled. I not only could not see anything I would drop, I started dreaming of how much more I could read.

Index

About the Authors

Jean Scott, the Queen of Comps, is the country's best-known low-rolling casino player. Her first book, *The Frugal Gambler*, was a national bestseller. She has appeared on countless television and radio programs about gambling and her written work has been published in numerous gambling magazines. She lives in Las Vegas with her husband Brad.

Angela Sparks, the Frugal Princess, is Jean Scott's daughter. A chip off the frugal block, she is following in her mother's footsteps and becoming an expert low roller in her own right. She lives with her career Army Ranger husband Steve and two grade-school children near Ft. Benning, Georgia, until Uncle Sam decides to send them elsewhere. She keeps busy with volunteer work and substitute assignments in the school system.